5940 0399 ✓

HITTING ROCK BOTTOM

Hitting Rock Bottom

DISCLAIMER

This book is designed to provide accurate and authoritative information as of the date written in regard to the subject matter covered but should not be construed as professional advice on any specific facts or circumstances. It is sold with the understanding that the publisher, author, editor, and other contributors are not engaged in rendering professional services. While every attempt has been made to provide accurate information, neither the author, the publisher nor the contributors can be held accountable for any error or omission.

LIBRARY OF CONGRESS

CATALOGING-IN-PUBLICATION DATA

ISBN: 978-0-9988777-0-9 (hardback)
          978-0-9988777-1-6 (paperback)
          978-0-9988777-2-3 (ebook)

Printed in the United States of America

HITTING ROCK BOTTOM

NEW BEGINNINGS FOR AT-RISK YOUTH

THE ALDER GROVE ACADEMY EXPERIMENT

BY GARY J. ROSE, PH.D.

ACKNOWLEDGEMENTS

I did not anticipate it would take this long from the closing of the Alder Grove Academy to get my cadet's and former student's stories into print.

Many of my cadets experienced similar backgrounds and problems: truancy, drug/alcohol usage, probation, ward of the courts, credit deficient or failing grades, lack of parental supervision, or parents who could not positively deal with son's or daughter's rebellious antics.

Most of the cadets were associated with the Placer County high schools and middle schools. The academy was their last shot at turning their lives around.

Most of them agreed while in the academy program, that if they could share how they turned their lives around, perhaps they could save at least one child from destroying his or her life.

My cadets and I believe that the Alder Grove Academy was a success. However, it required a lot of dedication from many individuals for us to thrived for 2 ½ years; had it not been for them, the academy would have failed.

I am very grateful to Joan Berry, the former director of the Placer County Office of Education Alternative Education department who entrusted me to create the academy when - at the time - many educational administrations shunned military style institutions. It was her inspiration that led to its creation.

Paul McDaniel taught me how to structure the academy: he spent almost 30 years in the Air Force and survived three tours in Vietnam. "Santa," as many cadets called him, relished drills and ceremonies as well as teachings the polishing of boots and selecting the best every Friday. I don't know many individuals who would give up Christmas Eves to visit kids at the hall to spread joy and goodies. But that is what Paul and his departed wife did each Christmas Eve. He was very inspirational in teaching U.S. Government and the U.S. Constitution to our 7th and 8th graders, who, upon passing his exam, proudly displayed their awards he issued. I extend a thank you to Paul.

Michelle (Ms. M) – Thank God for her presence, especially in times of need, when we had wall-to-wall cadets and little staff. Her care of all of us when we were sick or down in the dumps, kept the program alive and vital. I am so grateful for all the she did behind the scenes. I have often said that teaching is the easy job; it is the teacher's aide that performs the tough job, and they often do it for little pay or recognition. I am sure our female cadets will long remember "Mom" and their chats during "girl's circle."

Tom Grayson – I should ask, "Did we have fun or what?" Tom came once a week and taught life skills to cadets. He "pushed their buttons" to foster coping skills since many suffered from anger management issues. Tom would be tipped-off by older cadets when a "new booty" arrived. Tom welcomed the newcomer, and then drill him/her (trying to find their anger buttons), much to the delight of cadets who had endured a similar inquisition when they arrived.

Jenny and Beverly – They came to the academy later and had to handle a range of duties and responsibilities, and they deserve a note of appreciation. Their extra pairs of eyes and ears prevented many potential problems from arising.

Sergeants Howell and Hewitt – They brought inspiration, leadership, and determination to make the Alder Grove Academy a worthwhile institution turning many at-risk students's lives around. I want to offer you a thank you from the bottom of my heart. Their one-on-one conversations with cadets, positively changed lives and futures. They are both my heroes, and I want to thank them for their service to our country.

Denise Gibbon, my literary attorney and confidant – I want to extend a hearty "thank you" to her for continually motivating and reminding me that "we" had a good book, and that it would take time to bring it to fruition. Her inspiration, drive, and commitment – both to me and the cadets – made this book a reality, and for that we are all eternally grateful. I consider her a close friend.

Lara Nelson – She helped in the initial formatting of the manuscript, "picking my brain" for my motivation, teaching styles and reasons for teaching at-risk students for so many years. Thank you Lara for putting my reminiscing into words. Through your questions, many fond memories returned and were incorporated into the book.

Debra Lum – She edited entries for grammar or spelling errors late into the production of the manuscript with Denise. Debra was always available to me as a friend and someone with whom I could bounce off ideas. I thank you Deb.

R'tor John Maghuyop – book formatter and graphic designer. John helped me produce my first book and did such a fantastic job, that without hesitation, I sought his expertise again in formatting this book, incorporating pictures and cover designs. Thank you so much John. Get ready for book four.

To my law enforcement brothers and sisters, the probation officers I had the privilege to work with, both in juvenile hall and out of the street, the Auburn Police Department and Placer County Sheriffs Department – You provided valuable support, and without whom the Academy would not have had so many success stories. I extend a warm thank you. Just showing up for a cup of coffee and donut, showed the cadets that law enforcement is not "the bad guy," but instead is a system that wants to see them succeed made a difference.

Finally, my cadets and former students - You learned from me, and I learned from you. I was honored to have been your teacher and mentor. I could not be prouder to see so many of you mature into hard working individuals with careers; parents raising children; graduates from colleges, universities or trade schools; defenders of our nation.

Let us remember Albert, Josh, and Jose, to whom this book is dedicated, and help keep their memories alive.

To you all: the memories you shared in the writing of this book will forever live in my heart and mind. I wish the best for all of you in the future, and I will keep you in my prayers.

I will never, ever, forget you!

In memory of
Alder Grove Academy Cadets
Josh Pavlov, Albert Torres, and Jose Portillo,
and with best wishes for Alder Grove
Academy Cadet Noe Perez
on life's journey.

TABLE OF CONTENTS

PART III
THE PRICE OF CELEBRITY

PART IV
LOOKING BACK

PART V
A FINAL WARNING

INTRODUCTORY NOTE TO OUR READERS

I taught at-risk teens at juvenile delinquent facilities for many years before the Placer County Office of Education ("PCOE") gave me the opportunity to establish the Alder Grove Academy ("AGA"). Of the many students I taught, some were fortunate enough to attend the AGA as cadets. Although this book was inspired by the AGA experience and the contributions of those cadets, I want every reader to know that *all my students* contributed to my experience and growth as a teacher and I thank them all for what they taught me.

The AGA experiment involved numerous at-risk cadets at three different sites in Placer County, California over a two and one-half year period. At one point, forty-two male and female cadets of different ethnic and socio-economic backgrounds qualified for the program. Although cadets and I sometimes refer to AGA-1, AGA-2 and AGA-3, these names merely refer to three sequential locations while the AGA constituted one program.

As a teacher of at-risk teens, I had been profoundly affected by the book *Freedom Writers* as well as the movie based upon it. I shared that book and film as well as others like it with my students, including *Dangerous Minds*, *Stand and Deliver*, *Gridiron Gang* and *Lean on Me*. My students and those who later became cadets agreed that if they, too, shared their stories, other teenagers headed down the wrong path might avoid the mistakes that they had made and create a better life for themselves. Thus, we offer this book to both the teens who might be on the wrong path and the adults in their lives who want to help them.

The name "Alder Grove" will appear often in these pages. It is important to understand that I taught at what was known as the Alder Grove Community School both before the PCOE sponsored the creation of the Alder Grove Academy and after its closure. Though my staff and I often used many of the same educational methodologies at both the community school and the academy, the academy program was distinguished by a number of important factors described in this book.

The students and cadets who played an integral role in the development of the AGA program before and while it existed have now reached adulthood. Nevertheless, I decided that the authorship of their teenage journals should remain anonymous to protect their privacy. Adult authors in the *Looking Back* section are identified with their real names or nicknames they have chosen.

I have modified and divided some of the cadet and student entries, distributing parts of the same journals throughout the book. However, as often as possible, I use the students' actual text, including some profanity, so that other teenagers taking the time to read this book can better relate to their stories. Though several teen journals and adult contributors report many of the same incidents, I've included most of those passages because they meant so much to us all. Those who attended AGA are distinguished, wherever possible, as "cadets."

My students, cadets, staff and I offer our stories freely in hopes of saving at least one at-risk teenager from a life of heartbreak, addiction or incarceration.

Thank you for your interest and commitment to at-risk children.

Dr. Gary J. Rose

PART I

A MATTER OF BELONGING

THE ALDER GROVE ACADEMY CADET OATH

I solemnly vow upon my honor as a cadet and citizen, to adhere to the rules and regulations of the Alder Grove Academy, and to adopt the Academy's mission and goals into my everyday life.

I pledge to be honest in thought, word, and deed, to strive toward my highest learning effort and avail myself of every opportunity to learn to my highest capacity.

I will do this by maintaining unimpeachable integrity of behavior to bring honor upon the Alder Grove Academy and the Placer County Office of Education.

I shall endeavor to give thoughtful, intelligent obedience to the commands of my superiors, to obey the Constitution and laws of my country, state and county in a way that will set my behavior for the remainder of my life.

There are two types of education…
One should teach us how to make a living,
and the other how to live.

–JOHN ADAMS, SECOND PRESIDENT
OF THE UNITED STATES (1735-1826).

CHAPTER 1

WHAT IT LOOKS LIKE
AT ROCK BOTTOM

Today Mr. Rose said something that really, really inspired me. I don't remember his exact words, but it was something about how we haven't reached rock bottom yet. He is always honest with us and he said that he realizes many of us cadets haven't reached the bottom of our screw-ups. He went around the room and after asking certain people if it was okay to share their backgrounds, he pointed out how some of them have not reached rock bottom yet and probably won't until they're faced with prison time.

–Journal #5, 16-year-old female

For many years, I taught teenagers who society describes as being "at-risk." It always struck me that the term was inadequate because the risk isn't only theirs but society's as well. These are youth who can destroy the future not only for themselves but for their families, neighbors and many other innocent victims. They drink, take drugs, steal, assault others and sometimes commit murder. And in the midst of the chaos and despair they may cause themselves and others, some are desperate to change but don't see a way to either re-direct their lives or cope with what they've done.

One of my first at-risk students, Reggie, was one of those who longed to start over. I met Reggie while on my first teaching assignment at a local high school after performing undercover police work for over two and a half years. A class clown, Reggie struggled academically but still gave me his best. He called me one day to tell me that he had been caught vandalizing the tires of several vehicles. He wanted to make restitution to the victims.

I told Reggie not to contact the victims, that the juvenile court would administer restitution and that, in the meantime, he should try to stay out of trouble. He continued to insist he had to make amends while I insisted he should leave it to the court. A short time later, Reggie was found by his mother hanging from a tree in their front yard. I was shocked and heartbroken for both him and his mother. What I hadn't realized was how important it was to Reggie to clean the slate, how he was crying out for help, and how desperate he was for a new start.

Change for these kids is particularly difficult. Often, they have to hit rock bottom before they even try. Hitting rock bottom is personal. For some, it could mean getting caught and released for shoplifting or intoxication while for others, it could mean a drug overdose or using a lethal weapon to commit a crime.

The overall theme in my classes at the juvenile hall facility ("JDF" or "the hall") and later, at the Alder Grove Academy ("AGA"), was that there would soon be no more free rides—the second and third opportunities that we so often give those under eighteen in our juvenile delinquent system. They were nearing adulthood, a time when they would be held accountable for their actions and inactions.

What I taught was what I believed then and now. Choices matter and poor choices lead to poor outcomes. As difficult as their lives might seem, they were the masters of change. It was still possible to make choices that would lead to a better, happier future—one where they were successfully accountable to themselves and society.

Accountability

There are three skills that are the foundation for teaching accountability—order, structure and discipline.[1] Most at-risk children lack adult models and resources exemplifying at least one of these three skills if not all three.

Too often, we associate order, structure and discipline only with military and police institutions. In reality, they also underpin personal relationships, good parenting, and a healthy work life. But it all starts with parents or other guardians.

---

1 The latter is two-pronged: first, one must be self-disciplined to accomplish one's goals and, second, having an understanding of self-discipline, one learns to respect society's need to use disciplinary techniques to maintain a civil society.

Without adults who can demonstrate accountability in daily life, most children have no idea that accountability is a sustaining principle for healthy personal growth.

Some of my peers criticized my approach to at-risk teens as overly strict or even militaristic. Interestingly, the same teachers often complained of disciplinary problems while I had few. I won't bother to deny that I have a cop mentality when it comes to determining who, among my students or cadets, might be more likely to spend their lives in poverty, drug rehab programs or prison. But I also have a teacher mentality when it comes to using law enforcement principles to effect change among troubled youth. This was the bases on my doctoral dissertation and the topic of my first book.

I don't pretend to offer a panacea for all at-risk teens—there were many I failed to help. However, I learned early in my teaching career that many of my students substituted one or more of their teachers or staff for one or both of the parental figures that had eluded or disappointed them in the past. While students often described me as a "father" figure, they regarded one of my female aides as being a "mother." So it wasn't surprising that the staff and students regarded themselves as members of a family. Though most of them might not be able to articulate why they used these terms, I think it amounts to familial shorthand for the love and leadership these children seek.

Clubs and Gangs

There is no mystery to a child's longing for family. If they can't receive a healthy balance of love, encouragement and discipline within the family, they look for it elsewhere. Too often, elsewhere is not membership in the Boy Scouts, 4-H or on a baseball team but, instead, with other peers who experiment with drugs, alcohol, sex or crime.

It's a matter of belonging. Working organizations, whether they are gangs or clubs[2]–including the armed forces, police and those with beneficial social purposes—are strikingly similar structurally. Membership usually requires allegiance to a group purpose, willingness to be ranked or qualified, participation in programs, rewards of some kind, wearing uniforms or demonstrating affiliation with some form of physical indicia, i.e., scarves, pins, tattoos, t-shirts or even bumper stickers. Quitting the organization may be simple—you stop showing up or cease paying dues—or rather complicated. Not complying with orders might lead to exclusion or penalties of either a civil or criminal nature depending on the purpose of the organization.

The police and military are based on the same concepts— brotherhood and sisterhood, mutual support of acceptable behavior and goals, and a system whereby disobedience results in a range of disciplinary measures or exclusion.

---

2 For our purposes, I'm using the words "club" and "gang" to distinguish two types of groups whose memberships include teenagers. Though this oversimplifies whether any particular group or organization has a criminal purpose, I refer here to clubs as organizations that help teenagers become mature and responsible citizens in a civil society while gangs promote various degrees of disruptive, destructive or criminal conduct.

In the Classroom

In the classroom, I believe in teaching from a place where parenting and military and police standards intersect. There were many who claimed that my approach was too extreme, too stern, and that these children needed a more conventional approach. But the reason that these students became my responsibility was because the conventional high school educator could not relate to them. These teens were simply unable to engage productively in a traditional educational environment. As a result, they were suspended or expelled and sent to the juvenile hall or AGA because they caused classroom disturbances, confronted authority, refused to attend school and were periodically arrested for alcohol and drug use, assault or other crimes. For these kids, the conventional approach clearly did not work.

In a 2006 poll, respondents rated fighting, violence and gangs in American schools as the most pressing problems facing their public schools and pointed to lack of discipline as a significant secondary problem. A nationwide survey of teachers, students and police at around the same time found that all constituencies believed schools were being compromised by disruptive, aggressive behaviors and classroom violence. In spite of our recognition of these classroom issues, teachers rarely receive the training they need in classroom management and the de-escalation of violence.

As any good police officer on the beat will attest, on-the-job conflict management skills are extraordinarily valuable. Though our current political and social struggles may cause some to disagree, well-trained police and properly administered police departments, in particular, have an arsenal of strategies for de-escalation, community involvement and leadership. So why not utilize retired and working police to train our teachers to use the same skills? The same rationale can be used to hire former military personnel as educators.

I am not suggesting that we turn our teachers into a police force. What I do suggest is that teachers have the opportunity to learn particular skills that would help them establish their authority in the classroom. Similarly, active or retired members of the armed services are ideally suited for many elements of teaching. Moreover, they excel at community building, organized physical activities and leadership. Why not put them to use as well?

By utilizing some of the principles promulgated by societally beneficial organizations—principles that I applied at the JDF, the Alder Grove Community School and the Alder Grove Academy–we can forge better and more cohesive classroom management practices, new community bonds, stronger schools and, ultimately, turn more troubled teens into happier, better educated and civic-minded citizens.

What sculpture is to a block of marble,
education is to the human soul.

–Joseph Addison, English politician
and writer (1671-1719).

CHAPTER 2

JOURNALS–IN THE BEGINNING

We got a new teacher named Mr. Rose and he is a lot stricter than that dumbass other teacher we used to have. He was a cop before he became a teacher and he's coming from the JDF.

He is asking us to write our life story so that maybe we could help other kids like us. If anyone is reading this I hope that I can help, but I am not a good role model since I got arrested by the cops for drinking. I have not written for a long time since I got arrested by the cops. You see I don't want to be here or at any school. I just want to get drunk or high and the hell with the world. The other day I brought in my water bottle and I had vodka inside. We never had our stuff checked until now because of what I did.

Mr. Rose gave us a writing assignment. I was already drunk and can't remember what the shit we were supposed to be writing on. Anyway Mr. Rose starts walking down the rows of desks and looks at my essay. Hell, my letters even looked strange to me, so I guess I shouldn't have been surprised when Old Cop Rose stops and looks down at my paper. He must have smelled the booze or seen my red eyes. Anyway I got hella scared and jumped up and started to run to the back of our old classroom.[3]

I ran past Ms. M's office and finally reached the back door. It seemed to take forever to reach it. Once outside I ran towards the drainage ditch and the creek that was by the school. I jumped into the water and hid under the bridge expecting Mr. Rose to be coming after me. But no one came and I stayed there for I don't know how long and then got out and dried off.

I found out later that Rose did not chase me but instead broke down laughing. I guess while I was trying to run down the hallway to the back of the class I was banging into the walls.

Now that I am back, we cannot bring anything into the classroom if it is open. Mr. Rose also searches us. He can be mean, too. A girl (no one likes her) came to class with a Starbucks coffee. Mr. Rose told her to either drink it outside or throw it out. She refused so Rose grabbed the cup and poured it out. She got pissed off and he suspended her. From that point on all of us knew he was not going to put up with our shit.

–Journal 32, 16 year-old male

---

3 "Hella" could mean "hell, yes" or "hell of a good–" or "hell of a lot of–" The students also used the term "hecka" to signify the same phrases but substituting "heck" for "hell"

It all started not too long after my sister and I joined the kids at Alder Grove Community School—this was before it became a military academy. Since day one, before Mr. Rose arrived, I felt as if I was just sitting in a room with a teacher but not learning diddlysquat.

I would go home every day with the same answer to my mother's question: "How are you, honey? Did you learn anything in school today?" I always replied with "NO." I know it may sound strange to tell your mom that you learned nothing at school, but it was the truth. I would go there and just eat or paint. Isn't that what kindergartners do? Am I right or wrong? Frankly, I'm surprised that we didn't have a naptime too!

To my dismay, they told us that we were going to have to suffer with him for the rest of the year. But that all changed when the teacher left. I think that was one of the happiest days of my life!

I remember sitting patiently in my chair, thinking about who the next teacher would be. All I knew was that he was coming from juvenile hall. Everyone mentioned a "Mr. Rose," but I had no idea who they were talking about since I had never been caught and placed in juvie. I just had random thoughts going through my head, wondering whether or not he was going to be a good teacher and just hoping—for all of our sakes—that he was going to teach us more than art education.

Sure enough, a smiling, jolly (and life-changing!) Mr. Gary Rose came struttin' in. From the moment he walked through that door to the second he opened his mouth and introduced himself, I knew I was going to like him. Within one week, I went from a teacher who didn't teach me anything to the most excellent teacher in my life. If anyone else has had him for a teacher, you have my guarantee that they'd say the same thing.

—Journal #5, 16-year-old female

I was expelled from Placer High School for truancy and fighting and I was sent to Alder Grove Community School before it became an academy. They had a teacher here who only had us do art stuff all day long. I think most of us hated it.

One day, Ms. M told us that our teacher was leaving and a new teacher was coming over from juvenile hall. None of us knew who the new teacher was, but we were ready for someone new. Ms. M said we would love him. We said, "We'll see."

The first day I walked in and saw him and heard him, I knew we would have a totally different teacher. His name was Mr. Rose and besides being a teacher, he also used to be a cop. He told us that he had heard about some of the problems at the school and that he had no idea how long he would be here. (He also said that we would not be doing art!)

After a few weeks, we realized that Mr. Rose was a no-nonsense kind of person. He was quick to jump on us if we started acting out and he also praised us when we performed as expected. But this was nothing compared to what was going to happen at the school after he returned from a trip to Russia. When he got back, he showed us pictures of a country we never heard of called Belarus. He had met his girlfriend there and she and her family took Mr. Rose to a part of the country where the Nazis had gathered up all of the townspeople and burned them alive.

I will always remember him saying that history must be studied since it tries to repeat itself. He talked about the skinheads he had had in juvenile hall and how he put them in a foxhole with a black soldier and how the other person's color, race, or religion did not matter as long as they stayed awake to protect each other.

–Journal #16, 17-year-old male

I was sent to the first Alder Grove Community School before it was a military school. I had been expelled for fighting and later I was accused of trying to extort money from another student. Whatever the circumstances were, I was expelled and sent to Alder Grove Community School.

When I first arrived there was an older teacher there who had been there for years but then she left. What followed was a string of teachers. Then one day

Ms. M told the class that the next day we would have a new teacher named Mr. Rose who was coming over from juvenile hall. I heard Fernando announce that he knew Mr. Rose and that we would really like him BUT be ready because he was a former police sergeant and did not tolerate people who did not give their all. I thought, "We shall see."

The next day, Mr. Rose showed up. In fact, he was already at school way before any of us and had our agenda printed on the board. Wow! We now had to do algebra, English, science, history, economics and he wrote, that "if we earned it," we would get P/E.[4]

Before I knew it, we were actually doing schoolwork and the time flew by. You had to pay attention because if he thought you weren't paying attention, he called on you. I had a hard time staying awake in class because I stayed up late the night before.

---

4 "PE" or "P/E" refers to "physical education," i.e., organized sports and exercise or some kind of recess outside.

The word got around to those students who had been cutting class that we had a no nonsense teacher and that they had better start showing up for class. He even told us the first day that he had been informed that there were a few trouble makers in the class and that once he found out who they were, they would be out of here. I don't know how he did it, but the next day after he made that statement, probation showed up and took a student away. It was like Mr. Rose was a man of his word.

–Journal #31, 16-year-old-male

I came into this world on the twenty-fifth of December—I'm a Christmas baby—but I feel I was cursed from the day I was born.

We had very little money while I was growing up. I always had to wear second-hand clothes. Sometimes I would wear the same clothes for two weeks before I would wash them. I took a lot of shit at school for being a poor, white-trash slob. I never had any real friends. I was the kid that had to run home after school so I wouldn't get beat up.

I was raised in the Auburn Greens—that's where they put all the trash that other cities and towns don't want. It was the perfect place for organized crime. The Mexican Mafia ran the drug movement through the Greens, and I saw drug use and gang violence on a daily basis.

When I was in the fourth grade, I was introduced to weed and alcohol. I loved it but I always wanted more, so I learned how to steal for profit so I could support myself. As time went on, I made decent pocket money and I started to dress nice. I learned that fear was a way to earn respect. Girls treated me better and I loved it.

By the sixth grade, I was getting high and fighting every day. For the first time in my life, I felt good about who I was. I can remember always getting drunk at the river with my cousin when I was eleven years old. We would go to different parties every night. I had so much fun. Sometimes, I would go days at a time without food or sleep.

I eventually started selling dope for the Mexican Mafia so I could supply my habit. I was making good money, but most of what I made went right back to them. When I was twelve years old, I started to rob houses. I was living the good life and for once I thought that I had *real* friends. I had it all—money, power, and a woman.

I got arrested five days after my thirteenth birthday because one of my so-called "friends" snitched on me for burglary. I served fifty days in juvenile hall. Because I was so small, I was put in with the little kids in C-Unit (A-Unit was for the big boys—the ones on their way to the California Youth Authority).

When I got out, I was placed on probation, given a 6:00 PM curfew and was drug-tested every week. I still smoked pot and dope every day. I fooled my probation officer for three months before I got caught for a dirty drug test.

During the time I was out, I tried to blow up a car with a pipe bomb because the owner owed me $5,000. As I was strapping the pipe bomb to the gas tank, the cops showed up and I had to run. I thought that I got away clean, but the cops found my fingerprints and I went back to juvenile hall. I got a good lawyer, though, so I only got sixty-five days.

I was out for ten days when I got arrested again. I went back to juvenile hall for robbery. This time, I had to do forty-five days in the hall. After that, I was locked up here and there for a few days at a time but I never got locked up for selling dope.

I was finally placed in R.A.F.T. (Rap Around Family Therapy). I was given five chances to get my life together, but I would smoke dope every night and I wasted my five chances pretty quickly. Not long after my fourteenth birthday, I was arrested for a dirty test for meth and I was sent to a juvenile detention facility called Fouts Springs for nine months.

—Journal #3, 17 year-old male

He who opens a school door, closes a prison.

–Victor Hugo, French author, poet,
and playwright (1802-1885).

CHAPTER 3

FROM ANIMALS TO CUPCAKES

I've played a number of roles in law enforcement over the years, but as well as I felt I did those jobs and as much as I enjoyed them, few things compared to the challenge of being a high school teacher for the kids I called the "A–Unit Animals" at the Placer County JDF.

These were older male juvenile delinquents. You never know if you can connect with high-risk students who are very manipulative. They will look you in the eye and say how thankful they are for all the help and education you have given them and then turn right around, commit a crime, and violate their probation.

Perhaps because of their youth, some crimes have more to do with self-sabotage than establishing a criminal record. One young man broke into one of our schools and got stuck in the air conditioning duct where the police and fire units rescued him. Another committed a home burglary and dropped his wallet inside the house.

Unfortunately, most juvenile criminal activities do not have amusing endings which might mark the end of a brief, errant streak. Instead, they often amount to repeated acts that include the sale or use of narcotics, car theft, weapons possession, burglary, arson, assault and battery and gang-related violence.

My A-Unit boys often continued to commit crimes after their release and were frequently returned, albeit involuntarily, to the hall in Auburn. Probation officers did not count these violations of probation as a new offense, but I did. When one of my students would return to the hall after promising me that he would not get in trouble again, I called him a liar as soon as he re-entered the classroom.

I am sure many of my colleagues in education would frown at such a tactic, but it worked more than once. When accused of lying, a student would hang his head and look at the floor instead of at me. With few exceptions, most would later apologize to me.

Of the other units at the JDF in Auburn, the two I was most involved with were the C-Unit and "Max."

Nicknamed the "Cupcake Unit," C-Unit housed females—most of whom loved the name–and younger, less sophisticated males. However, the girls in C-Unit were often in custody because they had committed crimes as serious as their A-Unit counterparts. I recall only three females joining the A-Unit boys for school. Though they had a teacher, they caused problems and had to be placed in the A-unit for their education.

Life outcomes for the girls were as unpredictable as for the boys. One young lady was in C-Unit for using morphine prescribed for her grandmother who was in hospice. The granddaughter had been expected to supervise its use for her grandmother. Fortunately, her deviant behavior amounted to a teenage hiccup and she went on to marry a submariner and have a family.

Another girl was in C-Unit for possession of cocaine. When she joined a California Conservation Corps fire unit, she received an award for bravery in a firestorm. Later though, she was convicted and sent to prison after being arrested when she acted as a "mule" for her drug-dealing boyfriend.

Hardcore and Sophisticated

Probation was pretty good at determining what males needed to be placed in C-Unit or A-Unit. Though we often referred to kids as "hardcore" or "sophisticated," they aren't always easy to distinguish.

I regard hardcore kids as those who are destined for prison. Many are gang members or come from a family where one or more relations are serving time. Hardcore delinquents expect to spend their adult life incarcerated and seldom care how many charges result from beating up someone they dislike. Their alpha male dominance is all-important.

Sophisticated describes those alpha males who are bullies or predators in relation to the weaker, more naïve boys. The latter are in custody for stupid crimes like shoplifting, petty theft, or hitting a teacher. Because the alpha males don't want additional charges brought against them, they often manipulate the less experienced offenders to commit a crime on their behalf.

As "bad" as they were, the boys in A-Unit couldn't compete with the Max-Unit which housed the most violent and hardened offenders regardless of their sex. Their offenses included rape, child molestation, armed robbery, home invasion, attempted murder, assault with a deadly weapon, major drug deals, kidnapping and felony assault among others. Each delinquent had his own room containing a toilet and sink. There was a common area outside of these cells that doubled as a "dayroom" and the classroom. At times, the Max unit became the unit to house those who were extremely ill, pregnant girls, suicidal individuals, and those kids who would be assaulted if housed in general housing.

Nurture and Discipline

I have always admired Principal Joe Clark and the way he turned around East Side High School, but it was one of his quotes that I not only firmly believe in, but also followed at all three academies. That quote of *"discipline is not an enemy of enthusiasm"* is so true, and became the foundation for our academies operating under the principles of order, structure and discipline.

When I first worked at the hall, students were allowed to lay on blankets in the classroom and would sleep instead of doing their classwork. I believed they played on the softness of some of the well-meaning teachers who treated them as younger and more innocent children who should be nurtured.

I didn't necessarily disagree with my peers' analysis— many of these kids had been abandoned or were abused. They desperately needed love and attention. But I also believed that nurture without age-appropriate discipline and consistent expectations of behavioral adjustments condemned at-risk kids to an at-risk adulthood.

So I put a stop to laying on blankets on the floor and to sleeping during class. If they did not do the work I assigned, I sent them to their rooms, denied them physical exercise with the rest of the class, and wrote a letter to the court.

That got their attention.

The Great Debate

As a substitute teacher for the Alternative Education Department at PCOE, my friend and fellow teacher of delinquents, Paul McDaniel, was often in charge of the Cupcake Unit while I taught the A-Unit and Max-Unit boys.

Paul and I had become close friends and confidants. While my background was in law enforcement, Paul had been a sergeant with the United States Air Force and served in Vietnam on three occasions. Our similar career experiences led to similar educational philosophies. We both believed that by integrating consistent disciplinary measures with a challenging academic routine, many of the nation's at-risk teens could learn to be accountable for their lives.

During one summer at the hall, we decided to demonstrate just how academically capable the kids could be and have some fun at the same time. We agreed to hold a debate between my Animals (A-Unit) and the Cupcake Unit (C-Unit). Food tends to motivate kids that age so we promised that the winning team would enjoy a feast of sandwiches and drinks. To pay for the food and other expenses, the probation office requested donations from Placer County public defenders and private attorneys who had represented some of the kids.

In the enclosed exercise yard, we set up a long table for each team. Before the debate, the girls learned that the boys had made a poster to stretch across the front of their table stating "A-Unit Animals." Not to be outdone, the girls made a poster identifying themselves as the "Cupcake Unit." The local press showed up, as did some attorneys, the Juvenile Justice Department, and members of the probation office.

Each unit had over 150 historical events to remember including issues surrounding each event. The audience soon realized that the kids loved showing off what they knew. While the debate was in progress, a probation officer approached one of the best female debaters and told her that she had to leave the debate because she was due to be released immediately. Instead of leaving, the young woman requested that the probation officer contact her parents and the court to request permission to *stay locked up* until the debate was over. Fortunately, permission was granted.

A teaching assistant in the Cupcake Unit had kept track of the points and announced that the girls had won by one-half point. But in the midst of the girls celebrating their victory, someone calculated the points again and discovered that the boys had won instead.

At first the boys wanted to claim victory, fearing that they were being cheated. But Paul and I persuaded them to be gracious about the mistake and that we were all winners. Their grumbling subsided considerably when they realized that we had ordered enough sandwiches and drinks for both the winners and losers.

Later, I found out that a local reporter had taken twenty of the debate questions back to her office and quizzed her "educated" co-workers for the answers. They only got three right.

Painful as it may be, a significant emotional event can be the catalyst for choosing a direction that serves us–and those around us–more effectively. Look for the learning.

–Louisa May Alcott, American novelist and poet, author of "Little Women" (1832-1888).

CHAPTER 4

JOURNALS–WHERE WE COME FROM

The first time I ever did Triple C, me and my homeboy was just kicking it, smoking some herb.[5] He asked me if I had ever done Skittles. I said no, so we went and stole a box of them and a bottle of whisky. We popped the pills and drank the whole bottle. What I did that night was what I was missing my whole life. On Triple C, *I was God*.

---

5   For the uninitiated, Triple C is also known as Coreciden HPB, an addictive over the counter drug. See "Triple C, Addictive Cold Medicine, Being Abused by Teens," Jason Knowles and Barb Markoff, ABC 7, Eyewitness News, November 25, 2014.

I could steal anything, talk my way out of anything, and I didn't really have to sleep.

Me and my buddies found this abandoned house where we could keep all our stolen shit, smoke and party. I was never home after that—it was like I was always fighting with my family anyway. I was popping pills, smoking, and getting wasted pretty much every day. I had more alcohol than I needed, but I just kept stealing more.

I was tripping really bad on all the drugs one day because I had taken at least forty-five—maybe more. I remember I pretty much woke up in Taco Tree over by 84 Lumber. I took more drugs while my buddy went to buy two super-nachos. Me and another friend weren't hungry, so we walked up to 84 Lumber to use their phone. The guy who was working there was being hella cool—he knew I was tripping bad. I told my friends that they could leave because I was gonna call my mom and she'd pick me up, but I knew I wasn't gonna call her.

I called a buddy whose house was right nearby. He said I could go ahead and walk over to his place and chill in his room. He came home later with this kid—we called him "Ass Master." When I was looking at him, he turned into a big fat weasel. I got hella scared of him. Then I decided that I wanted to go to my buddy's house in the Greens, which is through Chana Park.

I told my other buddies I wasn't gonna go with them. I tried to make it to the Greens, but suddenly I couldn't walk. I somehow made it to one friend's house and he pretty much carried my ass all the way through the park.

When I got to my other friend's house in the Greens, I chilled there for a while. His mom knew what kind of shit I was doing and she knew everything that was up with my mom. I chilled there some more and then called my mom and she came and got me.

My life was all fun—it was all a big rush. But I finally got caught. Now, I'm trying to get my life back together.

–Journal #8, 17-year-old male

Back when I was a freshman in high school, I was a good student and I got everything done. Then, in my sophomore year, I started messing around with drugs, including Vicodin and Ecstasy. I have been clean for about eight months, but alcohol has been a big thing for me.

I got introduced to alcohol as a freshman and I got very drunk at age fourteen. My brother (who is two years older than me) drank too. We began drinking together—Wild Turkey, straight up.

When I was fifteen years old, I was messing around with a matchbook and some matches. I started a grass fire—the flames got out of hand and I couldn't stop it. The cops rolled up and then the fire trucks came. I got arrested for arson. They took me to city hall and fingerprinted me, then they called my parents.

I don't get along with my parents. I live with my dad and my dad's girlfriend. I feel like my dad's girlfriend hates me. They have a daughter, who is my half-sister. She's seven. My brother is twenty-one now and he's already out of the house. I think my dad's girlfriend wants to kick me out so that they can have their own little family. I don't even have a job or any transportation...

–Journal #11, 17-year-old male

My dad is in prison. He's been gone since I was twelve years old. He was arrested for trying to rape my sister. I live with my mother now. She has to work seven days a week just to support us.

I first did drugs when I was thirteen. I got the drugs from friends. I did marijuana, crystal meth, and cocaine but I have been clean for two years. I was also first arrested at age thirteen—for disturbing the peace. I threw popcorn on the floor at school. The vice-principal was called and he told me to pick it up. I said, "Fuck you. I'm not doing shit for you." I was sent to juvenile hall for a couple of hours.

The second time I was arrested it was for hitting the same vice-principal. I went back to school, but a couple of days later I got in trouble with the vice-principal *again*. I was on a bus and the vice-principal told me that I had to get off. I said, "Fuck you. I'm not going with you." I got up and smashed him in the face and spit on him. I was expelled. Most of my arrests have been for assault and battery and they were gang-related.

When I got out of juvenile hall, I started hanging out with the wrong people—gang members. I got drugs from them. The next thing I knew, I was a gang member, too. I hung out with them when they shot, stabbed and jumped people.

I don't like being a gang member. My mom really wants me to quit. I've been thinking about leaving but I worry that if I quit the gang, they will go after me or my family.

—Journal #9, 17-year-old Latino

Fouts Springs was considered the hardest locked boot camp facility in California. There were five white boys, fifteen Mexicans, and ninety-five blacks. When I was there, I considered myself a peckerwood. I was a skinny white kid and I didn't like blacks. Even though I only weighed 105 pounds, I was involved in a physical confrontation every day. I had no friends in the camp, but then one day a black kid actually saved me from getting jumped. From then on, I realized that I could like some blacks.

I dropped out of that camp after four months due to bad behavior. It was probably the hardest four months of my life. I was placed back in the hall and stayed in the A-Unit for three months before I was sent Camp Singer—another boot camp—for six months to a year. After seven months, I was eligible to graduate from Singer, but I didn't have a home to go back to, so I was placed in a foster home instead.

After just twelve hours, my new foster parents decided I wasn't welcome in their house. They felt that I was going to corrupt their family. It didn't matter, though, since I was arrested yet again and sent to a group home in Tahoe for one year.

I only stayed in Tahoe for three months. I would sneak out every night and get drunk. When the summer came to an end, I ran from Tahoe and I went back to my hometown of Auburn. I tracked down my girlfriend and I went to stay with her in Rocklin for a little while. I got back to smoking dope every day. I started to go off the deep end—and fast.

My girlfriend and I got into it over my drug use, so I left and moved back to Auburn. I ran into a friend of mine and he said I could stay with him but I had to quit smoking dope first. So I did stop for a while, but I started up again and was smoking weed and drinking all day, every day.

I was trying to stay out of custody long enough to spend the holidays with my family, but in December I was arrested by the Placer County Sheriff's Department. I was 16 years old. I was sent to Camp Singer for the second time. I completed the program in six months—with flying colors— and I was finally allowed to return home.

Once I got back home, I started drinking every night again like a fool. I thought that I was trading one evil for a lesser evil since I had given up dope for alcohol. I would steal so I could drink more. I got real drunk one day and came up with this bright idea about how to get some money. I stole a Sacramento Bee newspaper stand. Some guy watched me put the stand into the car and called the cops.

In September, I had to go before the judge yet again. I was told to go home and come back the following week to serve twenty days. I got off easy this time and felt I had to celebrate my good luck. So, I went out and stole a bottle of Captain Morgan. I got caught by a UPS driver who took down my license plate number. The cops pulled me over and arrested me at gunpoint. This stunt got me locked up for another eight months—this was on top of my twenty days. I got out two weeks before summer break.

The first day I got out, I went to a meeting with Narcotics Anonymous. I wanted something different this time around. I would go to a meeting every day and it worked for a little while, but then I would start to drink again. We had a birthday party for one of my friends and everyone was drinking and having fun, so I had to have at least one beer. Then I had another, and another, and so on. From that day on, I was drinking every day.

–Journal #3, 17-year-old male

Every morning I wake up with my mother yelling at me. I know she means well—she only yells at me so I can get my life straightened out.

My stepdad is a different story. He's an alcoholic jackass and I hate him with all of my heart. He verbally abuses my mother on a daily basis. Every day after work, he goes to the bar down the street from our house and drinks for about three hours. Afterwards, he comes home and treats everyone like shit. Every time I see him, I want to beat the crap out of him because of the way he treats my mom and the rest of us.

He is the reason I get up so early and come to school. He's also the reason I don't go home until ten or eleven at night. I just don't want to be at home when he's awake—I don't want to deal with his shit.

So, because of him, I am often out on the street and having a great time. Every day is like a big party for me and my friends—and until I reach what Mr. Rose calls "rock bottom," that is the way it is going to be. Just going around, looking for a party, looking for a babe…that's pretty much my life right now. I think Mr. Rose is right—only *you* can decide if you want to clean up your act.

–Journal #22, 17-year-old male

I was expelled from E.V. Cain Middle School. I had been in the bathroom, talking on my cell phone with a friend, before school started. I was calling another friend, telling her to come to school, when the bell rang, so I had to hang up my phone and go to class.

When I went in to my first period class, my teacher said that the vice-principal wanted to see me in his office right away. I had a feeling it was something bad. I went to his office and when I sat down, he told me that I was on in-school suspension.

I asked him why and he said that because I hadn't come in for after-school detention, I was now on in-school suspension—whatever the hell *that* was.

So, I was sent to ALC (that's a class for bad kids). I had to sit in a cubby. I couldn't turn around or stand up or I would get into trouble. Later, at lunch, I had to walk down to the cafeteria with a teacher because I had to eat with her. She was the person that was watching me. A couple of minutes later, two of my girlfriends came up to me and said that they were also in trouble with the vice-principal. They said that he was going to call the police and that they would probably have to go to juvenile hall because they had drugs on them.

I told them that they could say it was all my fault and they agreed. I realize now that what I said was a mistake but I wanted them to like me. Sure enough, the vice-principal called me in and had me give him all of my stuff.

A police officer came to the school. He asked me a lot of questions, and I answered them all. I was surprised because the officer left me alone for about twenty minutes. Then he came back in, took out his handcuffs and told me I was under arrest. I was scared. Tears started running down my face and I was shaking. I knew this was the biggest mistake I'd ever made but we always learn from our mistakes, right?

The cop took me and one of my girlfriends to juvenile hall. A probation officer separated us and I got searched by a female probation officer. Then I had my picture taken—first my left side, then my right side, then I looked straight ahead.

The probation officer also scanned my hand and fingers. After that, the probation officer took my shoes and socks and they put me in a small room by myself. It was very cold there. Later, I got to call my mom so that she could pick me up. She did not come for a long time, so I had to stay in juvie for seven hours. I was *so* happy to see my mom.

Three days later, my mom and dad and I went to E.V. Cain to see if I was suspended or expelled. I asked when I could come back to school and they said, "Not until January."

My parents tried to homeschool me. It only lasted for one month. My parents regretted making the choice of homeschool because I got up and walked around whenever I wanted to. Sometimes I did my assigned work, but I mostly hung around outside. I really pissed off my parents, but I didn't care.

–Journal #13, 15-year-old Latina

Education is our only political safety.
Outside of this ark all is deluge.

–Horace Mann, American educational reformer
dedicated to modernizing U.S. society (1796-1859).

CHAPTER 5

WE ALL BLEED

It was November, 2005. After working for several months, I'd finally agreed to much-needed knee surgery. While inserting a breathing tube down my throat before surgery, the anesthesiologist had discovered that my vocal cords were inflamed. I wasn't surprised since my voice had become quite raspy. She urged me to give my voice a break while I recovered from knee surgery. As a classroom teacher of twenty high-risk juvenile offenders, I didn't bother to ask how I was supposed to go to work and not raise my voice.

Still, I had no choice but to stay at home and be quiet for a few days since I couldn't walk without crutches. Paul McDaniel, a close friend and our primary substitute teacher for Alternative Education at the hall, stopped by to see how I was doing recovery wise.

He was also there to discuss what we'd do for the kids housed at the juvenile hall facility over Christmas. Inspite of our law enforcement and military backgrounds, we believed that everyone, no matter how callous or hardened, is always a little bit of a kid during the holidays. Even when we were confident that particular JDF teens would end up in prison later in life, it saddened us to see them incarcerated over the holidays and not even receive visits from friends and family.

So Paul and I had played the parts of Santa and his elf, respectively, for a number of years at the local JDF. With a year-round white beard, Paul was a natural as Santa and I always enjoyed seeing how delighted students were to see me dressed as Santa's elf.

Santa and his elf would enter the room with a cart holding Christmas treats, and then Santa (Paul) would ask if the kids had been naughty or nice. Then, acting surprised in his realization that the kids were in the JDF, would say, "Hey, wait a minute…why are you guys in here?"

Pretending that we were embarrassed about being in the JDF with "bad" kids, Santa and I would head for the door while the kids laughed at Santa's mistake. But Paul and I would stop at the threshold and, with some help from JDF staff, start serving egg-nog, root-beer floats, ice cream, cake, and candy. We'd also give them some inexpensive gifts including books, puzzles and some table games that could be used by all the students for their break times. What is most powerful is that the kids have always remembered our effort. As older teens and adults, they have thanked both of us time and again.

While we talked about our Christmas Eve routine, we half-watched and listened to the morning television news and, in particular, for any news about the murder of a California Highway Patrolman the day before. Thirty-seven years old and a 16-year veteran of the highway patrol, Officer Andy

Stevens had been working a stretch of road near Woodland, California when he'd pulled two vehicles over. A farmer on a tractor watched as Officer Stevens waved the first vehicle on and approached the second. According to the farmer, shortly after the officer reached the driver's side of the vehicle, a shot rang out and Stevens fell to the ground. The car raced away. Stevens died immediately, a bullet through his head.

Officer Stevens' murder was on both our minds. Although Paul and I were dedicated to helping troubled kids make better choices, we also want the bad guys caught and punished, especially when they kill cops who are just doing their job.

Law enforcement was in my family's blood. My uncle was an officer with the Pleasanton Police Department in California. After hearing stories about his work I was inspired to join. My brother, three cousins, son and daughter were or are in law enforcement. My sister was the secretary for a local chief of police.

Though I was no longer a cop and didn't know Officer Stevens, my law enforcement background as well as that of my family made his death personal. Among those of us who are or were committed to law enforcement, when one cop bleeds, we all bleed.

"We have a breaking news item concerning the killing of CHP Officer Andy Stevens." The broadcaster's words cut through my conversation with Paul. "Two individuals have been taken into custody in the parking lot of a hotel in the City of Rocklin."

Who's the idiot, I wondered? A picture of a handcuffed young man with a shaved head appeared on the screen. Two anxious looking cops were on either side of him.

The broadcaster went on. "The police have identified the alleged shooter and his girlfriend—"

I didn't hear anything more. "Oh shit!" I said. "Is that who I think it is?"

"Sure enough," Paul said.

I felt sick. One of my former students had been arrested for the murder of a cop.

What we learn from others becomes
our own reflection.

–Ralph Waldo Emerson, American
essayist and poet (1803-1882).

CHAPTER 6

JOURNALS–FAMILY TIES

I never get too close to anyone because I am scared that they'll leave me like my dad did. I'm scared that someone will act mad at me and kick me down the stairs like my dad did. I'm scared that when I *do* get close to someone, they'll turn on me. I believe that everyone's insecurities and doubts come from their childhood. If traumatic things happen to a person when they're little, it affects how they grow up. It affects how they treat other people. It affects what they believe and how they live their lives.

When I was around six years old, my mom and dad separated. I don't exactly remember why or how it happened, but I do remember a few things. One day, when my mom and I got home, we noticed that our front door was slightly open. We walked in and found that the house had been completely trashed. Lamps were broken, chairs were thrown across the room, and picture frames were shattered into a million pieces.

My dad had this skateboard that he really cherished—it was broken in half and stuck into the wall. There was honey all over the kitchen floor and eggs had been cracked open and left on the kitchen counter. We went upstairs and saw that my mom's bed was slashed in a million different places. There were feathers everywhere. Nothing had been stolen—everything was just trashed. Everything was a mess except for me and my sister's room. It was spotless. Even though I was only six, I knew it was my dad who did it.

After all that, my mom, my sister, and I moved into an apartment that was on the third story. By now, I was in the first grade and suddenly my life changed forever. I had gone to a friend's house after school—something I did every day. We jumped on his trampoline for a while, then his mother came out and told me that my mom had had an accident. I didn't understand what was going on at the time. Things are still kind of a blur. They took me to the hospital and I went in to see my mom. Everyone said that she only had a broken arm, but she was just lying there in a hospital bed and she wouldn't wake up. I was confused and no one told me anything. She finally woke up a few days later, but she couldn't talk, walk, or even move.

My grandma came down and took care of me and my sister. My mom came home in a wheelchair a while later. Because I was so young, I didn't know what to think. As I got older, I learned that the part of her brain that controls her motor function is slowly deteriorating. She went to the Mayo Clinic a few years back but they found nothing. I guess we'll never know.

We've lived with my mother's disability for almost eleven years now. She talks like she is basically drunk and she has to walk with a walker. She also shakes really bad when she tries to concentrate or write. She's doing well, though, and I still love her.

–Journal #10, 17-year-old female

I grew up in Southern California. My dad passed away two weeks before my first birthday—he was in a car accident while driving home from work. My mother raised me all by herself with the exception of two boyfriends she has had since my father passed away. As far back as I can remember, it was me, my mom and my sister living in a small townhouse. We lived there for the first fifteen years of my life.

When I was younger, I played every sport you can imagine, and I always made the All-Star teams for baseball and basketball. I started having problems when I was in the third grade. There were four of us who always hung out together, and we always seemed to get into trouble. One of my friends was a redneck. We always tried to fight the Mexicans. People probably thought we were racists. Every lunch, we would go over to the field and stare them down. We acted like we owned the school. By the fifth grade, we actually started to fight them. We thought we were tough if we beat them down.

I started smoking pot in the eighth grade. By the end of the year, I was snorting cocaine in the bathroom between classes. One day me and my friends got loaded with cocaine. We were walking through a neighborhood, looking for a house to rob. We found a random house that had about three days' worth of newspapers piled up in the driveway. We went around the back to break in but we found an open window. We all got inside the house and checked it out to make sure no one was home. No one was, so we went upstairs to see what kind of valuable stuff might be there. The house was a pig sty. One room had porno magazines stacked from the floor to the ceiling. Then we found about $10,000 worth of watches.

Okay, I will finish this another day. I need to go outside and get rid of some anger.

—Journal #20, 17-year-old male

My life is sometimes a deep struggle, but my parents are the best. My mom is very encouraging and supports me. She has always been there for me, even when I fucked up. She's been depressed throughout most of my life—for reasons that I didn't understand until now. She had stress with work and with me constantly disobeying her. She was also fighting with my dad a lot. They are on their way to a divorce, which seems like the best move for them. They seem happier now.

My dad is a real tough guy. He told me his life story and how he had a hard time with gangs, family problems, and drugs. I didn't have a hard time like he did. Everything that happened to me has already happened to him, so he knows how it feels.

He's a hell of a hard worker and he pushes me to do better, but he isn't a very loving guy—he was raised differently. When I disobey him, I get knocked around. My dad can be really helpful sometimes, though. He gives hella good advice to me and my friends. He was a Blood (gang member) at one point in his life and he will tell it to you like it is.

—Journal #12, 17-year-old Black male

My mom and dad are both drunks and when they leave for work, I just help myself. They never notice that some of the alcohol is missing since they probably think the other one drank it.

My mom and dad fight a lot. Usually it is after they are drinking. Sometimes they leave me in charge of my baby sister and they go to the bar. Then they come home shit faced and start to fight. A lot of times I am already asleep because I am drunk or got a hold of some pot. They start to yell so loud that it wakes me and my sister up. Then my dad swears at my mom as he goes out the door and drives off. He already has one DUI and I hope sometimes that the cops will arrest him again and force him to go to counseling. He won't change anyway.

–Journal #32, 16 year-old male

You know, a lot has happened since I've been here. Like way back when I ran a mile in 6:36 seconds and now we run 2-3 miles a week. It sucks, I hate running. We are in the 2nd quarter now and report cards just came out. Listen to this, we had to take a three- hour exam. It was hard, and my home life sucks because I live in a trailer way out in Colfax. I'm away from all of my friends but it's ok because I can see them at school or call them. I also have a girlfriend now and I like her a lot. Sometimes I feel like just giving up. I have until next month to see if I can go back to my old school. I don't know if I want too and I might just stick it out here.

I do hate the army getting in our faces and everything I do just seems to get me angry, but I know they are doing it to help me for when I become an adult. I like Mr. Rose and everything and I still love this school. I guess I am all mixed up inside.

Every Thursday, Tom Grayson comes in and he is really cool. I like him a lot. He too, gets in everyone's face but we all know that he, Mr. Rose and the army wants us to have some coping skills especially those of us with anger issues.

I've met a lot of people here, even a close friend, Sabrina. We all came here for different reasons. Mine is pretty easy since I just need to pay a fine.

Mr. Rose is trying to get the county to pay for a field trip down to San Jose to see the Winchester Mystery House. That would be great since I have heard all the stories of the house and seen Mr. Rose's video.

Mr. Rose just gave us an assignment in which we must listen to the lyrics of the song *Eve of Destruction* and we have to find out who it was written by, sang by, when it was published, and what the lyrics mean.

Whoever wins will go with Mr. Rose to a 5-star restaurant. It is going to be cool. I sure hope I can win. We also just completed our CPR training and got a new metal for our uniforms. I was excited to learn how to save people.

I will always remember that will doing the test on the dummies, Mr. Rose would joke with us that if he ever needed CPR, he wanted us to just let him die…then he would start to laugh.

–Journal #37–16 year old male

The things which hurt, instruct.

−Benjamin Franklin, American statesman, scientist and philosopher (1706-1790).

CHAPTER 7

YOU CAN'T SAVE EVERYONE

"You can't save everyone," Paul reminded me after we learned about Brendt Volarvich's arrest. I knew he was right–I'd said the same thing to Joan Berry, the Director of the Alternative Education Department and our supervisor, not too long before. She was always concerned about the welfare of all of our students, almost to a fault. I used to joke with her that she never met a felon she didn't think she could save.

If I'm honest with myself, though, I was as hopeful as Joan. I suspect I started using the phrase to help swallow my failure to bond with some kids. You think you have them on the right path, they promise they've changed, and then they commit another crime.

Then why was I so distressed about Brendt? Why be surprised? Was it because a law enforcement officer was the victim?

I have attended two cop funerals and no matter how hardened you think you are, you get choked up, especially seeing those family members left behind. Because I belonged to an elite family of law enforcement, there was no doubt it cut more deeply. Usually, I condemn any asshole who senselessly shoots down any officer and firmly believe that hell is too good for the killer. It should have been no different when I heard about Officer Stevens' death except for one crucial fact.

I'd had an opportunity to help the killer change his life.

When you know these kids by name, by voice, by the bravado and bull-shit they use to disguise their fears, sometimes you think you just might be the one who can reach at least a few of them. After all, you're not their bad parent—a druggie or convict, absent, indifferent, mentally unstable, or abusive. And you're not the decent parent who is beset by poverty or illness and lacks the time to monitor the same child he is trying desperately to feed.

But perhaps I had never known enough about Brendt.

Although he had accumulated an impressive list of offenses by the time we met at the hall, he hadn't stood out as irredeemable. At sixteen, most of his incarceration was based on "VOP," violation of probation by using drugs or alcohol. Sure, I stood over his desk while lecturing the class, stood close enough to grab him by the shoulders and try to warn him of what might lay ahead. But I wasn't in the business of corporeal punishment even in a juvenile hall classroom.

There was more that bothered me about Brendt and it was the very thing that should have given us a reason to bond. His father, Dennis Volarvich, had been a cop.

Years before, Dennis had left the Los Altos Police Department and was hired by the Santa Clara County District Attorney's office. He was forced to resign after having an affair with the widow of a murder victim. He then worked as a private investigator for four years. When Brendt was only twelve, Dennis attempted to rob a Bank of America branch in Fremont, California. After a forty minute police standoff, he shot himself.[6]

All cops hear stories in the news about rogue cops, and we know how it tarnishes law enforcement and causes society to distrust our profession. Still, members of law enforcement have to police each other and not hesitate to see to it that bad apples are removed from the profession. I recall seeing and reading the news about Dennis and wondering how a cop could become so bad.

Though I tried to draw Brendt out about his feelings in regard to his father and the tragic end to Dennis' life, he never opened up to me. Looking back on it, I believe he had repressed that pain. I recall that he rarely laughed but was never angry, either. Although he didn't cause any problems, he did not want to be engaged in the classroom or even participate in sports. He did just enough to get by and was a ward who seemed older than most of the other kids in the unit.

Brendt had mystified me and I now knew what I'd only suspected before—that I'd never made an impression that could compare to the devil that drove him. He probably regarded my effort to bond as substantial as smoke. With the benefit of hindsight, I believe he knew he was going in the wrong direction and clearly understood that his actions had consequences, but he no longer cared.

---

6 http://www.sfgate.com/news/article/Ex-Cop-Kills-Himself-After-Bank-Robbery-Former-2818394.php

Until the day he was arrested, I had believed that my "old school" educational philosophy would eventually get the attention of other educators and show them that discipline does work. As confident as I'd been that I could usually tell who had a chance to change their life and who did not, I had to admit that my confidence had been misplaced when it came to Brendt. I should have pushed harder to break down his walls, to show him that there was something worth caring about. Now, a good man was dead and his wife was a widow. And though Brendt deserved whatever punishment the state bestowed, his life was now cut short as well.

How could I boast that my approach to troubled teens was best when one of my kids had gone out and murdered a fellow police officer? I'd had a lot of careers in my life but I had taken teaching as seriously as I'd taken any.

For the first time in years, I wondered if I should quit teaching at-risk kids. Who was I to think I could make a difference?

You Do What You Can

"Mr. Rose," one of my students said when I entered the A-Unit classroom at the hall a few days later, "did you hear about Volarvich?"

Limping slightly but glad to be without my crutches, I nodded and walked slowly to my desk where I placed my briefcase. I could envision exactly where Brendt used to sit. Then, I hadn't been sure if he was listening or scheming about what he wanted to do when he got out. Now I knew I'd been right to doubt where his mind had been.

Officer Stevens' murder had released a tsunami of questions that I wasn't prepared to answer. Did I want to be here anymore? Did I have any more energy to give to kids who often continued to commit crimes? Could I still make a difference or was this one tragic event telling me that I'd lost both the battle and the war? I didn't need the money and the pay wasn't that great in Placer County anyway. As I had over the weekend, I got upset. But this time I had an audience.

I have a speech I give every class about the broken or dysfunctional homes they might be coming from. The theme is clear and direct—deal with it. After Officer Stevens' death and Brendt's failure to deal with his family's problems, I repeated this speech with new urgency. I told them that although they did not get a chance to decide who their parents would be, they had to deal with it or society would deal with them once they were eighteen.

As adults, they would not be given the breaks they had received as juveniles. And whether they knew Brendt or not, I used him as an example of someone whose failure to deal with his father's mistakes became his excuse for messing up his own life. I reminded them that they had to strive to be better people for themselves and those they loved without excuses. And if they wanted children, did they want to give those children the type of life they were leading or something better?

Finally, I admitted to my A-Unit animals that I wasn't sure they were worth the time.

How long I stood on my soap box I don't know, but my students soon answered the questions that were haunting me. It was my turn to listen and be reminded why I'd taken them on in the first place. Several of them asked me not to give up on them just because Brendt screwed up. They reminded me of how many of their parents had given up on them—how could I do the same?

I looked around the room knowing that most came from dysfunctional families where either one or both of their parents were in prison, had abandoned them, or was economically destitute, sick or dead. Whatever guardian was left did not know how to hold their ward accountable without being too authoritarian, making them into an unsupervised buddy, or ignoring them.

Many had no one in their lives who gave a damn about them. Their role models were the so-called celebrities they saw on television, heard on the radio or reached out to on social media–the misogynists and violent rappers, the overpaid sports and movie stars, and sex symbols who rotated through expensive drug treatment programs.

No, you can't save them all but you don't give up either. You do what you can.

I decided to stay. As Joe Montana once said, he would quit when he stopped having fun. I was still having fun.

The surest test of discipline is its absence.

—CLARA BARTON, PIONEERING NURSE WHO FOUNDED
THE AMERICAN RED CROSS (1821-1912).

CHAPTER 8

A MESSAGE FROM DEATH ROW TO AT-RISK TEENS

By Brendt Volarvich, San Quentin Prison, Death Row, November 17, 2014

I was one of Mr. Gary Rose's students when I was in the Placer County Juvenile Hall and I'm now on California's Death Row. This letter was *completely* my idea to write to you–Mr. Rose's students and other at-risk teens. I want to tell any teenager who will listen how important it is that you change your lives for the better.

Nine years ago today, I made the worst series of choices I've ever made and ended another man's life as well as my own. Wish it could've been the other way around–that Officer Stevens got me instead. I know that's a strange statement to hear but it's the truth and it's much preferable to this prison. I know, now that my head is clear, that the man I shot wasn't trying to kill me. He didn't deserve to have me kill him.

You see, I feel guilty for what I did, but I can live with the guilt because it's like it happened to another person. I don't view the "me" who's writing this letter, the "me" Mr. Rose and others knew at the juvenile hall, as having killed a man.

When I was spun out on meth,[7] especially when I'd been awake more than seven to ten days, I became someone else, something else–a whole other guy took over, one who didn't have the morals or code of honor I like to believe I do have.

My childhood was good until I screwed it up. Things started going wrong before my father died. I had already begun to experiment with drugs, weed, meth and Ritalin plus smoking cigarettes. When I was twelve, my father, who had been a cop, killed himself after he committed a crime. Looking back, I think I shut down emotionally. I really started screwing up, acting out, whatever. Drug use became normal for me. My brother followed in my footsteps. My mom barely survived it initially, then pulled it together for our sakes. I don't know how she did it, but she did.

Following the last time I left the hall, I tried to join the Marine Corps. They were willing to take me but I had to get my juvenile record sealed by a judge. The judge was the same judge who had sentenced me for one of my last juvenile offenses. He didn't like me. The judge told the Marine officer that he would only seal my record if I did a whole year without getting in trouble.

I only lasted a month or two out before I was caught committing my first adult felony. When I look back at it now,

---

7 "Meth" is methamphetamine, a man-made chemical.

it was as if I was on a collision course with death or prison. I couldn't give up the meth and the life that comes with it.

Later, after getting arrested for killing Officer Stevens, I didn't feel much of anything until I sobered up and slept for two weeks straight.

Then it hit me like a ton of bricks. Being charged with murder sucked. I wanted to explain that I didn't mean to kill Officer Stevens. I simply panicked, thinking he was trying to kill me. In my mind it was self-defense. You keep thinking you'll wake up and it'll all be a bad dream. Then you come to accept it. At least I do because I'm adaptable to bad situations. Lots of practice.

Only after I started my prison term did I learn how drugs and alcohol severely restrict blood flow to centers of the brain that control or affect empathy, impulse control, and decision making. By using meth, my brain chemistry was affected and irreversibly changed. Though I now understand how badly meth screwed my life up, it's no surprise that nine years later, I still crave meth.

This is not an excuse. I'm not saying I wasn't to blame. I was. I chose to carry a gun while dangerously paranoid and delusional. I'm not asking for no punishment for what I did—I wrongly killed an innocent man—but because of the meth, I never planned to murder him.

Being sentenced to death was a relief. But before I face the executioner, I've had to face life on Death Row.

This place really gets to you. It's been three years since I got to hug my mother, before that it was five years. You're surrounded by sickos, sociopaths and psychopaths. You have to always be on guard, you can't trust anyone. The only good thing here is that there is never a cell mate living with you on Death Row which is just fine by me! I don't think I could live with another guy, especially if it was a child rapist or a rapist in general. I absolutely abhor people like that.

I hate the choices and decisions I've got to make in this so called "life" I live behind prison walls. But I put myself here, so I can only blame my own dumb-ass self. If I could, I'd volunteer to be executed this very day. Death is preferable to life in prison, especially in this unit.

If I could get you and other teens like you to listen, I'd tell you this.

Don't turn away from your parents, teachers, and loved ones! Take it from a guy who's been in your exact spot or worse. Those who are trying to help save you are right. You are headed for prison, rehab, death, and misery. It's only a matter of time.

I know how you think. You think that you're different, that it won't happen like that for you. But you're not invincible or immune to drugs and the life of crime or "the Game." It will bring misery and heartache to you, your family, friends, and loved ones—supreme unhappiness. Believe me. I know.

PART II

STAND AND DELIVER

If you are planning for a year, sow rice; if you are planning for a decade, plant trees; if you are planning for a lifetime, educate people.

—CHINESE PROVERB

CHAPTER 9

BLUEPRINT FOR AN ACADEMY

In April 2007, my supervisor, Joan Berry, requested that I meet with her after school. I had no knowledge as to the subject matter but suspected that I might be scolded for something related to my classroom methods which many other teachers and administrators questioned.

About three months before, Joan had asked me to join her and two other teachers for a visit to Mather Academy, a public, boot-camp style school for troubled teens in a neighboring county.

Joan and I were both impressed from the moment we saw a cadet raising the flag outside the Mather Academy. The teachers were civilians but two former U.S. Army personnel handled the discipline and physical training. They, like the commander of the school, wore traditional green camouflage uniforms. The cadets wore the same uniforms but the other teachers did not.

When we entered the classrooms to observe, I was struck by the level of student engagement. I noticed that the cadets turned to stare at us for only a few seconds before they returned their attention to their teacher. After class, I asked to speak to a female student with corporal stripes. It was striking that as soon as she approached us, she stood at attention. After I instructed her to be "at ease," she relaxed her posture and enthusiastically answered our questions about Mather.

The two major forms of discipline were having to run a long distance or what they called "digging the hole." The cadet who was disciplined on that day was given a shovel and, under the watchful eye of the disciplinary sergeant, was told to dig a hole in the ground. The hole was supposed to be 2'x4' and once the hole was created, the cadet could return to class. The next cadet who faced discipline had to then fill the hole.

I was inspired by the overall result—students who were engaged in the classroom and did not display the behavior problems that the teachers I worked with constantly complained about.

That had been three months ago.

When I met Joan in her office just before the Easter break, she challenged me to create a military-style school like Mather.

I had my orders and I longed to deliver.

Academy Accountability

The primary and short-term goal of what Joan and I intended to call the Alder Grove Academy would be to help errant teens successfully return to a traditional high school environment. But we knew there was a long-term goal underlying our primary task—to transform at-risk teens into productive and crime-free youth who could eventually make mature social and work-life decisions.

How would we do it?

Paul and I were convinced the answer lay in the context of a military environment. And though discipline is important in a military atmosphere, we envisioned it only as a necessary complement to a challenging academic component. We hadn't come to this conclusion in a vacuum but based on years of teaching juvenile delinquents and experimenting with techniques we'd learned during our respective careers in the military and civilian law enforcement.

Even in our delinquent-filled classrooms, we had seen how the delivery of consistent and clear instructions and discipline often resulted in behavioral changes, changes that introduced at-risk kids to the self-discipline necessary for making better choices. Mather was one example of the impact of such an environment. After observing and meeting some of the students there, it convinced me that teens, too, sense the potential benefits of a military environment, that it can give them what their parents and guardians are often unable to teach them–accountability for their own behavior.

We agreed to build the program with three specific, measureable daily student commitments: to develop physical skills through physical training ("PT") and physical education ("PE"), to complete all school-assigned activities, and to perform academic assignments responsibly. We believed that even limited mastery of these skills would increase student readiness for adulthood, one where they were equipped to demonstrate physical and intellectual discipline, to abide by rules, to obey as well as assume authority, and most important, to challenge their own anti-social norms and behavior.

During Easter break, I checked websites such as West Point, several private military style institutions, boot camps, and lockdown detention facilities and thought more about what I had seen at Mather. Though each boot-camp style school offered something important, it was obvious that our academy would have few predecessors. My students would not come from wealthy families that had the means and desire to spend thousands of dollars for their child to attend a military-style institution.

Instead, they would be those that traditional schools no longer wanted on their campuses: students with attendance problems, expulsions for drug offenses, weapon charges, fights, gang involvement, and threats to teachers and staff.

Uniforms would matter. Not only would they make everyone equal but they would also establish pride in appearance. Many of my more impoverished kids had stolen clothes from retail stores so that they could fit in socially while attending traditional schools where it was important to wear the latest fashion. This passion to belong by looking like one's peers is also typical within gangs. Wearing a uniform would correct this problem.

I devised a blueprint where ranking structure would play a special role in motivating students and reinforce the family concept. Each cadet would be accountable to their platoon and each platoon to the academy. My hope and intention was that it would teach the students to get along with each other regardless of gang affiliation or race since they would sink or swim together.

The Student Spin for the Academy

After Easter break, I informed my class at the Alder Grove Community School of the directive to create a military style school based on order, structure and, when necessary, discipline. To my amazement, most of the students, male and female, loved the idea of a military style school and especially wearing a uniform and combat boots.

Though I was the final arbiter, wherever possible I wanted to give my future cadets the opportunity to put their own spin on the academy so I gave them the opportunity to make some decisions about their lives as cadets.

On the internet, I had found a website selling BDUs–Battle Dress Uniforms. I projected the various uniform designs on our classroom whiteboard. It took my future cadets some time to agree about what uniforms they would wear but they unanimously agreed that I should wear a black version of their BDU.

They also accepted the concept that appearance was important so it was also agreed that their hair could not touch the collar of their uniform. The males agreed to cut their hair military-style or place it in a ponytail and the girls with long hair were to help one another put their hair in a bun.

When it came to creating their "Cadet Oath" and conduct code, I downloaded several examples from other schools for them to review. We then broke up into groups so they could make changes until they were ready to vote for a final version. Again, I was surprised to see how quickly they understood how to use the templates to create rules, regulations, and a ranking structure.

Everyone agreed that they would divide themselves into three platoons–red, white and blue. They also agreed about the rules for proper behavior in the class during all phases of the day—before school, in the locker room, during breakfast and lunch, and in the classroom. They even decided that the football was not to be thrown until we reached the field, and that food or other objects would not be thrown inside or outside.

I had always been fascinated by the Spartan civilization and had introduced the subject to the students. Most of the students had identified with a Spartan lifestyle when we studied ancient Greek cultures, so it wasn't surprising that our future cadets and I decided a Spartan helmet would be the academy logo and a Spartan the mascot.

Meantime, I purchased the uniforms as well as the emblems and stripes that would distinguish cadet ranks—private, corporal, sergeant and staff sergeant–and ordered shoulder patches and baseball hats with the Spartan helmet design.

When I presented a summary of what we'd accomplished to Joan, she could not believe we had completed so much in just one week. Though I didn't have all the answers for the program, her ongoing confidence in getting it approved encouraged me to make one more purchase—the boots.

I knew many of the kids couldn't afford them but our local Big 5 Sporting Goods store gave me a 10% discount. Polishing boots was all part of accountability and although I had yet to involve the military, I hoped to have a member of the armed forces determine who shined their boots best.

Teachers who inspire know that teaching
is like cultivating a garden, and those who
would have nothing to do with thorns must
never attempt to gather flowers.

–Author Unknown

CHAPTER 10

JOURNALS–SOME SORT OF MILITARY SCHOOL

When I arrived in class after Easter break, Mr. Rose had his PowerPoint projector on and he showed us some different military uniforms. We asked him what this was all about, but he would only say, "You'll see." Once everyone else arrived, he told us about a meeting he had with his boss about the possibility of creating a military-style boot camp school. He said the armed forces might be a partner in the program.

Before I knew it, we were all asking questions and making suggestions. Mr. Rose told us that we still had to get approval from the Superintendent of Schools before the school could officially become the Alder Grove Academy. He said that it would be *our* academy and therefore we had to work as a team to put it all together. He asked us to come up with a presentation for the Superintendent and her staff—to convince them that we really wanted a military-style school.

One of the things we had to decide on was a type of uniform. We got into a big argument because none of us could agree on what type we should wear. The girls wanted the normal jungle-type uniform. Some of the guys wanted the type of uniform that the soldiers wore in Vietnam and others wanted the latest ones that were being used in the Middle East. Mr. Rose said that he's going to pay for the first set of BDUs that we will wear and he finally made us choose.

Next, Mr. Rose told us that we needed to come up with a presentation for the PCOE superintendent and her staff—to convince them that we really wanted a military-style school. We all started working together to decide what kind of questions they would ask us when they came to our school for the presentation.

—Journal #16, 17-year-old male

It was almost Easter break when Mr. Rose told us that he would be traveling back to Russia to study the Nazi killings that had taken place during World War II. I have to say that I could not wait for the break to get over to hear his stories of the trip.

When we returned, not only did he tell us about his trip, but he said that he had been asked to put together a process where we would be turning the community school into a military style boot camp academy.

At first, I thought "what the hell?" I didn't want to be part of the army and thought that the army would be trying to recruit us to fulfill their quota. I also wasn't thrilled with the idea of wearing camouflage instead of my street clothes.

But we all knew that we had better go along with the program and not get on Mr. Rose's bad side. Amazingly, he allowed us to choose our first uniforms since he was paying for it out of his own pocket. He had a PowerPoint presentation set up one morning showing different patterns of camouflage. Of course, the class could not come to a unanimous decision, so Mr. Rose paused and said "Ok, since I am paying for this, I will allow you to pick from three styles." The girls wanted something totally different than most of the guys. In fact, us guys had to choose from either the Desert Storm brown uniform or the Special Forces Vietnam green forest style.

—Journal #31, 15 year-old male

I was sent to this school that is called the Alder Grove Community School because of truancy and coming to school drunk.

My last day here. I get to go back to my regular school. They are going to be changing this school into some sort of military school with the army. When I first heard that, I said I am glad that I am leaving. But listening to the other students that are staying here, they seem to really be excited. I kind of like the idea of uniforms but with all the booze in me, I would probably die running with the army.

I think it is a good idea though. We all fucked up and that is why we were sent here to begin with. It seems like old man Rose will not let us screw up and holds us accountable. I learned a lot from him and it was a lot different than that other teacher. One of my friends is a wanna-be gangster. I tried to tell him he was stupid but he did not listen. Well he got shot the other day. He is ok but he could have died.

When Mr. Rose heard about it, he said something that I will never forget. When he was a cop he said that the sad part about gang shootings is not the dead gang member, it is the hurt he saw on the faces of their loved ones at the funerals he attended. He said that part of growing up is to be able to stand on your own, not having to be part of some damn gang.

I am going to miss him. I am sure the new military school will be able to change a lot of kids here.

–Journal #32, 16 year-old male

My story starts out when I was locked up in the Placer County Juvenile hall for second degree armed robbery and an assault on another minor my age. While I was in juvenile hall, we were told we were going to get a new teacher named Mr. Rose. At first I thought that he was an asshole towards me and all the students in the A-unit. He made us do a lot of work in his class and you had better pay attention. God help you if he caught you sleeping. He would take the biggest book he had and slam it on your desk. No one slept through that. In less than a month I started to like him and on his weekly tests, I was surprised how my grades were improving.

One day I returned to the classroom after going to court. The assistant D.A. (district attorney) wanted to send me away to boot camp for 18-24 months. Mr. Rose seemed to realize that I was upset and came over to talk to me. He started telling me about a new school he was starting up. I asked him if I would be able to go there as an alternative instead of the boot camp school. He told me that he would write a letter to the judge and we will see what happens.

After about another month the judge sentenced me and told me that I would be going to Mr. Rose's court and community school (Alder Grove) instead of boot camp. Neither Mr. Rose nor I realized at that time, that soon, his school would also be a boot camp style institution.

I still had to do 115 days at JDF (juvenile hall). I soon got out but again screwed up and had to do another 45 days. You see, me and my "friends" decided to rob a house. After we robbed the house the owner found out that we did it because one of guys I was with, told the guy's daughter!

Then the daughter called my friend and started threatening him, and he called me and said he was giving all the stuff back. So, I told him that he was a "dumb fuck" for admitting to it. Then I told him that he better not say anything about me when he gives the stuff back. He told me that the old guy (friend) that helped rob the house, was also giving he stuff back. I called them both "bitches."

The word got back that I was talking shit about the other guy and he started threatening me. I told him that I would beat his ass and he replied that he would put me in the hospital.

A couple of days later, I told him to meet me somewhere but he didn't want to. Then, around five or six days later, he called me and told me to meet him at the park. I started to call some friends so that we could jump the guy. I told my friends to bring some bats and crow bars. I grabbed a baseball bat and I went to the park but he wasn't there. I called him and told him to hurry the fuck up. About 10 minutes later he shows up with around four or five car loads of people and when they stopped, they all got out of their cars and went after me.

My friends still weren't there because they lived on the other side of town, so I took off and the guy started catching up with me. Then I got hit in the head while I was running. I fell to the ground and all of his friends ran up and started beating me with bats and kicking me in the face and everywhere else on my body. I thought I was going to die.

Then they finally stopped and I grabbed the baseball bat I brought with me and I went after the guy who I was supposed to fight in the first place. I hit him over his head and he dropped to the floor while my head was bleeding. I felt really dazed but I didn't care if I killed him.

Fortunately I didn't but I did crack his skull on the side. I hit him a few more times but then his friends started coming towards me. All toll, five people went to the hospital that night. I had to get five stitches in the back of my head. The guy I hit had to have some staples and stitches.

When my probation officer found out, he tried to find out who did this to me. Later that night, I learned that he arrested but later bailed out of jail. As soon as that shit got out, he started saying shit again and I told him that I would be willing to fight him again but instead, I ended up in JDF.

If you want to know anything personal about me, here goes. I was born in Sacramento, California. I am the only Russian in the academy. I'm 15 years old and I have a big family. I have four sisters and two brothers. I'm the middle child and the first born in America.

I grew up listening to rap and hanging out with older kids that were always in out of Sacramento juvenile hall. Some of my friends joined gangs and then everything just kept getting worse for me like when I started hanging out with gang members. Whenever they saw a rival gang member, they would start talking shit back and forth. Most of the time it ended up with a fight.

I started going with my friends whenever they were going to beat up someone or it they wanted to steal a car. We also pick-pocketed people, rob houses, or just go to a party and get drunk.

The first time I ever got caught by the cops was when I stole a pair of shoes from Sport Authority. All the cops did was take me home and they told my parents what I did. My mom started screaming at me and I just left my house and started kickin it with the same "friends" that I later got in trouble with. Because I had just got off for the earlier theft, threatening to fight the same guy from earlier, resulted in me being charged with another crime and back to juvie I went. I served the weekend and upon my release, moved to Roseville and then Rocklin, Placer County.

Going to the Alder Grove Academy and doing well there, is all that stands between me and serving time at the California Youth Authority (prison for juveniles).

Mr. Rose has gone to bat for me and I must show him how appreciative I am by turning my life around. He always talks about burning bridges and hitting rock bottom. I think I have, but as he always says, "talk is cheap." Mr. Rose put his neck out for me just to get me into this academy on one condition tied into the court. They both put me on zero tolerance. The judge told me that if he ever sees me in his courtroom again, he will send me away for the maximum confinement which would be 6 years!

–Journal #38–15-year-old male

Hey, it is me again. I want to write today about how I feel about Mr. Rose, my teacher. When I first met him I knew right away that he was a very tough person, but the more I am with him, the more I know that he is a real fair guy. Mr. Rose will do whatever he promises he will do for us. He was a former police sergeant with the Milpitas Police Department. He is one of the best teachers I have ever had in my whole school career. He has a different way of teaching. He makes it fun and always finds a way to teach us if we don't understand. He just makes everything easier.

Again, when I first met him, I wondered who this guy was dressed in black. I was actually a little scared of him, but then I knew that everything he was doing for us, was for the best. He lived and breathed for this academy and is giving his life for it. It has become the best school in the county as far as I care.

–Journal #4–Jose Portillo

Mr. Rose has worked at the county's juvenile hall for almost 8 years before he came to Alder Grove. I learned from my friend Alex, that he was a former police sergeant and that he did not take shit in his classroom. I remember the first day I met Mr. Rose because I tried to give him shit that he was once a police officer. I will never do that again. He jumped all over me and I knew I had made a big mistake. Now he has become, without a doubt, the best teacher I have ever had.

Before I met him, my life was shit. I was getting to gangs, drugs, stealing, just fucking up pretty much.

I have been with Mr. Rose for 2 years now. My parents have never seen me get such good grades and believe me, he makes you earn them. My parents have also said that I have really matured. Part of it for sure, was because Mr. Rose was very demanding in his classroom. If you swore, and that was a big problem for me, he made you do push-ups. Before I knew it, I was in great shape because I was always getting caught swearing. My mother said that I am now a man. God I feel so proud…but it would not have happened if I had not attended Alder Grove Academy. Mr. Rose and the academy literally saved my life. I am so proud to be one of the first cadets and helped create the academy.

–Journal #16–17-year-old male

Today, January 25, 2008, my uncle, wow, my favorite uncle, got out of jail at 12:00. I couldn't see him because he got deported and they took his American citizenship away. My uncle was in jail for around 17 years. He used to be a big time drug dealer. I haven't seen my uncle in like 3 years. I lived with my uncle for one year because my mom and dad were going through their divorce and I didn't want to live with either of them, so I went to live with my uncle.

My uncle always gave me everything I needed and always took me places with him. My uncle treated me like his own son. I think my uncle is very happy to get out of jail. He is going to eat so much Mexican food that he is probably going to gain a couple of pounds. I can't wait till summer so I could see my uncle again.

–Journal #4–Jose Portillo

Well, when I was in second grade, I lived in Del Paso Heights. I lived there for about a year or two but we moved because my mom met someone. This someone, when I first met him, seemed cool because he took me and my sister to this store and told us to whistle whenever we saw something we wanted.

We moved to his two-bedroom house in Colfax. He had a really nice house but it was only two bedrooms so me, my brother, my sister and his daughter had to live in his barn. The barn was horrible. It had no bathrooms so in the middle of the night, we had to walk over to the house to use the bathroom. Most of the time the door was locked, and when we knocked they would rarely let us in. So instead, we had to go to the bathroom outside.

My mom's boyfriend is an alcoholic and through the years we lived there, my mom became one too. One day my man and her boyfriend, went to a bar and when they returned, he did not have my mom. He just went to sleep. My neighbors went and picked up my mom at the bar and I took my mom's hand as she stumbled down our hill to get to our house.

She was really drunk and could barely stand. We made it to the house and her boyfriend woke up. They started fighting like they do all the time. This time, it was way worse and that mother fucker hit my mom when I was right there, and she went unconscious because she hit the floor.

I ran up to her crying like I never had cried before. I called my sister at our neighbors and my sister fainted. The neighbors called the cops. My mom got taken away in a helicopter and went to the hospital. Her boyfriend got arrested. Their relationship still wasn't over. He got out in a year and they got married. About a year or two later, my sister was dying her hair and she got a little bit of dye on the door. My mom's boyfriend went crazy. He flipped out and my mom and him fought and we finally moved out.

That was the best day of my life. We moved to an apartment and started over with nothing. We lived in Colfax for about two or three years and then we moved Auburn.

Everything was going good in my life until the day something happened that would change my life forever. I was walking home from school one day and there was a package outside of my house. I opened it and there was some pills and I took them to school. There I overdosed. I wanted to go a day without stress. I wanted to feel good, so I took some, but I took way too much. I had to go to the hospital cause it was so bad.

The day I thought I was gonna have no stress or troubles ended up being exactly opposite. About a week after that, my mom took me to a psychologist. I did not take those pills to kill me but my mom thought so. I got expelled from school and was sent to Alder Grove.

It became the best school I've ever attended. Ever since the day I overdosed, my mom does not trust me, but I'm doing good and she thinks I am still doing bad.

At Alder Grove, I met Kasey. She became my best friend. We are the Bopsey Twins as Mr. Rose calls us. Kasey smokes but I don't, but because of that, my mom thinks I do. She searches my backpack all the time and she says she gonna buy me a drug testing kit, but she hasn't yet.

I hope she does so I can prove her wrong. My mom says that I need to understand that if someone I hangout with smokes, that I makes other people thing I do too. I don't really care what everyone else thinks. I don't smoke and that's that. And, I don't care is Kasey smokes, since she is my best friend.

–Journal #41–16-year-old female

A letter to Oprah

Dear Oprah,

I am currently a senior at the Alder Grove Academy and a big fan or your show. I know you're a busy person, but I come to you asking a big favor. My fellow classsmates and I have put together a book about our lives, our choices, and the program that changed everything for the better.

We were known as the rejects of society that were thought to end up in either jails, prisons, or dead. This was until a man named Gary Rose come into our lives and gave us a second chance. He is the man that helped bring us together and helped us rise above just being a statistic.

We have become the Alder Grove Academy Spartans and we want to help inspire teens and young adults with our stories. The book ranges from the past to our present and the situations we had been through that made our lives what they are today.

We really need your help to get our story out in the world, so please help us help others.

Sincerely,
Albert Torres

Dear Ophra Winfrey,

Hello, my name is Kasey. I am a cadet at the Alder Grove Academy. We are writing this letter to show you our story. Every cadet and Mr. Rose has written in this book. It is an inspiring, sometimes tragic, wonderful book. It tells about the sad and painful past some of us have had or some of our happy childhood memories. It talks about present things happening here in our academy. Boyfiends, girlfriends, parents, everything that has impacted our lives.

Some of the cadets have had parents leave them, endured drug problems, been in and out of juvenile hall, and almost hit rock bottom. Our teacher, Mr. Rose, has been the best thing to happen to some of us. He has a certain way of teaching and understanding his students. He maybe an ass sometimes, but that's why he is so respected. A lot of kids in our class have parents that aren't good enough, so Mr. Rose is like a father to some of them. He has a lot of heart and a lot of guts to pull off somethings that would be so hard for other teachers.

I hope that you take the time to read this over and read our book once it is published. Our story will inspire some kids and have a positive effect that will make a difference and make some think about what might come in their future.

Thank you Oprah.
Cadet Kasey

Today, Mr. Rose gave us an assignment about burning bridges and if we could go back and change it, what would we change.

One of my burning bridges would be when I was going to Whitney High School and was doing a bunch of drugs. My grades were straight F's and my mom was one of the people who tried to help me. But I didn't care and told her to fuck off. She got sick of trying to help me and not having any control over me, she kicked me out. I had lived with my mom most of my life so she made me live with my dad. I love my dad and I like living with him but me and my mom are way closer and have a different relationship now. I am doing good and not doing drugs or anything while living with my dad. He says I can't live with her (my mom) any more so it kinda sucks, but now, when I go to my mom's. which is all the time, it is even better hanging out with her because we are even closer than before.

–Journal #28–17-year-old female

In my life, I've been to many schools. Constantly moving and trying to make new friends, it wasn't always easy for me. My dad was always caught up on drugs. He would come home late at night all strung out and start hitting my mom. Some days were worse than others and there were the occasional days where if felt as if nothing was wrong.

As a six-year-old little girl, I felt so helpless. Why won't he listen to me when I asked him to stop? I'd ask myself, what am I doing wrong to make him hate us so much and want to do drugs instead of being with us.

My dad gave me hate, hate for men who can't own up to their responsibilities, hate for drugs, hate for the people who are so weak and unable to just to say no to the drugs.

My mom and dad split up for the final time after me and my sister asked her too. She told us she was sorry and she never wanted us to get hurt. She just wanted us to have a normal life in a normal family, and if she had known we wanted him to be out of our lives, it would have happened a long time ago.

When we left him, that is when the constant moving happened. I would move from school to school, house to house, and meet mom's boyfriends. Auburn, California, is the place I've lived for the longest time. I've lived here for six years. This place is where I met my best friends. This is the place I had my first love. This is the town where I pretty much had the best times of my life.

I went to E.V. Cain for seventh and eighth grade, then I began my journey on to high school. I went to Placer High but I pretty much stopped going. When it comes to school, I have no motivation to go. I'm not like all these other kids. I don't just go and do drugs constantly. I just can't motivate myself. So, after Placer, I went to Maidu, a home school. I ended up going to one of my meetings and then just not going for around three months until they finally dropped me.

After that it was the year of my sophomore summer. When school started back up again, I was enrolled in Chana Continuation school. Once again, it wasn't for me.

Yes, I had friends there but honestly they were going nowhere and doing nothing themselves in the long run. After about a month, I got kicked out of Chana and that's when they sent me to the Alder Grove. It was not an academy, just a court and community school and Mr. Rose was not there yet. The teacher who was there never really made us do any work. But even without having to do work, it was starting to get old.

I was constantly in court. "Amada, your truancy problem is not getting any better." Well, honestly, what did they expect.

I come to school for six hours, basically do nothing, and I wasn't going for it anymore. So I figured I might as well stay home with my boyfriend, or friends, and do something fun.

I would only come to school when I knew a man by the name of Tom Grayson was going to be there. Tom is the anger management instructor. I have more respect for that man then I do my own father. He'd talk to us about real stuff. He showed me that not all guys are assholes. The most important thing is he taught me that I am a wonderful person and the best day was the day I was born.

The day Mr. Rose came to our rescue. I was late. I walked in and Ms. M was there and she told me a little about what was going on. I think that there was about 16 of us in the classroom when he arrived. To be honest, I don't remember what the hell he talked about. It was weird listening to a true teacher.

Mr. Rose's style of teaching actually made sense to me. I actually started to attend school not only because of the courts saying I "had" too, but because I actually wanted too. Don't get me wrong; I was still late. Come one now, I was 16 at the time, and I'm not about to wake up at 7 A.M. to be on time by 8 A.M. It is just sooooo early! I guess I am the kinda girl who has always and who will always HATE mornings.

–Journal #39–17-year-old female

Gee how times has passed by. It seems like it was just yesterday that I entered the Alder Grove Academy. Now it is time to say goodbye. I loved being in Mr. Rose's class here in the academy. He is easily my favorite teacher in my nine years of school so far. It sucked being a new bootie last year. I miss last year! I miss all of the people that were here. I didn't really mind the uniforms last year but they kinda got annoying. P.E. was ALWAYS fun! Football was really fun! Josh was the clown of the class last year. I hated U.S. history and World history before I came here? Now they are both two of my favorite subjects. I have GREAT grades now!

It's a lot easier than I thought it would be for my freshman year. Math is a lot easier than when I had my 8th grade teacher help me.

I am going to MISS YOU when you leave. I wanted to cry when I found out you were leaving. I'm going to miss the doughnuts when you are gone. I will love you forever and always.

–Journal # 40–14-year-old female

Tell me and I forget, teach me and I may
remember, involve me and I learn.

–Xun Kuang, Chinese Confucian
philosopher (312-230 BC).

CHAPTER 11

MARSHALING OUR FORCES

As I'd already told the kids, the superintendent and attorney for the education office were to visit the classroom in the course of deciding whether to approve the creation of the academy. In anticipation of that visit, I told my students to prepare a presentation for the school district officials.

First, I asked the kids to write down on a piece of paper why they wanted an academy. Second, I asked them to put themselves in the place of the attorney and superintendent and see if they could anticipate the questions that the visitors might ask.

After they formulated their questions, the students picked three peers, two males and one female, who would answer the visitors' questions. Acting as the attorney or superintendent, I asked the questions we expected the administrators to ask and the three student representatives rehearsed their responses.

When the superintendent and attorney arrived, they sat near the back of the class while the student representatives followed the script that the class had prepared. Fortunately, the uniforms and boots had arrived and our future cadets had put them on for our presentation. I can't help but think that the absence of baggy pants, short-shorts and gang colors impressed our guests from the start.

Everything went as we expected until the attorney asked a question we weren't prepared for. How do you think a new student would feel, he asked, when coming to class for the first time and seeing the other students in uniforms?

There was a brief silence in the classroom.

To my amazement, one of our newest students raised her hand and said she could answer the question. She told the attorney that wearing the same clothing as the other students would make her feel like she wanted to be part of the team. He nodded his head and smiled, and I knew we had won them over if, indeed, they had even needed to be won over. If we did not get approval, it wouldn't be the fault of the students.

Within an hour, the superintendent and attorney appeared at Joan's office door and gave her the "thumbs up" sign. I was soon advised that I was the Site Supervisor and Director of the Alder Grove Academy.

Clearly, our visitors were as impressed with the future cadets as I was.

At the Donut Shop

My next task was to determine which branch of the military would consider working with a group of at-risk teenagers who lacked proper role models. Being the stereotypical cop, I decided to go where all cops go to contemplate issues—the donut shop. Over a cup of coffee and a chocolate donut, I felt prepared to deal with the problem.

The National Guard had already turned me down. I had rejected the Marines because they were being scrutinized by their administration following some incidents involving their forces and juvenile delinquents. Though I hadn't approached the Navy or Air Force, I had a gut feeling that my students, many of whom had neither seen the Pacific Ocean nor could afford to fly, would not find it easy to relate to those who spent most of their lives either at sea or in flight.

It wasn't until I was sipping my second cup of coffee that I glanced across the parking lot and saw what I'd never noticed before—a U.S. Army recruiting office.

There, I met Sergeant Howell and his corporal. I must have made a good impression because Sergeant Howell got very excited about the project. The sergeant warned me that his commander would make the final decision but Sergeant Howell believed participating at the academy would be a great way to give back to the community.

I floated out of their office confident that I had all the pieces I needed to make a military-style academy a success. My optimism was justified. Sergeant Howell received formal approval and soon thereafter Joan sent a letter to the army confirming their partnership with our academy.

The Alder Grove Academy was no longer just an idea. With less than eighteen cadets, none of us could have imagined that we would eventually have forty-two cadets and have to add green, orange and purple platoons to our original red, white and blue.

Our deeds determine us as much as we
determine our deeds.

–GEORGE ELIOT, ENGLISH WOMAN NOVELIST,
JOURNALIST, TRANSLATOR (1819-1880).

CHAPTER 12

JOURNALS–RISE AND SHINE

Big day today! Our uniforms arrived and so did our boots. It was crazy. The girls headed off to their bathroom to get changed, and the boys used the main classroom. Then the big bosses from P.C.O.E. showed up and we gave them our presentation. They only asked us a few questions, but after they left—within a few minutes— Ms. M. told Mr. Rose that they gave his boss the go-ahead. We are now the AGA!

–Journal #16, 17-year-old male

There are a lot of people who are fighting this new academy thing and what it represents, but I'm starting to see a change in everybody's attitude here. Just last week, we stepped up our PT training with Sergeant Howell and ran two miles as a class. (By the way, Mr. Rose runs the two miles with us even though we know he has bad knees. It's like he has told us—you can talk the talk as long as you walk the walk.)

–Journal #11, 17-year-old male

I wasn't sure what to expect the first day of school at the new Alder Grove Academy. I started out as a platoon leader because Mr. Rose trusted me to get the job done. I took my job seriously and I gave it my all. Someone like me learns how to take advantage of a good situation—I had nothing when I was growing up, so now I have to work with what I can and I make the best of it. After two weeks, I was promoted to staff sergeant.

In the academy, it goes like this: you start out as a private, then you're

promoted to private first class, then corporal, then sergeant, and then staff sergeant. As staff sergeant, I have to lead by example. I always have to be on top of my game. For example, if I tell my cadets to do something, I have to be willing to do it myself.

–Journal #3–Jose Portillo

Today we were playing softball down on our football field and I have to admit, I wasn't paying attention. I was in the outfield and I heard a lot of the students yelling my name. Then I felt a sharp pain on the top of my head. The ball hit me and it really hurt. Everyone started laughing, including Mr. Rose. He came over to see if I was all right. It *did* hurt, but I didn't want to show it. The student that hit the ball also came running up to me to make sure I was all right. Guess I need to pay more attention, huh?

–Journal , #28, 16-year-old female

We all got into our platoons and Mr. McDaniel made us stand for inspection. Most of us did okay, but some of those that don't take the academy seriously just screwed off until Mr. McDaniel and Mr. Rose jumped down their throats.

Today was a fun day. Mr. McDaniel is trying to teach us how to march. We might even be able to compete and win an award! First, we had to stand on what we call our parade grounds. This is the area that has some basketball courts and we sometimes play Frisbee down there, too. The army will be with us tomorrow, so Mr. Rose and Mr. McDaniel would like us to know some of the moves before they get here. It is more Mr. McDaniel, since he was in the Air Force for a long time. You see, Mr. McDaniel is a close friend of Mr. Rose. They worked together at juvenile hall. Mr. McDaniel looks like Santa and sometimes we joke with him about that.

Marching is not as easy as you might think. Some of the other students don't know their right from their left. We seem to know how to come to attention and where to put our arms out to get the right spacing between us but then, when Mr. McDaniel said to turn right or left, a lot of us banged into each other because we went in the wrong direction.

Mr. Rose, Ms. M. and Ms. Jenny like to watch us march and we can hear them laughing when we screw up. Sometimes Mr. McDaniel makes us screw up on purpose by saying too many commands at the same time. It's been fun learning how to do everything.

–Journal #30, 17 year-old male

Everything is going good at home and at school. Last week, I asked the army for help—they said that I could call them anytime I needed to. I talked to Sergeant Howell about a problem that I have—it's a gang problem outside of school. I didn't want to bring my problem to the academy, so he and

I talked about it. They know that I don't have a lot of other choices. They know that I'm facing the CYA (California Youth Authority), and I *really* don't want to go there.

—Journal #9, 17-year-old Latino

I have been out of the hall for a little over two weeks now, and I think I'm doing pretty good so far. Alder Grove Academy has taught me to be more responsible for my actions. I have never made sergeant and I feel bad for letting my platoon down, especially when I run. But, that said, my attendance here is way up and my grades are great.

Mr. Rose really knows how to push our buttons. He tries to make us angry sometimes. He tells us that we need to know our anger buttons so we can develop good coping skills. I wish I had him as a teacher when I was younger. I don't think I would have gotten into so much trouble.

One thing about him—he does not give up on us. He does get mad, though. Boy, does he get mad! But we realize it's because we've let him down in some way. Can you believe he sometimes comes to work at 4:30 a.m. just to get all of our notes and stuff ready? He even has some of the guys come in to review algebra during what he calls his "Breakfast Club." Those students go to Costco and buy pancakes, syrup and sausage and while they are eating, Mr. Rose teaches them algebra. I never heard of a teacher doing that and the kids he works with are doing much better with their math.

—Journal #14, 17-year-old male

I think I am changing each and every day into something better. I try and try to keep this going, but people constantly judge me and put me down. I've finally learned to ignore it and move on. Just like racism. I deal with that and I'm used to it—being hated because of my color. Like Mr. Rose says to us, "I don't care if you like me or not but you *will* respect me, as I will you."

I know there are gonna be racists and I will have to deal with it, but I'm not a racist. I don't give a fuck what you look like. It doesn't matter. There are always gonna-be Whites, Mexicans, Blacks, Chinese, etc., in the world. Shit, it don't bother me one bit. We all have hard times and our own problems to worry about.

Everyone here at Alder Grove has a story to tell. They've all been in deep situations. We've learned that you should never give up, even when it looks like all is lost. You've gotta keep your head up. You don't wanna end up in jail or prison where you gotta watch your back and sleep with one eye open. Once you're in prison, you start thinking about what you could have done differently in your life.

Mr. Rose has given me the same advice my father has— "You gotta choose your friends wisely. You need to know who to trust and who will really watch your back." I was constantly screwed over by friends—mostly girlfriends—but I got a girl now that I can trust. You really have to make the right choices in life because it *does* affect you.

–Journal #12, 17-year-old Black male

Most of the students here have a lot of respect for Mr. Rose because he was a police officer. I know that sounds crazy, right? I mean, here we are, most of us on probation after being arrested by the cops, yet we feel real close to him. He doesn't bullshit us. We know that if we ask him a question, he will give us a straight answer. Sometimes he will ask us if we REALLY want to hear the answer, meaning we will *not* like it.

Mr. Rose showed me that I was not a failure when it came to algebra. He told us all that, frankly, he never uses algebra outside of the classroom. But he said that the state and the feds want us to learn it so we can think "abstractly." I think we already think abstractly in Mr. Rose's class because—like in history—after we learn something, he asks us to consider whether it could happen again. Also, if we give an answer too quickly, he will make us defend what we say. (And if we joke around, then we have push-ups to do.)

–Journal #26, 17-year-old male

I was born in Santa Cruz by the beach boardwalk. I moved to Auburn after I was born. I love to skate, but unfortunately skating brought me to the Alder Grove Academy. I actually think this school is a good school. The uniforms are bitchin. Hopefully this school will straighten me out. I think it will. I like how there are only two classrooms, meaning less students and less drama. Placer High had hella drama and I also like the fact that I get to leave here at 1:30.

I ended up at AGA because me and my friends too off with some skateboards and because I cut class too much. Honestly, I wish I was back at Placer with my friends. I regret doing all the dumb shit I have done; what Mr. Rose calls "burning bridges." Now, when school is through, I must walk to my grandpa's welding shop. I do get to skate everyday now since I go to AGA. I was pretty good before I got into all this trouble. I was even sponsored, but now that the cops took my good board, I will have to get really good again.

We do a lot of work in Mr. Rose's class. We cover at least eight subjects and then have to take a weekly test we call "payday." It takes us at least 2-3 hours to complete, but we like the challenge. My grades are starting to improve. I really like

PT with the army and PE is very intense. Whether is it flag football or softball, almost all of the cadets really get into it.

—Journal #42, 16-year-old male

Wow! I got my grades today, and I got mostly B's and a few C's. I have just completed my second month here and I have learned a lot of stuff. In fact, I think I have learned more here in two months than I would have learned at my other high school in an entire year. Yes, part of it is that I have been coming to school—I don't want to lose any merits, so I have to be here in time to raise the flag. Now, if I could just stop the damn weed, I think I would be okay.

—Journal #22, 17-year-old male

What was worst initially was that we had to wear black combat boots which we had to polish on our own. I hated it until one day, one of our youngest cadets came up to me and with a big smile on his face. He said, "Hey, check out the shine of my boots!" I noticed that everyone but me was really getting into the competition set up by Mr. McDaniel (he taught us how to polish our boots) to see who had the best polished boots.

—Journal 31, 16-year-old male

What sculpture is to a block of marble,
education is to the human soul.

–Joseph Addison, English politician
and writer (1672-1719).

CHAPTER 13

TURNING TROUBLED
TEENS INTO CADETS

The key elements required for the program were committed cadets, support and merit systems, and disciplinary procedures. Ideally, those elements would enable every cadet to improve his academic standing, social skills, and physical health.

The Cadet Commitment

Though new cadet trainees had not participated in creating the rules and regulations agreed to and initiated by the first academy class, we believed that the creation and approval of these rules by the first group of cadets made a deep impression on the trainees who followed. Like the Spartans they would study in our history classes, the cadets had to meet not only my standards but standards represented by an oath cadets had created.

Student Support Systems

As much as we believed that our program could give cadets a foundation for adulthood, we also knew troubled teens would need additional support systems to help them achieve these goals.

In order to make sure each student stayed on course, we created what we dubbed a "rehab" plan though the plan had nothing to do with drugs or alcohol unless drugs or alcohol was an issue. The plan outlined the reason for the student's referral to AGA and laid out how the cadet's behavior needed to change before they could return to their traditional school. Usually, it included individual and group counseling. At the beginning of AGA-1, when the numbers were lower, I read every file. But as the AGA grew, I left this up to my assistant, Michelle Segarra, who would inform me as to what a particular student might need and why he was at AGA.

The teaching staff, working in conjunction with the Special Education Unit, determined the suitable individual plan for those students who qualified as special education students. Those who lacked adequate credits for their grade level were placed in a general education development (GED) program to enable them to earn a degree comparable to a high school diploma.[8]

---

8   In the United States, "GED" is often thought to stand for a "general education degree" or "diploma." However, the American Council on Education coined the term to identify tests of "general educational development" that measure proficiency in science, mathematics, social studies, reading, and writing. Passing the GED test gives those who do not complete high school or who do

The army also provided additional support. Sergeant Howell and Staff Sergeant Hewitt shared my interest in creating a buddy system based on the "battle-buddy" program I had heard about during the Viet Nam War. With their help, we assigned an established cadet as a "battle buddy" for every new cadet to guide the latter through the academy's requirements and also help them academically when needed. Their sergeant was also responsible to keeping track of the progress of their assigned cadets that made up their platoon.

The Merit System

Each cadet would receive one hundred merit points when he began the program. Every infraction would result in losing one or more of their points. Infractions included tardiness, lack of proper uniform, swearing, throwing food, and verbal or physical disrespect of the teaching staff or fellow cadets. Major violations, like answering back to me or my aides, could result in the loss of several points. Ultimately, I would decide how many points were withdrawn.

Leadership grades would be based on the following scale: 90%—100% = A, 80%—89% = B, 70%—79% = C, and so forth. Cadets could earn points if the army was impressed with the appearance of their boots and uniform during inspections or for displaying leadership qualities.

Cadets were to take care of cadets. Each cadet-sergeant was responsible for the cadets under his or her command.

---

not meet requirements for a high school diploma, the opportunity to earn their high school equivalency credential.

When the cadets realized that I gave sergeants additional responsibilities, they either strived to become a sergeant or accepted the fact that they were not ready to handle the additional burden.

Though one could be rewarded for exhibiting leadership qualities, I made it clear that a choice not to lead was a legitimate choice and not a reason for self-consciousness or belittlement. We are all blessed with different skills. I always pointed out that there were police officers who loved being patrol officers and never wanted to be considered for management.

Discipline

Discipline would be imposed on any cadet who violated school rules or failed to live up to the Cadet Code of Conduct. The army could impose discipline during PT which would consist of routine physical drills and ceremonies. The teaching staff could also institute discipline if a simple request to "knock it off" did not suffice. In addition, sergeant cadets could discipline their fellow cadets with my approval.

Disciplinary measures included losing merit points, pushups, sit-ups, or a run. Alternatively, each cadet was offered the opportunity to write a five-page essay. Not surprisingly, *no one* ever requested that option.

If one advances confidently in the direction of his dreams, and endeavors to live the life which he has imagined, he will meet with success unexpected in common hours.

–HENRY DAVID THOREAU, AMERICAN ESSAYIST, POET, PHILOSOPHER, AND ABOLITIONIST (1817-1862).

CHAPTER 14

JOURNALS–FORWARD MARCH

Two days ago, we had our first drill and ceremonies with the U.S. Army. It wasn't bad. In fact, it was kind of fun. Sometimes I think I'm dreaming because I used to hate this life and I didn't want to be here. I had a lot of friends at Placer High.

I've made a lot of bad decisions, but I'm here to be better. Mr. Rose shows you that no matter what the situation, you can find a solution. And you can't give up because he will not let you. No matter where you are, he will not give up on you. For me, he is like the father I never had. With a teacher like Mr. Rose, I know that I will make it.

–Journal #34, 16-year-old Latino

The army came today and we had to "fall in." They were surprised that we knew a lot of the stuff they were going to teach us. I told them that Mr. McDaniel had been working with us.

—Journal #30, 17-year-old male

It's just before lunch, and it's been a rough first week for me at the new academy. School isn't half-bad but if I don't get my act together, then I may not be staying very long. It's not that I'm dumb or don't pay attention in class. I'm just having trouble getting to school on time.

Unfortunately, I still haven't stopped drinking—I just do it when I get home or on the way here. Sometimes in my other schools, the kids carried flasks with them. They would sit in the back of the classroom and nip on them. You can't try that here, though, because Mr. Rose seems to see *everything*.

I don't think I am an alcoholic since I feel I could leave it alone if I had to. I've slowed down and cut back a lot. I know quitting is a decision I have to make by myself…I have to *want* to quit.

—Journal #11, 17-year-old male

Mr. McDaniel came to our class today and taught us how to shine our combat boots. It was really fun learning how to get them shiny. We will be having a contest soon so that Mr. McDaniel can see if we did a good job.

—Journal #16, 17-year-old male

PT is great. The army stresses that we have to work as a team, not as a bunch of individuals. We wear army shirts and our own Spartan helmet shorts. We play baseball and football—and we love it when it rains. Mr. Rose says that if the U.S. Armed Forces can do it in the rain, then so can we. Rain, snow, heat, wind, fog—it doesn't matter. If we earned PE, we get to play. But if we start acting out or piss him off, we lose the privilege of PE and in we go.

–Journal #14, 17-year-old male

Well, my drinking and drug use have finally caught up with me—they caused me to be late for school and also led to truancy. I was expelled from Colfax High School, and here I am in my first week at Alder Grove Academy. My mom and dad got a divorce and it was tough on me and my sister. So, I made a lot of dumbass choices when it came to my friends and experimenting with pot and booze.

This school is a lot different than I thought. We heard about a military school while I was going to Colfax, but I never thought I would end up here. On my first day, Ms. M welcomed me and my dad. She gave us an overview of what the school was all about. Then she introduced me to Mr. Rose. He was really nice but I could also tell, just from the way he spoke, that he was a "for-real" person. He seemed very intense and I liked what he had to say.

I hated the idea of having to wear a military uniform, but now I don't mind. In fact, it makes my life in the morning a lot easier—I just do my hair and makeup and I'm ready to go. I'm a private, but I think I would eventually be a good sergeant. I'm in the orange platoon. There are only four of us now, but that's because we are the newest platoon (more and more people are coming to this school).

Some of the kids here—they're called cadets—didn't like it at first, but they told me it's the best school now. Many of them could have gone back to their regular schools, but they don't want to. Not me—once I can, I am getting out of here so I can be with my friends.

—Journal #15, 16-year-old Latina

The academy has stopped getting food from Placer High School. The new food, in my opinion, costs us too much money for what we get. If you want breakfast, its two dollars and all you get is a muffin, a banana and expired milk. For three dollars at lunch, you get shit. Unless your parents filled out a form for free food, you have to pay. Unfortunately, mine were too proud so I have to eat scraps.

—Journal #23, 16-year-old male

We have been very busy here at the academy. Mr. Rose has really challenged us and we love to reach the bars he has set for us. I can't believe that I have earned a PT award for running a timed mile with the army! The guys had to do it in 8 minutes and 30 seconds, and us girls had to complete it in 10 minutes and 30 seconds. We also had to do as many sit-ups and push-ups in one minute as they did. I've passed the CPR test and I have that award too.

We now run two miles on Mondays and Fridays, for a total of four miles a week, and my attendance is getting much better since Ms. Berry picks my sister and me up at our house. Academically, I am earning B's but Mr. Rose feels I could do better and I think he's right.

Something special happened today during our run. One of the other female cadets didn't want to run the mile for a medal (she's a little heavy). She said she couldn't do it, so why try? We all encouraged her to try her best, but none of us actually thought she could do it either. Then Mr. Rose had a talk with her. We couldn't hear everything he said, but he told her that he would run with her and help pace her so that she could win the medal.

Just like in a Hollywood movie, there is old Mr. Rose—who has bad knees already—running behind all of us with my girlfriend, encouraging her every time she had to stop and take a break. We could hear Mr. Rose tell her to take some breaths and then he got her to start running again. When the class and the army soldiers saw them coming toward the finish line, we all started clapping and yelling for her to keep going. I started to cry. I hoped that she could finish under time and she did.

The whole class circled around her and congratulated her. She couldn't speak because she was out of breath. The army told her that she had completed the mile run under the time limit and would earn a PT award. And there was Mr. Rose—out of breath and sweating. He started joking with us and asked for an ambulance. My girlfriend went over and gave him a hug.

–Journal #5, 16-year-old female

Over time Mr. Rose got to know us individually He used to joke with me since I always had a hard time staying awake in class. He would walk up to my desk without me realizing it, pick up the biggest book he could find, and slam it on my desk. Yes, he woke me up.

–Journal #31, 16-year-old male

I used to go to Placer High School. I guess I was kind of the tough guy. I fought a lot of people—for just about any reason. And it got me in trouble most of the time. I got caught up doing a bunch of bullshit–fights, drugs, and doing my own thing. I have never gone to juvenile hall, though, and I don't plan to.

My life got harder and harder until I got sent to Alder Grove Academy for fighting and putting this guy in the hospital. Since I've been at Alder Grove, I am doing much better. They push me to my potential—they don't put up with any bullshit. I was a loser, and now I'm on top. I've got great grades and I'm on track to graduate. I've learned how to handle situations. I've learned how to *focus*. I've also started showing respect to people and my parents have given me more trust.

—Journal #12, 17-year-old Black male

I love my mom but sometimes I feel she doesn't care about me. She always talks to her friends in secret and exchanges things with them in a way that I couldn't see. She had a lot of pills in her room but they were all prescription. She was always tired and never wanted to eat anything. I gave her massages but she still moaned with pain. Every night I would go to bed crying, wondering what was wrong with my mom and if she was going to die.

My stepdad had bought a new computer and it was huge. The screen on it was bigger than a television. One day I wanted to play games on it so bad but it was in my mom's room and she was in there with her friend who was our next-door neighbor. I hated her since she would always eat our food.

A few hours later she came out and my mom was there by herself and I wanted to get on that computer so bad that it was killing me. So, I finally built up my courage and went in her room without knocking on the door. I pushed the door open and I couldn't see my mom. I looked down and I saw one of her hands on the other side of the bed shaking. I leaped over the bed as fast as I could and my mom was having a seizure. I remembered seeing my stepdad slap my mother when she had other seizures so I slapped her a few times in the face. After a few minutes, she gasped for air and begin squeezing my arm and woke up. I was so scared. She finally told me that she was doing drugs with the neighbor who just left.

I was so disappointed. The one person who told me not to do drugs - the one person who told me to always stay healthy and be a leader and not a follower or fall under peer pressure–all those rules and my own mother almost died. I almost lost my mother!

If it wasn't for that damn computer and my desire to play games on it, my mother would probably not be here right now. So, when I saw my stepdad later, I thanked him so much for that stupid computer he bought.

–Journal #35 16- year- old black male

It's my fourth week here at AGA, but I am still technically a "new booty." I feel like I am fitting in more each day. I still have to wear the old military uniform, not the new digital ones that the other students get to wear, but I really like the idea of the uniforms. It saves me time in the morning since I don't have to decide what to wear. Having to wear the same uniform also makes us all equal—I think that some of the students here come from families that are poorer than mine.

We've *all* made stupid choices. Although we are supposed to be the toughest kids in the county and undisciplined, I have really met some great kids here. These cadets have been through a lot in their short lives. Many of them have been victims of child abuse and sexual abuse, and some of their parents have been in prison. It has only been a month, but being here has shown me how lucky I am to have the life I have.

–Journal #17, 17-year-old female

The other day I broke my ankle. That day was awesome. Class was great and we had fun at P.E. Mr. Rose had received complaints from customers who used the post office that was one building down from where AGA #2 was located. You see, there were so many cadets now, that when we walked either home or to the bus stop, we blocked the exit parking lot of the post office. To eliminate this problem, Mr. Rose told all of us that from now on, when we left the school, we were to go right, not left. But my dumbass self, decided to violate the rule and went in the wrong direction. I slapped Dillion on the back of his head saying "oh lay" and fell and broke my ankle. It looked hella cool; my leg pointing one way and my ankle the other way. I had to go to the hospital and they gave me Vicodin and some morphine. Of course, with all the drugs in me, I felt happy and hella good.

–Journal #36–16-year-old Latino male

It is almost Thanksgiving. We are going to have a big Thanksgiving dinner here at school. All of us are supposed to bring in something to eat. Before we eat, we are going to have our first Turkey Bowl—three platoons versus three platoons. Our Staff Sergeant is the captain of one of the teams. The winners get a chocolate cake that Mr. Rose bought for us— there's a big turkey on the top of it.

–Journal #28, 16 year-old female

We had a bitchin' Christmas party at the Academy. One of the girls actually made some handmade pies. One was chocolate and she made it especially for Mr. Rose. Ms. M bought a nice jacket for Mr. Rose—she said it was from us— and the parents of one of our female cadets bought Mr. Rose a quart-size bottle of Grey Goose.

We are a little upset with one of the other cadets. He conned Mr. Rose into buying a jacket for his mother. She was supposedly dying, but she wasn't really. The cadet had asked Mr. Rose if he could do some yard work at Mr. Rose's house, but Mr. Rose told him that he already had someone who did that kind of stuff for him. Mr. Rose asked the cadet why he needed money so quickly. He even asked the cadet if it was because he wanted to buy drugs for the holidays. (Mr. Rose is not afraid to get in your face and challenge you).

The cadet told Rose that his mother was dying of a brain tumor and he wanted to buy her a leather jacket. Mr. Rose then asked him if he knew how much a leather jacket cost. The cadet told Mr. Rose that it was not for a *real* leather coat—it was for a coat that his mother had seen at Target.

Believe it or not, Mr. Rose took the student to Target after school and he bought the jacket for him to give to his mother. He told the cadet not to worry about repaying him as long as he stayed out of trouble and continued to try hard in school.

Well, this kid got in trouble after Christmas and was put back in juvie. Then, ICE took him away. It was after he was booked into juvie that a few of us found out that his mom was not sick—he just wanted to get her a Christmas present and his mom put him up to asking Mr. Rose. What a bitch! Someone told Mr. Rose, but he didn't get mad. He just said something like, "Oh, well. I guess my cop skills are shot. I didn't see through all the bullshit he was saying. I hope they had a nice Christmas."

–Journal #29, 17-year-old Latino

It snowed yesterday and the football field still has some snow on it, so we all asked Mr. Rose if we could play football this afternoon. He told us—as usual—that we had to earn it. I sure hope we can.

Well, Mr. Rose did let us play football and we also had fumble drills. One of the girls was proud that her PE clothes were not dirty, but then a close friend of hers lifted her up and put her in a large mud puddle. We all laughed, including her.

I really don't want to go to Placer High School since I like it here now and I am doing good. But Mr. Rose and Ms. M told me that I need to experience a *real* high school and that there are a lot of things there that we don't have here, so I guess I will have to go.

—Journal #24, 14-year-old Latino

Treat people as if they were what they ought to be, and you help them to become what they are capable of becoming.

–Goethe, German writer and statesman (1749-1832).

CHAPTER 15

THE AGA PROGRAM PHASES

Phase One: The Observation Period

When a female or male cadet was referred to the academy, the academy director, a military staff member, and an instructional assistant interviewed them.

The cadet-applicant and their guardian were informed about the structure and environment of the academy, the dress code, the disciplinary structure, and what the academy administration hoped to accomplish in regard to making the student intellectually and physically fit.

A three-week evaluation period followed in which the cadet trainee was observed both in the classroom and during drills and ceremonies to determine if they were a suitable individual to advance to full cadet status.

If the cadet did poorly in the evaluation period, the cadet and cadet's guardian were informed that the student was at risk of being terminated from the program. The cadet or guardian could request a hearing and be reconsidered during an additional two-week observation period.

If accepted by the academy, and the minor and guardian agreed to enrollment, the academy issued the student a Cadet Trainee enrollment packet and a uniform. The uniform would be considered the property of the academy. New cadets were referred to as "new booty"—a term the army shared with us.

The Court and the Placer County Probation Department were notified at the end of Phase One if the cadet trainee was responding to training or if they were about to be terminated from the program and referred back to the respective agency that sent the cadet trainee to the academy.

Phases Two and Three: Education and Physical Health

Although traditional education took place in the classroom while physical education, drills and ceremonies, were conducted primarily by the military attachment, the educational and military phases were designed to complement one another. Strict discipline and accountability were to be enforced in both the classroom and on the parade grounds. This wasn't just theoretical—the military officers routinely sat in on classroom instruction and observed the cadets' behavior.

Army instructors explain what is expected of students during the military part of their training. Photo by former Alder Grove Staff.

Education

Many at-risk students I had taught at the hall and at Alder Grove Community

School had been credit deficient and below grade-level. Emotional issues that often included drug and alcohol use often had made it difficult to help a student become academically accountable. The academy cadets were no different.

My goal was to persuade cadets that moderate mastery of courses like algebra and English composition was necessary for a pay-off—for example, getting past the high school exit exam, the SAT or ACT college admissions exams, or entry exams for a trade-school or some branch of the armed forces.[9] Eventually, when most realized studying was not something that they could avoid just because they found it difficult, they decided to buckle down and apply themselves.

The results were usually gratifying. Because I posted grades, cadets were soon eager to compete academically against one another individually and as platoons. No matter what rank a cadet had earned, *everyone* had to maintain a 2.00 grade point average or face an academic warning and possible removal from the program.

Physical Health

At AGA-1, the introduction of the army and a regular physical education program resulted in an obvious improvement in the cadets' physical well-being. Many, especially during the first few weeks, suffered from muscular soreness from exercise and foot blisters from running with the army. Some coughed due to their cigarette smoking and a few stopped smoking because of the increased physical activity required by the army.

I am a strong believer in walking my talk. I would not ask my cadets to do something that I would not do, so when the students ran, I ran. When they performed physical education exercises, so did I. And when they attempted to earn an award for completing a mile run using army time as the target, I ran with the slowest runners to help them pace themselves.

---

9   SAT originally stood for the "Scholastic Aptitude Test" and ACT for the "American College Test." Now, however, SAT and ACT are brand names for the same college entry exams.

Drill competitions and simple rally races taught cadets how to think more

strategically. On one hand, they developed a sense of team consciousness when one platoon played against another. On the other, they learned to evaluate their platoon members' individual strengths and weaknesses in order to successfully compete against an opposing platoon.

Marching in unison is only one part of the military training cadets at Alder Grove Academy received. Photo by Gary Rose.

The man who removes a mountain begins by
carrying away small stones.

–CONFUCIUS, CHINESE TEACHER, EDITOR,
POLITICIAN AND PHILOSOPHER (551-479 BC)

CHAPTER 16

JOURNALS-MARCHING
IN UNISON

It's the second week of school and I have only 80 merits
or points left. You see, each cadet starts out with 100
merits or points in the beginning of each quarter. You get
demerits or lose points if you get into some type of trouble.
I managed to earn five merits back today after volunteering
to help the teaching staff. That was a relief because if you
lose 30 merits, then you're put on academic or disciplinary
probation—and if they put you on probation, they've got
grounds to expel you.

–Journal #11, 17-year-old male

I love skateboarding and that is what brought me here
to the Alder Grove Academy—me and my skateboarding
friends were cutting class too much. Honestly, I wish I was
back at Placer High. A lot of my friends are there. I really

regret doing all the dumb shit I did. Now I have to work at my grandpa's welding shop after school.

I think this school is pretty good. The uniforms are bitchin' and there's a lot less drama here. It's very no-nonsense—we work and play together as a team (in platoons). Hopefully, this school will straighten me up. I think it will. Right now, there are two classrooms. One has the seventh and eighth-grade kids and us high-school kids are in with Mr. Rose.

I get to skate every day now since I started going here. I used to be sponsored, but the police took my board so I couldn't skate for a while. I'm back to skating and trying to get good again.

This week went by really fast. When we played PE and PT with the army, it was really intense. Mr. Rose gets us all jacked up to play. He referees when we play softball and when we play football. This way, none of the idiot students can get away with anything.

–Journal #26, 17-year-old male

Yesterday the cops were at crack corner asking my friends if they knew where I was. Some kid that used to be at the academy said I spray-painted his neighbor's truck or something. If I get in trouble for that, I will go directly to placement.

–Journal #14, 17-year-old male

I am very proud because I am the first staff sergeant that the Alder Grove Academy has ever had. I've tried to be a good leader and do my best, but I am not perfect and I have my faults. Sometimes I feel like I'm letting the academy down because we are not a team yet and I don't know how to fix that. The class as a whole is trying to work together, but I have been struggling with my rank.

I have put so much work into this school and I feel I get nothing back but grief and stress. I work really hard, but I keep getting into trouble for giving discipline to the cadets who don't take care of themselves. I love being a leader as long as people at least put some effort into making the program work. I am just going to have to deal with the dummies and hope that they will turn it around. The only other solution is for Mr. Rose to see them messing up and kick them out.

When I finally talked to Mr. Rose, he told me that being a leader and a role model is not an easy job. He told me that when he first became a police sergeant, he also had a hard time since he was promoted over other individuals who had put in more hours on the street.

Mr. Rose always has a way of breaking things down for us—he shows us that what we do in our early years will help us when we become adults. I really hope I don't let him down.

–Journal #3, 17-year-old male

The reason I am here is because I got suspended from E.V. Cain. I really did not want to be here but once I heard it was an academy and the U.S. Army was part of it, I thought that it would be kinda cool. But still, there was a part of me that wasn't sure.

After a couple of weeks, I ran away from home. I was caught and sent to a halfway house. I did not like it very much and I wasn't sure if I was sure if Mr. Rose would let me return to the academy. My friends told me a few days later, that Mr. Rose would give me a second chance and I was so happy to hear that. I was still a little worried since I was not in the greatest physical shape and the thought of running and physical training with the army scared me.

When I returned, it was PT day but the army really made it fun. I was not the only one who was out of shape but as each day passes, I can do more and more.

Hello, it is me again. Today is our first day at the new site. I really like it here. My grades are up and if I tried hard, I may make the honor roll for the first time in my life. I am also proud in being able to run up to two miles with the army. Damian has been making up do sit-ups up hill and it is hard. Sometimes I think I am going to be sick.

I still have a lot of good memories from Cockroach high, like when Albert caught a pass and ran over a tree. I will always remember the last day when we had a big BBQ and played football all day. Then to see how tough we were, Mr. Rose challenged the whole class to run 2 miles. We all completed it, even Mr. Rose who said he was dying and wanted to know why no one called the ambulance.

I am getting better at push-ups and I am on the honor guard where we raise the flag in the morning by the administration building. We also ran up the dreaded hill to the cemetery to visit with Mr. Rose's dad. It was a real emotional moment that I will always remember. After our runs through the cemeteries, we got kicked out. Mr. Rose told them who we were, but they still would not give us permission.

Well I spoke too soon. Some of us cadets thought that by getting kicked out of the cemetery, we would not have to run anymore. Wrong! Mr. Rose said that they could prevent us from running in the cemetery, but the roadway is public… and so we were stuck with that dreaded hill.

Hello, it is Friday and today I got certified in CPR. I really enjoyed the class. I received a metal and a certificate. Since it is Friday, it is payday; our weekly test. It is three-hours long and covers a lot of subjects. The day starts out with coffee or chocolate and of course, donuts. I have ADD and the coffee really helps me.

My new goals is to become a sergeant of the green platoon. I will be more mature and first hope to become a corporal on the way up to sergeant. It might take a while, but I will try my hardest to achieve my goals.

Thanksgiving is getting close and we are going to have our own family Thanksgiving party! We will also have the first ever Turkey Bowl. Mr. Rose held a draft to see whose team we will be on. I sure hope my team wins.

—Journal #36–16-year-old Latino male

Mr. Rose is not only a great teacher but, in a way, he is also a father figure to me and my sister. He is the type of guy who "talks the talk and walks the walk," so you don't have high expectations that are going to be crushed. In other words, Mr. Rose will not tell you what you want to hear—he will be honest with you. If he knows that the truth might hurt you, he will first say, "With love in my heart." He has a personality that is welcoming and he has a way of talking to you that makes you feel like you can go to him in confidence with anything you want to, even if it's something you wouldn't want to tell a parent or even a friend.

There is only one time that I did not like Mr. Rose. You see, I am what you might call a "procrastinator." I'm the type of person who wants to be better and I want to follow through with my goals, but I never do it. It's like I have the thought in my head of changing my ways and wondering what it would be like to be a good kid with no drama, drugs, or violence—nothing. It is almost as if I have convinced myself that I can't have fun without any of those things.

Anyway, my point is that Mr. Rose changed that almost completely by ignoring me for a short time. He was upset with me and my sister for truancy, which is the reason I got kicked out of Placer High School—it's one of the top schools in Placer County. I started doing it again at Alder Grove Academy and he did not tolerate it. He told me that I was going off the deep end and he was right. I was slipping fast.

Don't get me wrong—I like going to school—it's just there's a part of me that doesn't want to wake up in the morning. (Hmm, I wonder why...) So finally, Mr. Rose and Ms. Berry had had enough. They arranged for me and my sister to appear before the Placer County Board of Education. They felt that my sister and I—and our mom— should have a little meeting. I've never really gotten into any big trouble before, especially with the police. I knew I had lucked out so far—even though I hung out with a bunch of idiots, I had never been caught for anything and I have never had to be locked up in juvenile hall like a lot of the other cadets here.

So, my mother drove my sister and me to the S.M.A.R.T. meeting. I was angry and hurt and I wanted to take out all of my frustration on those people because I just thought they were acting like they cared when they didn't. Boy, was I wrong. *Man*, was I wrong.

They figured out ways that I could sidetrack myself from doing the wrong things and focus on doing something that was fun, like a hobby. I love to cook and we found classes that I could take at Sierra College. I have so much that I want to do in life, but I never really thought about actually planning it out. I just thought I would go day to day. Little did I know that this is the least "best way" you could go. It is definitely better to plan your future. Now when I think of it, it's just using common sense—I had never considered that before. My life seems to have taken a turn for the better. I hope I don't screw it up.

–Journal #5, 16-year-old female

Today, when I woke up and got ready to go to school, I thought it was just going to be another day at the academy. When I arrived, I learned that our platoon sergeant was not there and Mr. Rose made me the sergeant until the real sergeant showed up. I had a team of cadets for the first time and that made me feel good. We went and played some football from 8:50 a.m. until 9:50 a.m.

When I play football, even though it is flag football, I like to give everything I have to the game. I play for blood, and I kind of showed it today. In football, I am everywhere. I'm Mexican and proud of who and what I am. I don't give up, so whoever wants to play with me—make sure you are ready because I am *always ready*, no matter where I am. I will be right there, waiting for a challenge!

–Journal #34, 16-year-old Latino

Mr. Rose got mad at me today because I was pushing and shoving in line. I thought he was going to put me on his PMP list. PMP is what Mr. Rose calls the Positive Motivation Platoon and he is in charge of it. You don't want to go on that platoon because they do not have *any* fun. It is very easy to be put on the PMP, but only Mr. Rose knows when you will not have to be on it anymore.

Here is an example of how it works. We're supposed to take our uniforms home with our PE clothes each Friday so that our mess hall doesn't stink too bad. Well, the other day two students—Mr. Rose called them knuckle-heads—

showed up without their uniforms. They said they didn't care if they each lost a merit. So, Mr. Rose put them in his PMP.

At lunchtime, our normal cafeteria food arrived but Mr. Rose had sent Ms. M. to McDonald's to pick up hamburgers and fries. While we ate the hamburgers and fries, the two other students in the PMP had to eat the crappy food we normally got. Then, when we went out to play PE, they had to pull weeds with Mr. Rose. They only had to stay in the PMP for one day, but they never forgot their uniforms after that.

–Journal #24, 14-year-old Latino

It's been over a month and a half and things have really changed for me. For one, I have a boyfriend here at school. He is really nice and I think I really love him. He was expelled for drugs and alcohol, and he has also some made stupid mistakes like me.

You won't believe it, but I am now a sergeant with my own platoon and we're the best! We have the second highest grade point average as a platoon and us girls kick butt when we play football and do fumble drills.

Mr. Rose is the best teacher I have ever had. He pushes us to do the best we can. Once we reach a bar that he has set for us, he moves it higher. Last week, we had a canned food drive for the poor. Since it is almost Christmas, everyone really tried hard to help their platoon win. The winning platoon was going to get $100 from Mr. Rose's own pocket. I think he is rich, though, so it won't hurt him. Anyway, we went to a lot of stores and they donated a lot of stuff to us—and my platoon won! We split up the money as equally as we could. I love Mr. Rose. He really inspires us.

–Journal #15, 16-year-old Latina

Well, we won the Turkey Bowl last week. It was cool the way our Staff Sergeant handled the cake presentation. Mr. Rose called all of us up front and congratulated us as the winners of the first AGA Turkey Bowl. We took a picture of us gathered around the cake. But then our Sergeant said that we would only take two-thirds of the cake and we shared the rest with all of the losers. That was kinda cool.

–Journal #28, 16-year-old female

Hi! I am 16 years old and although I was never arrested, I was sent to Alder Grove for truancy. I didn't like going to my other school since I didn't like the girls there. They all talked behind my back. They didn't like me, but they liked to talk about me. I will probably stay here at AGA until I graduate.

I have only done drugs a little bit. I've used weed and coke a couple of times. My mom smokes week medically, so I thought it would be ok and I tried it. I'm clean now.

My mom was 19 and my dad was 21 when I was born. They ended up giving me to my grandma. My entire life, I've felt abandoned and betrayed. When I was growing up I always felt like my mom and my dad left me. I had everything I needed, but I had a lot of anger toward my mom and dad. My mom and dad divorced and he has remarried with three kids. I've tried alcohol but I don't use it now. I don't like it. I recently got fired after being accused of stealing brownie mix.

While here at the academy, I am working towards getting my driver's license. Math is my favorite subject. Mr. Rose teaches it so that it is easy to understand.

It has been a long time since I have written in my journal. I've been promoted to platoon sergeant, and we have the highest attendance in the academy. I also have earned a lot of medals, but Butterball has more than any of us!

—Journal #13, 15-year-old Latina

I used to live in Los Angeles, but I moved to Auburn about four years ago because I used to get in a lot of trouble. I kind of had a lot of fun in Los Angeles...I had a lot of friends. One time, I got in *a lot* trouble.

Two days ago, I went to juvenile hall because I was behaving badly with my mom. I regret it, though, because she's really a good mom. When I returned to school, Mr. Rose got in my face. He told me he was disappointed in me, and he told me that I was a real "tough guy" for treating my mom bad. He then told the whole class a story about how we only get one set of parents and no matter how we might feel about them, we need to love them as much as we can because when they're gone, they are *gone*.

You see, he lost his dad a few years ago. He told us about how he and his family were all around his dad when his dad died. He told us that we should not think about bringing a child into this world unless we truly want to give them more than what we have. It really made me think.

I am going to try my best to behave and go to school. I'm going to try my best to graduate—both for my parents and for me. I want to *be* something in life.

—Journal #4, Jose Portillo, 16-year-old Latino male [GR Postscript: This student tragically lost his life a few years ago.]

I started at the Alder Grove Academy last year in March right after Mr. Rose got here. Before that it was a stupid lame school.

We cadets have been through a lot, good and bad. First, before we got approval to be an academy, we had to start off by deciding which uniforms to wear. Mr. Rose paid for those out of his own pocket since he was unsure if we would like to wear them every day.

A lot of kids kept going in and out of juvenile hall but once we became an academy most kids did not want to end up there and let Mr. Rose down.

–Journal #33, 17-year-old male

I did my first quarter test today. It was three hours long and in eight different subjects. I learned how to do CPR and I got my CPR pin. I liked it—it was fun. We also have a contest in English and whoever wins the contest, Mr. Rose is taking them to dinner at Applebee's.

I've had some problems at home with my mom. We got into a fight and she kicked me out, so I went to a friend's house to spend the night. I stayed there for four days. We tried to work it out, but the fighting started all over again. I think we've finally worked things out now and my mom and I are doing better. I also broke up with my girlfriend. It was over something stupid, but whatever.

I'm still doing the gangbanging shit but I don't know what to do about it. I know I need help. Things are going okay in school and I am getting good grades. It's only when I'm not at school and with my friends that I start having problems.

PT is hard but I love it. We are doing two to three miles and I like the challenge. I can't wait to do it again on Friday. I do get upset, though, with some of the people in class who do stupid things and cause us to lose PE.

–Journal #9, 17-year-old Latino

Well, here I am at Alder Grove Academy. My sister was already here, so I knew about the school from her. She looks out for me, which is nice.

I have never been placed in juvenile hall. Listening to some of the other students, it doesn't sound as bad as I thought. They all hate the food there and say that some of the probation officers are tougher than others. I hope that I never have to go there because I don't want to have to sleep in the same room with someone I don't know or like.

My sister said that Mr. Rose is an awesome teacher and almost all the kids here love him. He really makes us work hard. He brags that he is not a touchy-touchy, feely-feely type of guy, but my sister and I know that he cares about all of us. We just have to show him that we are doing our best. Don't try to con him or pull a fast one, though, because he *will* catch you!

I don't mind wearing the army uniforms—it's nice not having to worry about what I am going to wear each morning. I have a lot of favorite classes so far, especially history. We have to write hecka[10] notes but because we have so many subjects, we get to use our notes on our weekly test—we call it "Payday."

–*Journal #25, 14-year-old Latina*

My whole life, I was just an average student who got C's and D's because I didn't really care about my schoolwork. I just went to school to hang with my friends. I was always the funny kid in class, and I never got in trouble for it. I never really wanted a girlfriend either because there's no point in having one since all you do is break up. The only

---

10 "Hecka" is "a heck of a lot" or "heck of."

thing a person needs is "friends with benefits." But ever since I started at the Alder Grove Academy, I've been thinking of my work and weekly tests before anything else—how strange! After my first few tests, I was receiving B's and C's, but now I am getting straight A's.

–Journal #19, 16-year-old male

Today the army came and conducted PE. One of the sergeants was a female and I was so inspired. Seeing a woman in uniform was cool—and she could outdo some of the PE stuff our own guys couldn't even do!

Mr. Rose has taught me a lot—and not just school stuff like algebra, science and history. He's also taught us all about life. He even shared some of his cop experiences to show us where we were heading if we continue to make bad choices. He really makes me want to be all that I can be, and his stories about being a cop actually make me want to become one someday.

I haven't told anyone yet that I might want to be a cop or maybe go into the army. I think this academy has really changed me. I don't want to let you down, Mr. Rose. I promise to try and make the right decisions from now on.

–Journal #18, 16-year-old female

The school is the last expenditure
upon which America should be willing
to economize.

–Franklin D. Roosevelt, nicknamed "FDR,"
32nd president of the United States (1882-1945).

CHAPTER 17

GOING TO SCHOOL
SPARTAN-STYLE

One of our ongoing problems at the academy was our inability to acquire an adequate building. AGA-1 was housed where the original Alder Grove Community School had been located, in Dewitt Center, a large barrack-type wooden structure that had been built in 1943 as a general hospital for the U.S. Army.

The building showed its age. Because there were so many layers of linoleum, the floor groaned under our every step. When we returned from a weekend or extended holiday, the water in both the toilets and out of the faucets was a dark, muddy brown. On those days, we had to have bottled water delivered for drinking, making coffee and washing hands.

Between the classroom and our office were two large bathrooms—one for each sex–in the center of the building. The solid wooden doors gave you privacy but when you flushed a toilet, everyone in the building could hear the pipes groan and feel the floor shake.

There were power problems, too. If four devices were plugged in at the same time, all of the power would go out. Michelle would then restore power by unplugging one of the offending devices and resetting the circuit-breaker box so we could get back to business. Finally, based on many reported sightings of cockroaches, we dubbed the building "Cockroach High."

I told my cadets that we were going to start a school Spartan-style while Granite Bay High School, which had some of the wealthiest families in the county, was the "anti-Spartan" school. Most of my students, if not all, came from some of the poorer sections of the county so this dilapidated school did not faze them. We laughed about the brown water, the groaning or shaking of the building, and the terrible, incredibly loud buzzer. We soon purposefully broke it and created a more pleasing sounding device.

The cadets cleaned up after themselves—males and females–including the bathrooms. They tried to keep the new academy in the best shape that they could. It was our home and we treated it that way.

While at the first AGA, the cadets created a merit board for our original three platoons of red, white and blue. Soon, we had to expand the number of cadets in each platoon and we added another three—purple, orange and green. Each platoon had a sergeant with a colored arm band representing their platoon as well as a corporal. The rest of the cadets were either privates or privates first class. Those who were promoted were called up in front of the other students by army officers who gave the promoted students their new insignias and a letters of promotion.

The cadets loved the promotional ceremonies and it motivated many to work harder.

For marching drills, physical exercise and flag football, we marched approximately three city blocks to a grassy field near the Placer County Sheriff's Department for exercise. Fortunately, the field was the size of a standard NFL football field leaving us lots of room.

On the days that the army arrived, the uniformed cadets would "fall in" outside behind their respective platoon sergeant. Once inspections were completed, the platoons, two by two, marched with the army throughout the Dewitt complex and beyond. Passing motorists would honk their horns or salute which thrilled the cadets.

When we exercised on our own, the cadets followed the same routine but would change from their uniforms into exercise attire. Because we didn't have lockers or changing rooms, the girls used the bathrooms to change and the boys changed in the classroom. I played watchman so that the girls wouldn't spy on the boys; actually it was mostly the other way around.

AGA Grows Up

By the end of the first year at Cockroach High, AGA-1 had about twenty-eight cadets. The classroom was full. When school started up the next year, and just before we moved to AGA- 2, we had over thirty.

Our staff had grown as well. When I first arrived at the Alder Grove Community School, Michelle was the only other adult. Later, as student enrollment grew after becoming an academy, one additional aide, Jenny, was added to the roster. Jenny handled attendance, breakfast and lunch menus, and discipline when my back was turned. Michelle answered the phone calls, took formal attendance and prepared the paperwork for new and departing students.

The school district knew we had outgrown our first AGA facility. At the time, the county wanted to raze Cockroach High and use the property for other purposes. When the education office decided to request permission from the Auburn City

Council to move AGA to a second site, the same school district superintendent and school district attorney who had approved the original academy requested that I make a presentation to the city council. I asked my staff sergeant to accompany me to the meeting and also address the council about his experiences at AGA-1.

When the cadet finished his presentation to the council, one of the board members announced to the council and the audience that she was very impressed with our presentation and wished there had been such a program when her children were growing up. I wondered if her kids weren't ideal students either.

> "We are what we repeatedly do. Excellence, then, is not an act, but a habit."
>
> –ARISTOTLE

CHAPTER 18

JOURNALS–PROMOTIONS, PARTIES AND PENALTIES

I have now completed my first week here. Compared to all of my other schools, I think this one is great. It's very strict and has a bunch of rules—the students who were here before me put all of the rules together. We have a lot of platoons with different colors. One platoon is all girls and they are pretty tough at PT.

I am in the orange platoon. There are six of us. We used to have a female sergeant but now we have a male sergeant. I am just a private, but I think someday I would make a good sergeant.

We run a lot in this school with the army. They are really cool and we can go to any of them when we need to talk to someone other than Mr. Rose. We can earn medals and wear them on our uniforms. It's cool. I can't wait to get my first one—this might be next week when I get to try and run a timed mile.

I lost my temper the other day and Mr. Rose got upset with me. I thought he was going to yell at me but instead he let me finish yelling at another stupid student, then he just looked at me and said, "Are you done?" That was it. He didn't judge me. He just turned and walked away.

Everyone here loves Mr. Rose, but it is too early for me to tell how I feel. He is really strict and I would be afraid to make him mad. But one thing I think is nice about him is that he always teaches us in a way that helps us understand things. We have to take a weekly test that he calls "Payday." It covers a shitload of subjects, but we get to use our notes. We always know where we stand with our grades since we have to keep a record in our journal and our platoon sergeant also keeps a record.

—Journal #6, 15-year-old male

Today the army made us run up the hill behind the academy and into the graveyard. It is *all* uphill and a tough run. Mr. Rose runs with us and then back. We know it's killing his knees, but he has always told us that when we become supervisors we should never ask our employees to do something that we would not do ourselves.

The run down the hill is much easier, but the army said that we will soon do something called the Ranger Run. It sounds tough, but I know my platoon can do it.

—Journal #15, 16-year-old Latina

It is almost Christmas and everyone is acting like a bunch of idiots—or, as Mr. Rose says, we are acting like a bunch of squirrels. We are going to have a little Christmas lunch together today and a lot of students brought in some good eats. We bought a present for Mr. Rose. It is an army-type jacket. I think he'll like it.

My mom and dad asked me if I want to go back to my regular school and I told them no, but Mr. Rose has been telling all of us that we need to go back to Placer High since there are more opportunities for us there. I know he's right, but I will miss him.

—Journal #26, 17-year-old male

We had our Christmas party and I think Mr. Rose really liked the gift we got him! Actually, Ms. M got it for us. It is a camouflage jacket that looks great on him. I think he was almost ready to cry, but he thanked us and told us to "Get the hell out of here and have a safe and merry Christmas!"

—Journal #13, 15-year-old Latina

Hey, I passed my CPR test today and got a medal for my uniform!

I have also decided that I want to be a mechanic when I am through with school. I really like fixing things, especially bikes. On Monday, my friend brought his bike to my house to see if I could fix it, and I did.

—Journal #34, 16-year-old Latino male

The day I stepped into this classroom, my first impression was that it was going to be hell, even though I knew most of the kids here. I hated the uniform, but now I've gotten used to it—boots and all. I hated having to wear my hair in a ponytail, too, but now I sometimes do it at home or when I am skateboarding or boxing.

I used to think that polishing our boots was a waste of time, but now I polish my boots all the time, hoping to win the weekly "best-shined boots" award from the army. Everything feels normal to me now.

Mr. Rose is the best teacher I ever had. I like his way of teaching. He cares about you, both in school and out of school. He is like a second father for everybody in the academy. I can learn here because Mr. Rose has this thing where it seems like he can sense if the class understands what he is teaching. You have to pay attention, though, because he has this habit of calling on you and asking you questions. If you give a stupid answer—like you're not trying—he will make you do push-ups and the whole class counts while you do them.

This school is like my home away from home. At first I hated it with a passion, but I've grown to love it. Earlier in the year, I had the chance to go back to Placer High but I chose to come here instead. It's very open to everybody—it's like a family. We help each other. We can tell when someone is down and we help them through the day.

The U.S. Army made us select a "Battle Buddy" that we had to introduce ourselves to. We learned about where they came from and what got them into the academy. The army explained that our Battle Buddy would be our go-to person when we are having problems, including work in the classroom. Only Mr. Rose has a list of who everyone's Battle Buddy is. Mine has become a close friend. There are some kids who don't take it seriously but I think they will eventually leave the school anyway, so who gives a fuck about them? They're losers.

—Journal #4, Jose Portillo, 16-year-old Latino [GR
Postscript: This student tragically lost his life a few years ago.]

I'm tripping out right now because my mother is going into surgery for cancer in two days. I don't know what I'll do if I lose my mother and the hardest part is waiting and hoping that she'll be all right.

I gave up my staff sergeant position today. I handed my stripes to Mr. Rose. I was tired of one of the teaching assistants always coming off disrespectful. I worked hard getting this school started as well as doing well in class and showing respect for everyone.

—Journal #3, 17-year-old male

Mr. Rose talked about burning bridges today and asked how many of us can recall people—both family and friends—who have tried to help us go straight and yet we still let them down. He said that he knows some of us are on bridges that have shaky footing and unless we wake up soon and change our ways, those bridges are going to crash too.

It was after he spoke to us that I had a huge need to write this. I was so brainwashed into not giving a crap about anything but partying that I lost my friends (those that were my real friends). I stopped going to church a year ago, and I've lost contact with anyone and everyone I ever cared about. Even though I missed my associations with other people, I just disappeared from my life for a while. It hurt, but it didn't hurt as bad if I was on something. The thought of "What the hell am I doing?" crossed my mind sometimes, but never enough to impact my actions. No matter how much I would think about it, I couldn't care less.

I know that I am a good person. It's just that I've covered myself up with anger and partying for so long. I've been smoking, drinking and everything for the last four years. My true self just got lost somewhere and it took some good thoughts and a great teacher to find it again.

—Journal #5, 16-year-old female

We are celebrating Mr. McDaniel's birthday today. He is another teacher from the juvenile hall, like Mr. Rose. He is a big part of this organization. He helps us to maintain our uniforms and keep our boots shining.

—Journal #11, 17-year-old male

We are still in our old school, which we call "Cockroach High." We heard that we are going to be moving to a new school soon. I hope it has a place to continue to play football.

—Journal #16, 17-year-old male

My whole body hurts and I've been tired all day. I didn't bring my PT clothes yesterday, so I had to do a lot of leg-lifts and butterfly kicks as my "consequences."

For the past couple of weeks, I have been doing better. I now have a boyfriend—he's one of the few boys I've dated in the last two years. I told him that we are not gonna have sex and that if that's what he wants, he might as well go to the next girl.

I get to start at Sierra College early this year (in November). The cool thing is I'm only sixteen and in college already! I think it will be great. I want to study a lot of subjects, including anthropology, archeology, and history. I want to meet Professor DeFoe—he's known for being a great teacher and I hope I get to take one of his classes.

I wish I could be in college on my own right now. I am really excited about learning, especially the history of Egypt. I have been reading a lot of history books lately and Mr. Rose gave me a book about ancient Egypt—he said it was for me to keep. I think I want to be an Egyptologist or a paleontologist. Paleontology will be helpful when I go to tombs and search them—that's if I even find any bones. The most likely bones I will find are human bones and cat bones.

I truly think I could be successful in everything I want to do. I might even be a famous actress or archeologist one day!

–Journal #7, 16-year-old female

We got our grades today and some of my grades have gone down. Mr. Rose got upset with some of us because a few students complained when they saw their grades. He made a good point by having us say why we got an A or a B (because we earned it). Then he said, "The same applies when you *earn* a D or an F. Deal with it."

–Journal #25, 14-year-old Latina

I can't believe so many weeks have passed. I love it here. I told Ms. Berry that I do not want to go back to E.V. Cain Middle School. I told her that Mr. Rose is the best teacher I have ever had. My grades are all B's. I can finally understand algebra now! Mr. Rose makes it fun.

–Journal #13, 15-year-old Latina

I started going to Alder Grove Academy after being expelled from Chana High School. My buddies and I were fighting with a bunch of Southside gang members on school grounds. I'm not a gang member, but I was bored and I decided to do something stupid. I tried as hard as I could to stay at Chana, but they were tired of all the problems I was causing at the school.

I was finally placed in juvenile hall because I got into a fight with my girlfriend's stepdad after I had been drinking. I walked up to the front door of my girlfriend's house and her stepdad came out. He started bad-mouthing me on the porch, and then he pushed me. I almost fell down the stairs.

I don't remember too much after he pushed me, but I know I snapped. I guess I got so angry that I blacked out. The next thing I remember is riding my bike as fast as I could—I was trying to get away from the house. I was arrested and served twenty-nine days in juvenile hall before I was released on house arrest. This lasted for three weeks.

At some point, I got drunk in my house and blacked out again. When I woke up, I was back in juvenile hall. I was later released and they referred me to drug court. Drug court is a three-phase probation program. In phase one, we're required to go down to Roseville every Monday and Wednesday—we have to attend an anger management and moral reasoning group. Then, on every second and fourth Thursday, we have to go to court to find out how we're doing on the program.

We get drug tested two to three times a week and if anyone gets a dirty test, it's back to juvenile hall and the next drug court hearing.

—Journal #14, 17-year-old male

Today the third quarter is over and I have pretty good grades! I got all B's and C's, which is not bad since I am only an eighth-grader. I also passed my U.S. Constitution test and Mr. McDaniel gave me a medal to wear on my uniform.

It looks like some of the other cadets will be leaving us soon and returning to their regular school but most of us do not want to leave.

—Journal #24, 14-year-old Latino

I learned that my mom talked to Mr. Rose yesterday. Even *she* said that she has seen a huge difference in my attitude. She told him she was really proud of me.

—Journal #17, 17-year-old female

I cannot teach anybody anything. I can only make them think.

–Socrates, Greek philosopher (BC 469-BC 389).

CHAPTER 19

A PARADE OF PRIDE AT AGA-2

As unpleasant as Cockroach High had been, the new premises at AGA-2 presented new problems. Because of the way the inside of the building was laid out, there were spots where the kids could congregate for romance, collusion or combat and not be seen.

Even more important, we had no access to a physical exercise or training area.

What we did have was a parking lot a little wider than the classroom. When we played flag football among the parked cars, the landlord complained to Joan. We eventually damaged a car so the administration gave us bus tickets to transport the class to a dog park to play sports.

Three times a week the army would march us down the block and across the street to the main administration building for the PCOE where our platoons would form and our flag detail would raise the flag. From there, the only available places to run were up what we called the "dreaded hill" and through two nearby cemeteries. Eventually, we were forbidden to use both cemeteries. Finally, when the school day ended, students tended to gather in the post office parking lot next door. That, of course, led to more complaints.

This simply confirmed what my staff and I already knew—to accomplish AGA goals, we not only had to have adequate classroom space but a location to conduct physical training, drills and ceremonies, as well as sufficient staff to keep up with unpredictable teen behavior.

After only three or four months, we had over thirty students at AGA-2 and no space for more. Fortunately, I still had three staff members—Michelle, Beverly and Jenny. The administration also assigned a special education teacher to the site even though I did not have many students who needed her skills.

The cadets complained about rats but it proved to be a self-fulfilling prophecy. Though throwing food at one another was against the rules, some threw their lunch food into the rafters where we had our weightlifting equipment. The rats began to thrive.

Although I forbade that conduct once I found out about it, it was difficult not to feel some sympathy for the cadets. The food at AGA-1 and AGA-2 was bad. Initially, I had told the kids to shut up and be grateful that they had something to eat, but after a while even I started to refer to some of it as "mystery meat." Some days the lunch was so bad that it went directly into the garbage cans. On those occasions, I'd give some money to one of my three aids and she would bring us all lunch from the local McDonald's.

Times to Remember

We enjoyed several important victories at AGA-2.

- As time passed, more students wanted to stay in the AGA program instead of returning to their traditional high school. Although this created a problem because of our space limitations, it was a compliment to the program. Joan loved the fact that the cadets were doing better at AGA than they had at their traditional schools so she allowed them to stay on and matriculate in a PCOE ceremony.
- Meantime, proud as I was of our academic success, I tried to alleviate our space problems by encouraging some of the students who were doing well academically to return to their former high school and graduate with their friends. Most did as I suggested and their parents were grateful.
- Two former gangbangers did so well in regard to maintaining order, structure, and discipline that they both took the armed forces exam and scored high enough to join after graduation.
- One of the female students fell in love with archeology after we had a class in ancient civilizations and is still pursuing her dream in college.
- We had our first and only parade. I think it was Veteran's Day and school was out. Still, most of the cadets showed up ready to march with an American flag flying from an aluminum pole–not too fancy but they marched proudly in their green Special Forces uniforms and black combat boots. Our army volunteers followed in their Hummer. There was an ROTC school with

fancy flags and white rifles in front of us. But when we marched past the local Auburn population, my cadets and I were convinced we got the loudest applause.

- Because we had three staff members, we finally had time to pursue some community service activities including volunteering for the Salvation Army over the holidays. This also led to the academy competing with Placer High School in a food drive. I offered a cash prize of two hundred dollars to the platoon that could contribute the most food. Having persuaded a grocery store to donate a ton of *Top Ramen* to the cause, Sabrina's platoon made it possible for the academy to defeat Placer High School and win the cash prize.

Every great dream begins with a dreamer. Always remember, you have within you the strength, the patience, and the passion to reach for the stars to change the world.

—HARRIET TUBMAN, AFRICAN-AMERICAN ABOLITIONIST, SPY FOR THE U.S. ARMY DURING THE CIVIL WAR (BIRTH UNKNOWN–DIED 1913).

CHAPTER 20

JOURNALS–READING, WRITING AND RUNNING UP THE DREADED HILL

It's Friday today, and the first week at the new site is coming to a close. I'm glad that we changed locations. Maybe now I'll walk to school instead of taking two different buses.

We ran in the rain with the army this morning. Although I hate doing physical training, all of us are starting to see that we are getting better physically. Some of us have even stopped smoking. But I have recently lost some more merits for not being in uniform, so I don't know how long my stay will be here at the Academy.

—Journal #11, 17-year-old male

Mr. Rose got permission to use the huge grass field near Bell Road and it was there that the U.S. Army conducted physical training and Mr. Rose held PE. The army ran us a lot and Mr. Rose, bad knees and all, ran right behind us. We earned medals for almost everything and it really worked as a motivational tool. We had to run the Ranger run which was tough. We had to run a mile for time and Sergeants Howell and Hewitt along with Corporal Burubeltz cheered us on. I remember how proud one of my friends was when she ran with the help of Mr. Rose and earned a medal for finishing.

—Journal #31, 16-year-old male

I now have two medals! One is for my mile run—it's called the PT medal—and the other one is for volunteering to help one of the teaching assistants. It's like a community service award. I have never won an award before!

—Journal #6, 15-year-old male

It's been two weeks since I wrote and a lot has happened in that time. We did the CPR training with two probation officers—it was easy and fun. We've played a lot of good football, too, and the school is getting better. I am glad to be here. It's almost Halloween and that will be cool.

—Journal #8, 17-year-old male

The parade on Veteran's Day made me feel so proud that I am part of this school! Mr. Rose, Mr. McDaniel and Tom Grayson called out when we should march and the army followed us in a Humvee.

I feel torn, though, and often wonder what I should do. There are a lot of things I want to write, but I can't get the words to come out. Sometimes I'm doing good in school, and sometimes I'm not. I want to go back to my old school in Colfax or Placer, but I know I'll just get into more trouble. I want to stay here, too, because I have the best teacher I've ever had.

Mr. Rose is a great. He makes even boring subjects interesting and he loves to joke with us. He makes me want to stay. Maybe we can go to the Winchester Mystery House and Alcatraz—I hope so!

–Journal #7, 16-year-old female

Today something happened to Mr. Rose. We decided to run up the hill to the cemetery. It was a cold day and a little foggy, too, so most of us were already cold when we started out. (We all wear the same PT clothing—it's made up of a black shirt with a gold Spartan helmet and matching black shorts. Some of the girls wore sweats under their shirts and shorts to keep warm.)

Anyway, there we were, running up that damn hill, and Mr. Rose was at the rear. (We don't tell him this, but we are impressed that he runs with us even though he has had a shitload of knee operations.) At the top of the hill is the entrance to the cemetery. We had been asked not to run there—people were scared of us because our clothing is all black.

Mr. Rose had told us that most of the people buried in the cemetery were veterans from past wars. He had also told us that his dad is buried there. Once Mr. Rose reached all of us at the entrance, he asked us if we wanted to see where his dad was buried. We then followed him in and walked down to his father's grave. That's when it happened. Mr. Rose looked up into the sky and said something like, "Hey Dad, these are my cadets." Then he started to cry. He quickly caught himself, though, and started to walk away so we couldn't see the tears in his eyes.

Some of the girls, when they saw Mr. Rose cry, well, they started to cry too. Then some of the guys, including me, went up to Mr. Rose. Our Staff Sergeant put his arm around him and said that it was okay—and that Mr. Rose's dad must have been a great father. Mr. Rose then rejoined the rest of the group and acted tough again. He said, "Let's go. We have work to do." So, back down the hill we went.

—Journal #29, 17-year-old Latino

It's the first day at our new Alder Grove Academy (AGA-2) site. It is hella big. Today was also our first PT at the new site—we had to run two miles. In my heart, I said that no one was going to make me go down because I was born ready! We ran through the Auburn Cemetery, but after we completed the run we got kicked out and we can't run there again.

I can't believe that in two days we will have already completed our fourth week of school. I haven't missed a single day. I'm impressed that I'm a "Spartan"—something that I never dreamed could happen.

I love this school because I love challenges. I am not the smartest person in the class and my grades are not the greatest, but I know that I will try hard and I will keep doing so. Besides, Mr. Rose said that some of his best police officers only got C's in college. I am not giving up!

—Journal #34, 16-year-old Latino

Well, a lot has happened. The academy is moving—we'll no longer be next to Eisley's Nursery. The new site is supposedly going to be much better because it has a large football field that the guys here can hardly wait to play on it.

This place was okay, I guess. We had a small room that had some exercise equipment, but mostly we just hung out after lunch. I have a lot of memories here, though. We had the HILL that we had to run a lot. We also had an incident where one of the students tried to catch a football pass and he crashed into a parked car. He put a big dent in the side of a brand-new car and thought he was going to get in trouble. Mr. Rose told him not to worry and that maybe now the county would find us a place to play PE.

Mr. Rose took a picture of the damage and had Ms. M. send it to his boss. I guess his boss got really pissed, but Mr. Rose stood up to her. It worked, too—a few days later we started being bused to a park a long way away and we got to play both football and baseball.

One memory I will never forget is when we played our Mud Bowl football game. We chose teams based on our platoons and started to play. It rained a lot—the field was filled with mud and water—but Mr. Rose always says that if the army can do it, we can do it. When PE was over, we were covered with mud from head to toe. It was great. We all wanted to have our picture taken.

–Journal , #28, 16-year-old female

Wow, we have a lot of new Cadets—we must have almost forty kids now. Since the other teacher was sent to juvenile hall, we all attend class in Mr. Rose's room.

Hey, this weekend we got to march in a parade! Not all of us were there, but those of us that were had fun marching down the streets of Auburn. Mr. Rose, Mr. McDaniel and Tom Grayson called out our marching orders. There was another military school there, too. They had marching rifles and a bunch of flags. Compared to them, we were the ghetto school, but I was still proud of our Academy.

Guess what? Mr. Rose ordered a U.S. flag and a U.S. Army flag. He even ordered a special flag that shows our custom shoulder patch. They are all up by his desk. He also bought some marching rifles that are painted white, but he won't let us handle them because most of us are on probation and we could get in trouble. I hope I get to carry one of our flags the next time we are in a parade.

—Journal #30, 17-year-old male

There is another girl here at the academy that everyone thinks looks like my sister. We are such close friends that we kind of are. She made a mistake the other day and took an E that one of the other students had brought to school.[11] Someone told Mr. Rose that something was wrong with her and, the next thing I know, an ambulance and the Sheriff's Department showed up. They took the other student away, and then school was let out.

The following day, I learned that my girlfriend was eventually released from the hospital and that Mr. Rose went there to see her. Her mom is really pissed off and wants her out of the academy. But no matter where you go, if you want drugs, you can get them.

—Journal , #28, 16-year-old female

We took the CPR test and the whole class passed. I am also doing better now because my mother is done with surgery and it looks good. The doctor said that they think

---

11 "E" is a street name for what is also known as "ecstasy" or MDMA, a drug that is illegal to produce, possess or supply. MDMA stands for methylenedioxymethamphetamine and is a central nervous system stimulant and hallucinogenic.

they removed all of the cancer so she will not have to go through chemotherapy.

Today was all right, for the most part. I passed the weekly test by getting an A in each subject. At PE, we did fumble football drills. That's when Mr. Rose throws a football and we tackle each other so we can be the first to get back to where he is standing. It was fun to hit people and not get locked up for it!

—Journal #3, 17-year-old male

Even though I'm at the academy, I also have to go to drug court. In drug court, every dirty drug test is a sanction (or penalty) that is served in juvenile hall. The first sanction is for three days, the second is for seven days, and the third sanction will get you fourteen days.

If you continue to screw up and earn a fourth sanction, you get twenty-one days. If you get more than four sanctions, you could end up on home placement—this means you could be sent to a group home, boot camp, or rehab. Phase one lasts for two and a half months.

In phase two, we are required to go to Roseville every Monday to take a drug test. On Wednesdays, we have to go back to Roseville to attend a one-hour relapse prevention class. We also have to go to court once a month.

Curfew for phase two is 7:00 PM. Every Tuesday, I have to do one hour of counseling at my house. Phase two is also two and a half months long.

In phase three, we are still drug tested each Monday and we have to go to court once a month. Group is held on each Wednesday. This phase lasts three months. When you complete phase three, you get terminated from probation. If you fail the program, you are sent to placement.

I have screwed up so many times that I've been on drug court for over one and a half years and I am *still* on phase two. Part of the problem is that I went on the run while I was on probation. Now, I am on zero-tolerance probation. This means that if I get into *any* trouble, I go immediately to placement.

–Journal #14, 17-year-old male

After a few weeks on independent study, summer arrived. No school—great! But then summer ended and I still couldn't return to E.V. Cain after being expelled the semester before. The decision was made (by Ms. Berry) for me to attend Alder Grove Academy.

When I arrived, I was really scared. I was the smallest person in the school. We have to wear a uniform and combat boots, and we have to raise the flag each morning. The physical training is tough, but really fun. The army pushes us just as much as Mr. Rose.

Mr. Rose is great. He makes all of the subjects he teaches fun. But we do a hella lot of work. When we arrive in the morning, he has all six whiteboards filled with notes. "Payday" is on Friday when we have to take the weekly test. It covers all of the subjects we covered during the week. But after the test, if we've earned it, we have an extra-long PE session.

We now have six platoons, each with a different color. I am in a platoon with all girls, but I learned today that we will soon be getting *more* girls and therefore, we will have to change the platoons around.

–Journal #13, 15-year-old Latina

Today we were asked to write about our lives and experiences in the hopes that someday it might become a book that would help other students to not make the same mistakes we did.

It's easy to understand why Mr. Rose wants us to do this. Two movies have just come out that he likes. One was *Gridiron Gang* and the other was *Freedom Writers*. He had already made us watch *Stand and Deliver,* and that was pretty cool. He even has a picture of when he got to meet the teacher that movie was based on—Mr. Rose called him his "hero."

–Journal #16, 17-year-old male

I have completed almost one whole quarter at Alder Grove Academy—or AGA, as we call it. I am now a corporal. I don't know if I will make sergeant or not. I don't think I have won Mr. Rose's trust yet.

There are a lot of students in this class—there are over forty of us now. There are a lot of eighth-graders here also, and they act like a bunch of babies. The food is not bad, but sometimes Ms. M brings in some soup—it's really good.

On Friday, when we have our weekly test, Mr. Rose brings in donuts and we have either coffee or hot chocolate. It's really cool. I have never been in a school or had a teacher that did that. Mr. Rose said that he likes to run the class like a college classroom—but only as long as we show that we deserve it.

–Journal #21, 17-year-old Latino

We have been kicked out of the two cemeteries where we use to run. A woman from one of the cemeteries told Mr. Rose that people are concerned about seeing a bunch of kids, dressed all in black, running through the graveyard. She asked for us to stop. Mr. Rose tried to reason with her and said that his father and grandfather are both buried there, but she insisted.

Some of the cadets were glad that they did not have to run up the dreaded hill anymore, but Mr. Rose had other plans.

Sure, we couldn't run in the cemetery now, but the road leading up to it was still public property, so we continued to run up that damn hill!

Something happened to Mr. Rose today when he ran with us up the hill. It was his dad's birthday and he decided to show the class where his dad is buried. He knew he might get in trouble for running us into the cemetery since we had been kicked out, but he didn't care.

Before we entered the cemetery, he had all of us stand around him and he told us to please respect those buried here since most of them were veterans of our armed forces—in other words, no swearing, spitting, etc. We ran to the area by the flagpole and then he had us walk down to where his dad is. He read off the words on the headstone and then he looked up to heaven and said, "Dad, these are my cadets." Then he lost it and started to cry. I started to cry, too, as did many of the other girls. He walked away in embarrassment only to have our staff sergeant and some of the other cadets catch up to him and give him a hug. He apologized to us, but we told him he had nothing to apologize for.

—Journal #15, 16-year-old Latina

I am in a platoon with a girl sergeant and we kick butt in almost everything, including sports. Right now there are eleven girls and thirty-one guys. Some of them will be leaving soon because they get to go back to their regular school after they meet all of the AGA requirements.

A female army sergeant was at PT today and that really inspired me and one of the other female cadets. She was in great shape and told us about her life in the army. I may consider doing that.

—Journal #25, 14-year-old Latina

I have a lot of memories. One was when Albert ran into a tree after I threw a Joe Montana pass to him. This place has tremendously changed my life. I've improved physically and academically. I've also improved maturity-wise and behaving way better.

Mr. Rose can be an asshole sometimes, but because he pushed me to get to where I am now, I really don't want to leave the academy. Unfortunately, as Mr. Rose tells us, even though we are an academy, he cannot compete with our traditional schools and what they have to offer-and since I want to play sport, I know I have to leave.

Mr. Rose is by far, the best teacher I have ever had. We didn't share a lot of words with each other as I would have liked, but this school is still the best thing that ever happened to me. Thank you Mr. Rose for everything you have put me through. I will not let you down.

–Journal #33, 17-year-old male

Failure is only the opportunity to begin again more intelligently.

—Henry Ford, American industrialist, founder of Ford Motor Company, from "My Life and Work," 1922 (1863-1947).

CHAPTER 21

SPARTANS IN ACTION

If a cadet was going to change at all, it was at their own speed and in their own way—the difference might be subtle or marked.

Some improved academically. They had to take notes for their Friday exam which covered all the subjects of the week, regardless of grade level. Their exams included questions on U.S. or world history, economics, science, English, and algebra. Seeing a C, B or A for the first time usually increased a cadet's self-confidence.

For others, change came after receiving an award to display on their uniform. Some cadets confided that their commitment increased when their parents told them how proud they were of the changes their son or daughter had made in their lives.

Most who felt lost were reluctant to admit it to anyone at first. Sometimes, the girls would open up to Michelle, which caused us to set up a "Girls Day" at AGA-2 and AGA-3. Michelle routinely took the girls on a walk to discuss whatever might be troubling them. To release tension among the boys, we sometimes allowed them to play a rougher game of football.

Though both groups seemed to enjoy these opportunities, both sexes shared their uncertainty and discouragement with me through their journals where some referred to themselves and their classmates as kids nobody wanted.

Cupid in Combat

We had some very beautiful teenage girls in the AGA. Many of the girls were fully developed but lacked maturity. Others were not only fully developed but were much more socially mature than their male counterparts. Because some of the girls were as sexually active and aggressive as most of the boys, we never allowed certain male and female cadets to be together alone.

Though I allowed hand-holding during breaks, no physical signs of affection were allowed between lovebirds during classroom time.

Romantic break-ups were more difficult to control. There would be dirty glances, rude notes, and physical challenges. One summer day I reported to work and there was a phone call from Joan about a fight between two female cadets.

On the preceding evening, one cadet-couple had gotten drunk together behind the Big 5 Sporting Goods store. When they argued, the boyfriend wandered off and had sex with another female cadet. This started a fight between the females. No one was arrested but Joan called for a meeting to be held with the young women during our breakfast period.

I attended the meeting only briefly. As I left, I heard one of the young women yelling, "You bitch! You bitch!" I was confident Joan would resolve the matter much more effectively than I could. As Joan and I both expected, the same female cadets soon made peace and discovered new romances.

From Wannabees to Gangbangers

Parents and teachers share one particularly difficult task—how to help teenagers become more responsible at the same time that the adult stays in charge. It's an ongoing juggling act for any parent or teacher but especially for those dealing with at-risk teens. You give them one taste of adulthood while denying them another until you're confident they're ready to sample more of the menu.

So as often as I allowed and encouraged the cadets to set standards for the academy, I often had to make sure they knew I was the source of whatever liberties they enjoyed. The threat of gang violence was one of those times.

There were several members of rival gangs housed under the AGA roof at different times. Most were what we called "wannabes," but the probation office also placed recognized gangbangers at AGA.

Rival gang members who were housed in the county juvenile detention facility were always separated into areas called pods, each of which was patrolled by two probation officers. Yet, once released and put on probation, rival gang members were sent to my classroom, both before and while I taught at the academy, with no probation officers nearby. This might have been a compliment to my ability to control a classroom, but I would have preferred the help of at least one probation officer.

I watched the gang members in my classes closely and they respected that I

had gang experience as a former cop. I shared stories with them about how painful it was to have to tell a gang member's surviving parents and grandparents how sorry I was about the loss of their child after a gang killing. On the other hand, I'd also mock the absurdity of how gangs thought controlling bathrooms in a local park was a victory over their rivals.

Still, I never put one gang member up against a rival except in the heat of physical training or exercise sessions. On those occasions, they were so involved in the competition between platoons, they were content to sacrifice their gang affiliation for platoon loyalty.

When I sensed that there was some tension in the classroom between competing gangs, I took the opportunity to remind *every* cadet of our common purpose as well as my role in protecting the Alder Grove Academy family. I seldom varied the text.

This is *not* a democracy, I would announce. It is a dictatorship and I am the dictator. There will be no gang issues in this academy. There will be no gang colors. Our academy colors are camouflage. Our gang sign is the AGA patch. We are a family and, like most families, we will have problems but we will take care of our problems in-house, not outside. Finally, I warned, if I learned that any cadet was involved in a gang-related activity, I would do everything in my power to have them kicked out of the academy.

Though verbal assaults were common, I'm pleased to say we never had a gang-related incident and only one real fist fight. I like to think we took care of our problems like a normal family.

Right actions in the future are the best
apologies for bad actions in the past.

–TYRON EDWARDS, THEOLOGIAN, AUTHOR OF "A
DICTIONARY OF THOUGHTS" (1809-1894).

CHAPTER 22

JOURNALS–OF LOVE AND WAR

'm sad today. My boyfriend violated his probation and
he's back in the hall. I miss him. Mr. Rose heard that
probation is considering out-of-home placement, which
means I will not be able to see my boyfriend here.

I talked to Mr. Rose to see if he could do something. I
was mad at him when he said that "Some people have not
reached rock bottom." Then Mr. Rose asked the class to
write some letters to my boyfriend and he said he would see
that probation gave them to him in juvie.

I was still mad at Mr. Rose until I later learned that he
had written a letter to both probation and the judge, asking
that my boyfriend be given one last chance and they agreed.
Now I will have to really push my boyfriend to make the
right choices or I will lose him forever.

–Journal #15, 16-year-old Latina

Yesterday I got kicked out of the hall for some bullshit. I got a "dirty" for smoking but the stupid thing is, if I wasn't in CPS (Child Protective Services), then I would've been out in five days.

My stupid social worker and my P.O. (probation officer) are trying to send me to a stupid-ass group home in Loomis, California. I've been so stressed out, worrying that I'll never go home or come back to the academy to see all of my friends, especially my girlfriend.

They put me back into juvenile hall instead. I didn't know if I was going to get out or really be gone. They scheduled PRT (Placement Review Team) for the next Tuesday, so I had to stay longer in juvenile hall.

At the PRT meeting, my P.O. (probation officer) and my social worker said they wanted me to go to the group home. Then they went around and talked to my family and my counselor. My mom, my dad and both of my grandmas said how much they loved me and needed me. Then the PRT people said they were gonna put me on some R.A.F.T. thing (Rap Around Family Therapy), and I was so happy. You see, Mr. Rose had written me a letter. He stuck his neck out and said that I was doing well in most things in school and that I deserved another chance—on a thin leash.

That evening I got a letter from my girlfriend and a bunch of the kids from class. Mr. Rose asked them to write to me. It made me so happy, I almost started crying. I didn't sleep much—I was too stressed.

The next day, I went to court. I was still scared that I might not get out. The judge liked the letter from Mr. Rose, so he said yes and I got out. I went back to the academy and saw everyone and they said how much they missed me and how boring it was without me.

I just held my girlfriend. It felt so good to see her again. Mr. Rose called me off to the side of the classroom and said that this was my last chance—he would not go to bat for me again and he hoped that I had finally reached rock bottom.

Later that night, I just broke down and started to cry. I don't know why. I might still have to spend eight years at a group home or boot camp. If I mess up one more time, I'm gone and I don't want that.

My mom is still in rehab and is finally starting to do well. My dad is doing everything he can now, even though I never used to see him. I'm scared, but I know I'm gonna do good because this is my last chance and I don't want to mess it up. I'm trying to get my life back together.

–Journal #8, 17-year-old male

Today has started out really bad. I am so fucking pissed off right now that I just want to snap! When I came to school, one of the other cadets asked me if I was dating some girl, which I am. He said, "Oh, my brother went out with her about ten times, off and on, and he still likes her." I asked who his brother was, and it turns out he's the same motherfucker that me and my girlfriend got into an argument about because I saw him flirting with her. She had told me not to worry about it, but she has driver's education every day from 3:00 PM to 6:00 PM for the next two weeks over at Placer High. And what do I find out? This guy has signed up for the same shit.

My girlfriend told me she had no idea that he had signed up for the same class. We have only been dating for three weeks, so who knows what the fuckin' truth is? I found out he was in her class when I went to pick her up one day and he was walking with her.

A part of me doesn't even want to have a relationship so I don't have to deal with shit like this, but then I am just running away from the situation and I know I will probably have to face similar situations in the future. I don't want to be controlling because I *do* like her.

She has told me that they are just good friends, but when I asked her how good, she just said, "Good," and told me that there was nothing else going on. Then I realized I hadn't *asked* her if there was something else going on. She was the one that brought it up—why? She offered to not speak to him anymore and I should've taken her up on it. I don't know how to handle this and I don't know if I *should* be dealing with it. I don't want to do something stupid and end up back in the hall. But I don't know how to control myself and it could be dangerous. I need to go outside and get rid of some of this anger.

–Journal #20, 17-year-old male

Well, me and my boyfriend broke up a while ago. Actually, we broke up the Saturday before Halloween. I figured out that all he really *did* want was sex, but I didn't give it up to him. So, we broke up. He was immature about the whole thing. Even though I'm dating nineteen and twenty-year olds, they aren't getting any more mature. Sometimes I wonder if there really is a guy out there for me because in my head right now, they're all the same.

I have a lot of friends that care about me, but all they ever do is drink and party, so that is all I do every night. I am never sober anymore. When I'm sober, I feel like everything comes crashing down. I'm like a woman in a little girl's body—I'm trying to grow older and get smarter. Soon, I'm going to be working at a tanning salon by my house and I'm really going to start trying to stay out of trouble.

–Journal #7, 16-year-old female

I was sent to this school because I got kicked out of my old school for truancy. I've only been in this school for a week and a half but so far it has been pretty good. I thought that the days here would go by slowly but it is just the opposite.

The dress code is strictly army. It's not that bad. Halfway through the day, we switch back into our regular clothes after PE or PT with the army. (I guess I should say that we only get to change into our street clothes *if* we earned the right to do so.)

Most everyone at this school has problems with drugs and or alcohol. For me, I don't mess around with the serious drugs—just weed and alcohol. I want to stop and don't know how much longer I'll still be doing drugs, etc.

Some of the cadets here are gang members, former gang members, or what we call "wannabees." I am one of the very few who isn't any of these. At my last school, my problems were coming in late and getting into a couple of fights.

I do like this school. I already knew everyone who goes here and we all have a good time. Just a couple of days ago, though, we got to see two idiots get into a fight for no reason. The cops ended up coming and the two that got into the fight were suspended for five days.

–Journal #22, 17-year-old male

Today two of our goof-off students got into a fight. It was pretty funny watching them bitch-slap each other. One of the students was fifteen and the kid he was fighting was only eleven—pretty pathetic, if you ask me.

–Journal #19, 16-year-old male

PART III

THE PRICE OF CELEBRITY

Who dares to teach must never cease to learn.

–JOHN COTTON DANA, AMERICAN LIBRARY
AND MUSEUM DIRECTOR (1856-1929).

CHAPTER 23

SPARTANS IN THE SPOTLIGHT AT AGA 3

I was off after another knee surgery when I found out the county was moving the academy again. The decision had been made to house AGA-3 at the rear of the old Alta Vista Elementary School close to a football field which was three ramps below the classrooms. We would occupy four classrooms, one set of bathrooms, and a room closer to the lower parking lot that would be used to house our uniforms.

For an academy, it was perfect. I loved AGA-3 for its layout and football field. We were away from neighbors and we had a drill pad and gardening area. I planned on using both for educational and disciplinary purposes. If we could remodel the kitchen, cadets could run it and we could host dinners, spaghetti feeds and other events for parents and the neighborhood. AGA could also sponsor drill competitions with other schools on the large asphalt basketball area.

As usual, I had a lot of plans.

Others loved AGA-3, too. We were often visited by a local middle school which regularly suspended or expelled many seventh and eighth-graders who were often referred to AGA. As the program at AGA-2 had become better known, we had hosted visitors from Yolo and El Dorado Counties. Observers continued to tour the premises at AGA-3. Our local newspaper, the *Auburn Journal*, sent reporters to see who the students were who were marching around in uniforms.

On a weekly basis, parents with their children stopped at the school to see about enrolling their son or daughter. But it wasn't just parents who were looking for a military type school with high academic standards—their teen offspring also wanted to attend. Parents and students alike were often disappointed to discover that they could not join the academy unless they were kicked out of their traditional schools or committed a crime!

Nevertheless, our cadet population reached forty-two which gave us the highest attendance of any of our county's alternative education sites—not bad when we supposedly had the worst of the worst.

The Downside of Success

While we enjoyed our celebrity status, it also led to some serious and unexpected problems.

Because of the program's success, the probation department, and the juvenile court judges started sending us too many students who were more committed to drugs, crime, alcoholism and gangs than they were to transformation. These were students who did not fit the mold of a cadet and were unwilling to make an effort to adapt to the culture of the academy. I sometimes felt that the administration believed that any student dressed in camouflage would make a successful transition to the academy.

This wasn't entirely the administration's fault. I have to admit that Joan and her superiors did not have a lot of choices—the California Education Code required every county to find a place for students who had been suspended or expelled from their traditional middle schools and high schools. Complicating this further was Joan's departure. She was replaced by a new supervisor who was no more able than I was to alleviate our student population problems.

The unfortunate result for those of us at AGA-3 was that we lost control of the admissions process.

I remember two boys, in particular, who had been frequent house guests at the juvenile hall and had both recently been expelled for bringing drugs and alcohol onto their school campus. They were referred to AGA without interviews and arrived on the same day. When I issued them uniforms, I could tell they were never going to complete the program.

Sure enough, just before I started class, they asked an aid for permission to use the bathroom. Due to the layout of the building and shortage of supervisory personnel, the two teens left the building. They had hidden their street clothes in some bushes near their traditional school. There, they changed and left their uniforms in the same bushes. Eventually, they got caught drunk near their former school campus.

I would have thought that this breach of protocol and outright disrespect for the academy would have resulted in their permanent expulsion and referral to another facility. Instead, after a three-day suspension, they were told to return to the academy where they continued to cause disruption.

As committed as my original group of cadets had been to change, newbies like these two wanted nothing more than to take up permanent residence at rock bottom. They had no respect for teachers, staff, or the army personnel and often came to school missing a part of their uniform or not wearing their boots. They also disrespected personal hygiene and their uniforms, sometimes forcing us to call their guardians to tell them that the cadet's uniform needed to be cleaned. Not surprisingly, many of these parents were as uncaring as their offspring.

I disciplined most new students who did not go along with the program hoping that they would eventually leave. Fortunately, since many of these uncommitted youth were already habitual truants, they were sometimes incarcerated within a short time of their arrival at AGA.

I wasn't the only one who was annoyed by uncooperative newcomers. Many of the older cadets who had been at the AGA sites with me were irritated with uncommitted cadets. It had become apparent to them that the county education officials were no longer promoting the program as Joan had— as an elite and transformative experience for troubled teens. As frustrated as I was, I always tried to persuade the senior cadets that we had to uphold our standards and trust that the county education office had our interests in mind. If Jaime Escalante from *Stand and Deliver* and Sean Porter in *Gridiron Gang* had survived their administrative challenges, so would we.

Nevertheless, I caught older cadets shouting in frustration at the less-than-enthused newbies to just drop out, that there was no way they were going to make it at AGA-3. Though some of the senior cadets told me they had complained to the PCOE about admitting uncommitted students into the AGA, to my knowledge, the administration never responded.

Uniforms on Crack Corner

One day, Sergeant Howell told me that they had been receiving some complaints of army personnel smoking marijuana and hanging out at a place in Auburn known "crack corner." When I investigated, I discovered that a few of our uncooperative but uniformed newbies were hanging out at crack corner after school with other known drug abusers. Whether the cadets were using drugs or not didn't really matter to the army. What mattered was that it appeared to the public that army personnel might be publicly purchasing and using drugs.

This forced me to modify AGA rules about when to wear our uniforms.

Because we now had individual lockers, the cadets were to come to school in their civilian clothes and change into their uniforms. They could no longer wear the uniform outside of the AGA grounds.

As necessary as it was to change the rules because of these particular students, it also reduced our profile in the community. In the past, I often heard how impressed the probation department and the juvenile judges were when my uniformed cadets appeared in court for their periodic probation meetings. Though I was confident that my cadets would still be respectful and well-spoken on those occasions, I also knew that appearing in baggy pants and t-shirts was going to tarnish an otherwise good impression.

AGA was also undercut by the recession. By late 2007, many men and women of military age had lost their jobs or were seeking work for the first time. Because so many individuals went to the army recruitment center to inquire about enlisting, the army had to reduce the number of hours its officers could contribute to AGA.

One Teacher and a Lot of Kids

At some point, my supervisor announced she needed another aide and teacher at JDF because of the increasing juvenile hall population. Because I still had three aides, I was told that I needed to decide which aide to keep and that the other teacher who taught the AGA's seventh and eighth graders would be reassigned. I expressed my displeasure with this reduction but the administration claimed that the PCOE did not have the funds to have three aides and two teachers at AGA.

The administration reassigned Beverly and reduced Michelle's hours. So now Jenny and I had forty-two cadets from the seventh through twelfth grades combined in one classroom—rival gang members, horny girls and boys, predators and prey—and Michelle in the office. With only two of us to administer the program, we had no time to continue to promote community service activities or to take our eyes off the cadets.

The most uncertain time of the day was at lunch when Jenny picked up our lunches from the high school. This left only me and Michelle. Later, PCOE required Michelle to be at the main office as of noon leaving me alone with the cadets while Jenny was gone.

Paul McDaniel and some of my colleagues voiced their concerns over my safety. While I had approximately forty cadets to teach, the teachers at the juvenile hall had no more than twenty students per unit and two full-time probation officers in the classroom. Also, we had a court and community school that had two full-time probation officers with a smaller population than AGA. The Juvenile Justice Council investigated this inequality but was told by the county probation department that they could not relocate either one of the officers because of contractual commitments. Though the probation office eventually acknowledged the unfairness of the situation, they advised us that they did not have the funds to place even one full-time probation officer on the AGA site.

Politics prevailed. Every time there was an event, the superintendent requested that our flag detail present the flag and lead the pledge.

The Contraband Caper

I am sure some of the cadets used our shortage of supervision as an opportunity to hide contraband. On only one occasion, though, I was able to do something about it.

One of my responsibilities was to make sure all the cadets changed into their civilian clothes and left the campus at the end of the day. One afternoon, Michelle informed me that she had seen one of the cadets stash something near a pine tree outside her window that morning. As the students were filing out to go home in one direction that afternoon, I saw one of the cadets make a left instead of a right which would have led down to the football field. I stood partially concealed at the other end of the building where I could watch him. He moved some pine needles and pulled out a small black plastic film canister and quickly put it in his right front pocket.

I waited for him to come around the corner where I was standing at the top of some stairs leading down to the basketball area. I told him to come up the stairs where I began searching him. When I touched his pants, I felt the canister and told him to give it to me.

Instead, he slapped my hand, knocking me off-balance and causing me to fall down a few steps. I watched him run off campus, struggling to pull up his civilian pants since he did not have a belt, and disappear into the adjacent neighborhood.

I limped back to the office with a twisted knee that had already been diagnosed as having a torn ligament and destined for surgery. Michelle called the sheriff's department and then, in spite of my protests, called an ambulance for me. I learned later that the other cadets later yelled at the offending cadet for hurting me.

Seeing much, suffering much, and studying much, are the three pillars of learning.

–Benjamin Disraeli, British politician and author (1804-1881).

CHAPTER 24

JOURNALS–THE WAY UP FROM ROCK BOTTOM

Today we had to turn in our future career path paper. I think I want to be a dental assistant, but I also think being a hairdresser would be fun…I don't know.

We also competed in an essay contest and my girlfriend and I were co-winners. Mr. Rose played a song for us from the 1960s called *The Eve of Destruction*. We had to research the meaning of the lyrics and if we wrote a great essay (which was selected by Ms. M and Mr. Rose), then we could go to Applebee's and order whatever we wanted!

–Journal , #28, 16-year-old female

Holy Shit! Today I took a placement exam and I placed in the twelfth-grade level. Not bad State of California, who says I will not graduate because of your stupid laws!

I have been in the academy for almost an entire school year. I was sent here for what the Placer County Office of Education calls truancy. (Really, I have a weak immune system but we never got a chronic illness form from the doctor.)

I like to play the guitar and paintball. I also smoke, drink and party. My parents were druggies. My mom's drug of choice was speed but she's been clean for nine years. My father was the same way. Both of them are doing okay now. My life is probably going to be a repeat of theirs minus the happy ending.

I don't care for this school and nothing really interests me. I think I know a lot more than most of my fellow students. I just go into zombie mode and wait until we are dismissed. I don't have enough credits to graduate, though. Even going to school three extra years with straight A's will not get me there—all thanks to that damn California school system. It's not because I am mentally challenged like everyone else seems to be at this school. In fact, surprisingly, I have been getting pretty good grades. Mr. Rose is kinda unique in how he handles the subject matter. Shit, we have some seventh-graders, a shitload of eighth-graders, and then all the rest of us are high school students. I don't know how Mr. Rose is able to teach all of us together, but my grades are getting better.

–Journal #23, 16-year-old male

Ugh! The Ranger Run is terrible! All of the platoons are placed together, two by two. In other words, we create a long line of cadets who are paired up and stand next to each other. With forty-two cadets, plus the army and Mr. Rose, we are a pretty long group of runners.

Anyway, here is how it is done. The army places the fastest runners in the academy at the back of the line. The slowest runners are in the front, near the start. The army tells us to start running at a slow pace and off we go. Eventually, one of the army sergeants blows a whistle and the two fastest runners in the back take off and run alongside the rest of us so they can get to the head of the line—then *they* set the pace. This goes on until everyone eventually makes it to front of the line. By the time I got to the front, I thought I was going to die.

I think we are all in the best shapes of our lives. We had a physical fitness test the other day and the army helped Mr. Rose evaluate us for some government survey. We actually beat out all of the other traditional schools. Mr. Rose was so proud of us.

–Journal #15, 16-year-old Latina

This place is a lot different than any school I have ever been at. You can earn medals for a lot of things. It is very strict here and we have to wear army clothes. We also have to wear combat boots.

Actually, I guess it's pretty cool. We all come to school in our normal clothes and we have to be here by 8:00 AM or we lose a merit and our grades will fall. After we get dressed in our uniforms, Mr. Rose tells us to form up into our platoons. Then we walk to the flagpole, where our honor guard raises the flag. After that, we walk back to the mess hall and have breakfast. On Fridays, we have our big test. It's hard unless you took good notes and paid attention. Mr. Rose normally brings in donuts on Friday—if we deserve it.

When the army comes, we usually have to run a mile or two. Sometimes they play Frisbee football with us. We also play a lot of sports and sometimes Mr. Rose has platoon competitions where we compete against the other platoons. I really like it when we have tug-of-war. And it's *really* fun to do PT in the rain.

–Journal #24, 14-year-old Latino

Great news! I scored real high on my Armed Forces exam. Mr. Rose calls me his "hero." I will be leaving for Kentucky for basic training upon graduating from the Alder Grove Academy. Mr. Rose is right—some of us really need a structured environment. I owe him so much. He jokes with me that sometimes I am very sleepy and he hopes that I don't fall asleep on duty and lose control of my tank.

—Journal #11, 17-year-old male

Today we were going down to play soccer. Mr. Rose doesn't really like soccer, but there are a lot of Mexicans in the class and they wanted to play. We all started to argue, but then Mr. Rose yelled at us and said that if we didn't stop it, we would just go back inside and do some more Algebra… so we shut up.

Anyway, in order to get down to the football field, you have to walk down a bunch of ramps. Before we reached the bottom of the ramps, one of our stupid cadets decided to do a Pelé move by trying to kick the soccer ball with his foot and leg above his head (Pelé is a famous soccer player). Well, the idiot didn't kick the ball. Instead, he landed on his shoulder and dislocated it. Mr. Rose had Ms. M call the ambulance and they took him away. What a stupid shit! At least Mr. Rose still allowed us to have PE.

—Journal #29, 17-year-old Latino

Last night, five of us cadets had to go with Mr. Rose to a party for some teachers. Actually the P.C.O.E. was holding a teacher-of-the-year awards ceremony and the big shots in charge of Mr. Rose asked if the academy's honor guard would come into the hotel and lead them in the Pledge of Allegiance. They had all of us hang out in the bar area and they bought us some soda until it was our time to march in. We did it on our own since Mr. Rose said we deserved the credit for doing it, not him.

I have to admit, I was a little scared of walking through the crowd and up to the stage area. I'm glad that I did not have to lead them in the pledge but, you know, I was proud to wear my uniform and I got to show off all of my medals. After we did our thing, Mr. Rose took all five of us to Applebee's for dinner.

–Journal #30, 17-year-old male

I took my first drink with some friends at age ten. I thought it would be a real sign of manhood if I downed some Captain Morgan rum. I didn't really like it, but it made me feel older than my ten years.

My mom and dad were drug users and alcoholics. They started kicking me out of the house when I was in the seventh grade. We used to live in a run-down, little crack house. I'll never forget it. There was no power or hot water—it was a miserable place to live.

I eventually got caught with drug paraphernalia. That was my first official crime. Then I got into a fight and put a kid in the hospital. It was all for good reason—at least that's what I told myself. The courts put me on probation. I ended up getting arrested when I was fourteen years old. I was charged with public drunkenness and resisting arrest, along with a number of probation violations.

I was sixteen when my older brother moved out. I had a job at the time and I told myself, "I'm not staying here any longer." One night I just left. Soon after that, the house burned down. My parents had accidentally set it on fire during one of their drunken sprees or drug highs. At first I lived with a couple of friends, then I moved from house to house or stayed in one of the parks. I never really knew where I was going to sleep at night.

Supporting myself wasn't difficult—whatever I needed to do, I did it. I sold drugs or I stole stuff and sold it. I broke into houses and cars. I didn't even have to hot-wire any of the cars. I simply found ones that already had keys in them. I'd find them in parking lots or alongside the road. Sometimes I would break windows to get into them. My friends and I would just drive them around for a few days.

I hope I can get into the army after I get out of Alder Grove Academy. I've been staying in foster care and doing odd jobs. I'm trying to stay out of trouble. I'm clean now and I have to stay clean. Otherwise, it's juvie hall for me. Or maybe worse—the California Youth Authority.

–Journal #1, Albert Torres, 17-year-old male [GR Postscript:
This student tragically lost his life a few years ago.]

Outside of AGA #2.

The beginning of the dreaded hill run.

The dreaded hill.

Entrance to the cemetery at the end of the dreaded hill.

Field were TurkeyBowl was held AGA #2.

Field of AGA #3.

Parade Grounds AGA #3.

AGA #3 classroom.

Mr. Rose's desk with Spartan helmet and Academy flag.

Jose Portillo - We all miss him.

Payday: Friday's exam and student hard at work.

189

Cadet displaying his earned metals for achievement.

Some of our female cadets.

Mr. Rose on the football field. Someone has to referee!

Paul McDaniel and Josh Pavlov conducting drills.

Returning to class after a grueling PT with the Army.

TurkeyBowl cake.

Psyched Up! First parade.

Female cadets – Halloween Party.

Albert at Halloween Party.

Winning the essay contest.

Boy with a black eye.

Bobbsey Twins.

Essay contest winners at Applebees.

Hanging out in Mr. Rose's Rumblebee.

Sabrina and the Teach before Christmas break.

Thanksgiving dinner mayhem.

Noe/Josh and the gang – Thanksgiving dinner.

Thanksgiving spread AGA #2.

Amanda and Brooke performing community service at post office.

Tom Grayson teaching Life Skills.

Boot shining before inspection.

Team work.

Breakfast Club before algebra practice - AGA #3.

Flag detail.

Inspections.

Jose during inspection.

CPR training - AGA #2.

When I was a boy on the
Mississippi River there was a proposition in a
township there to discontinue public schools
because they were too expensive.
An old farmer spoke up and said if they
stopped building the schools they would not
save anything, because every time a school
was closed a jail had to be built.

–MARK TWAIN, AMERICAN WRITER, AUTHOR OF
"THE ADVENTURES OF TOM SAWYER" (1835-1910).

CHAPTER 25

LIGHTS OUT,
A TIME TO REFLECT

In the spring of 2008, the PCOE informed me that they would close AGA-3 on June 3rd and the facility would again be known as the Alder Grove Community School. By that time, Joan had been replaced at least twice but no one in the PCOE leadership ranks had demonstrated their commitment to AGA.

How Closure May Have Been Justified

Because I was never given a clear reason for closure, I can only speculate how the PCOE justified it.

First, the administration might have believed the program was too costly. In my own view, the expenses were minimal. The county covered the initial cost of a cadet's clothing requirements which I had reduced to approximately $100 per unit. This included the uniform, desert-storm combat boots as well as their PE and work-out clothes. The return on that investment was considerable. It had become obvious to parents, probation officers, judges and community leaders that the cadets who adopted the program wholeheartedly loved their uniforms, medals and stripes. The uniform symbolized each cadet's commitment to change.

Second, the PCOE was unable to provide the one full-time probation officer we needed to continue to grow the cadet population. This, too, might have been a budgetary issue. If the PCOE had been able to find the funds to assign one or two probation officers to the academy, then I would have been able to better address the problems presented by non-compliant students and, in some cases, turn them around. As I mentioned before, the PCOE did not have a lot of choices when it came to the placement of seriously troubled teens.

Third, the academy's operations suffered during the last six months because the army personnel were too busy at the recruitment center to continue to contribute to the AGA program. Without an active military commitment, the PCOE might have believed that AGA could not deliver the full program we had promised.

The fourth reason for closing the academy could have been philosophical. Instead of a program like AGA, based on order, structure and discipline, there were some in the office of education who wanted to try and modify a student's behavior by utilizing a new form a behaviorism known as PBIS–Positive Behavior Interventions and Support. Though I understand that this program requires teacher retraining, behavioral specialists and social workers, the PCOE was willing to accommodate these expenses.

From Proud Cadets to Paper Tickets

I have to admit that I am not an expert in regard to PBIS, so my opinion of the program is based on what I've read and been told by parents and other educational professionals. With that disclaimer in mind, this is what I understand and have reason to believe.

The PBIS system relies on extrinsic motivation to alter student behavior. The teacher gives individual rewards— usually paper "money" tickets–to the student for good behavior. At the end of the week, the student might use the ticket to participate in a drawing for a prize or exchange it for candy, more play time or a movie. This approach to delinquent education inspires a number of unanswered questions for me.

When a teen accumulates one or more tickets, how does an instructor know whether the student has learned anything about so-called good behavior? More important–will the student still behave in the manner that earned him a ticket when the teacher isn't present to bestow a ticket?

I used to post academic awards and leadership certificates as well as attendance records which were parlayed into leadership grades. But I rewarded these based on cumulative, repeated and consistent changes in behavior, not random instances. Also, not every change was materially rewarded. Can a paper ticket replace observable student satisfaction and growth from social interaction and discussion? Most important, how does it replace the judgment of an adult who works with the student over an extended period of time?

In my fifteen years as a teacher for delinquents, I never had a situation where a big Mac, classroom lotteries and candy replaced or inspired the understanding and practice of *being* responsible, diligent, polite, generous or consistent in daily life without expectation of a reward. Professionally, I find it difficult to imagine how insignificant rewards for periodic demonstrations of teacher-pleasing behavior inspire good study habits, pride in one's improving grade point or a classroom atmosphere that encourages innate satisfaction in at least attempting to do the right thing.

And what about discipline? If a disruptive student doesn't care about paper tickets and doesn't earn the teacher's approbation, what then? Within two weeks of using PBIS, my successor suspended six teenagers. During three years with AGA, I suspended one. Were the six suspended students irredeemable or was PBIS inadequate to the task?

At-risk teens often do not understand why they behave as they do let alone how to identify and engage in healthy relationships with others. Before, during and after AGA, I have watched how the act of "learning," whether the topic was academic, physical, or psychological, can replace self-destructive behavior. As a professional educator, I believe it is the consistent and ongoing interaction between the student, teacher and other adults and peers that instructs, disciplines and inspires troubled teens. Unfortunately, not all educators or school districts are willing to make the kind of commitment troubled teens require of us.

Though I was encouraged to apply PBIS principles if I continued to teach for PCOE, I declined. After fifteen years of educating troubled teens, PBIS gave me no reason to alter my approach to changing the lives of at-risk youth.

What We Remember and Prize

In spite of the closure of AGA, the program substantially improved the lives of many cadets as well as making a favorable impression on the community.

- The Superior Court loved referring students to the academy and we often received praise from the bench when our cadets appeared in court with their progress reports.
- The county's education superintendent used the academy's uniformed flag detail at some of her events and representatives from other districts routinely visited the academy to learn how we ran our program.
- The number of cadets who passed their high school exit exam on their first attempt after studying at the academy had steadily increased.
- Many cadets asked permission to remain at AGA long after they had met the goals of their rehabilitation plan because they realized that they *could* succeed with enough discipline and structure. When I've had the good fortune to see them years later—successfully

employed and with families of their own—I can only
congratulate them on their foresight.

- During two years at AGA, the academy enjoyed the
best attendance record of any other county alternative
education site in spite of the influx of suspended
students who were sent to us from other sites.

Because of my staff, the army, PCOE's original
commitment and the ongoing enthusiasm of the teens
who longed to change their lives, AGA was an economical,
effective and popular program that proved itself to educators,
parents *and* students.

Forget conventionalisms; forget what the world thinks of you stepping out of your place. Think your best thoughts, speak your best words, and work your best works, looking to your own conscience for approval.

–SUSAN B. ANTHONY, ABOLITIONIST
AND SUFFRAGIST (1820-1906).

CHAPTER 26

JOURNALS–SAYING GOODBYE

Wow, this year has gone by so fast! It seems like just yesterday that we were at the old site (Cockroach High), planning out this whole military academy idea. We've had a lot of disappointments along the way; kids getting locked up, false promises about money from the county for field trips. But throughout it all, AGA has stayed together and has overcome many obstacles. Time and again, we've had disappointments, but I feel it was all worth it. We set the stage for future cadets to succeed in the academy if it ever starts up again. We showed them that they, too, could meet the challenge.

Not only has the academy taught us academics, but it has also taught us discipline and for many of us cadets, brought a sense of hope and accomplishments to our lives.

Throughout the year, we made many memories. We got the army involved in our program, which really set the stage and helped us get into a more structured disciplined military mode. We've run countless miles up and down the "hill," through the graveyard and even through rain and fog. It wasn't fun at all (to me at least), but after we ran I will admit I felt really good and really awake.

We played football almost every day which was most definitely the highlight of most of our days. Then we got kicked off of our first field which totally sucked, but eventually we devised a plan to ride the bus to the park and play there.

One time we played football which we called "the Mud Bowl." It had rained the day before and was still drizzling when we went out. The field was literally a huge bowl of mud. I tried not to get dirty but one of the boys tackled me and I got soaked. It was really cold but we still had a lot of fun.

Everyone's hair was matted with mud and our P.E. uniforms were completely covered in wet mud. It was one of the best memories that I have of the academy which I'll carry with me for a long time.

—17-year-old female

Today Mr. Rose told us that he is not sure if he will be coming back next year. I know that if he doesn't, I don't want to be here. I love him. I have a great dad, but Mr. Rose guides us in the right direction. I'm a little scared, however, because this school has a lot of structure and is strict—that is what all of us cadets here need. If I go back to my regular school, I hope I do not start making the wrong choices again.

—Journal #25, 14-year-old Latina

This is the best school year I've ever had because this is the first time I stayed in the same school the whole year. A lot of stuff happened throughout the year-good stuff and bad stuff.

I remember the first test I ever took since some of the questions already had some answers on it. Saige and I had the same answers and she was marked wrong for some of them and she tried to get me in trouble but Mr. Rose said it was too late to grade them over again.

Hella people got locked up again and a few of them aren't coming back. There's only one that I'll be missing though and that's Noe Perez. He is going to boot camp for about one year for a bad choice he made.

It's also great, knowing that I can do the most sit-ups in the school during P/T with the army. Other than that I hope I can graduate from here with a diploma from the Alder Grove Academy. I also want to wear those fancy new camouflage uniforms if the academy were to continue next year.

—17-year-old black male

Today is the last day of school and so far it has been good. I can remember the first day I came in and when I got into the classroom I saw a lot of kids dressed in camouflage and they were shinning their boots. Then I got my uniform and got to be introduced to Mr. Rose who now is a really good friend.

After a few weeks I started to meet other kids and made some cool friends. We all used to talk about what was happening in the world and just stuff like that. Then a few more weeks went by and just out of nowhere I got surrounded by a bunch of guys and they tried to throw me in the trash can. I fought and fought but they finally got me in there. So that's about the best times I can remember. I was finally accepted by the other cadets and now really belong to the Alder Grove Academy. I can't wait until tomorrow when we get to have sports all day. Gold platoon will win I hope.

—15-year-old male

I can't believe it's here. I don't really like this place but I'm definitely going to miss it (can't explain this). I remember the first time I became a staff sergeant at Cockroach High. I was still a private. This is the place I met my boyfriend. Now we have been together for almost eight months. I'll never forget all the memories he and I shared. I'll also never forget all our football games-especially the Turkey Bowl aka Mud Bowl. Everyone was covered with mud.

The worst thing that happened here was when Josh, me and another cadet got dropped off at the old site by our stubborn bus driver. We walked all the way to the new site and it took us about four hours!

Albert was one of the people I became most close with and…well, basically everyone else. Mr. Rose was a great teacher and I'll miss him a lot. We had our differences but we made it through them. That isn't even half of my memories. I am proud to say that I was a cadet at the first Alder Grove Academy.

—17 year-old Latina

This was the worst days ever in school. This year a lot of bad things happened to me both inside and outside of the academy.

But Mr. Rose has not given up on me or some of the other cadets. I missed two days of school so I will lose my perfect attendance this time, but I still have my other metals for attendance in the past and my grades and PT.

Because I missed some days and did not pay attention in class my grades have slipped a little and I hope that I can still get a new academic award. I'm kind of sad because I promised by mom that I was going to get a new academic medal. But because of that one week I went to LA and had fun, well, now I will pay the price.

Today is the last day of the academy. There is talk that Mr. Rose will be leaving Alder Grove Academy since it will not be an academy. I will really miss him. He is like my dad.

We had great times here and I will miss my fellow cadets. I wish them all well. I will miss the potluck dinners we had like a family. Mr. Rose gives a lot of us nicknames and because I am a little fat, he calls me Butter Ball and I love it. I also heard that he bought us a lot of trophies and I hope I get one.

−16-year-old Latino was awarded the Academy Mascot Award.

Today is the last day. I never thought that I would stay to the end. All the things that have happened since we left Cockroach High where the academy first started and all of the PT with the army really did pay off. I feel I am in the best shape of my life.

Moving to the new site was cool except everyone lost their AGA (Alder Grove Academy) spirit and motivation. A lot of new students have been coming into the academy and I think everything is going downhill because of their attitude. Knowing Mr. Rose though, he will build it back up.

Even though these new kids are screwing things up, I will always remember the good times we cadets had and I wish I could come back next year because I think Mr. Rose will make the academy even better and somehow get rid of the troublemakers.

I'm pretty sure it will be better, but as Mr. Rose tells us, it is time to move on to new and better things. I am pretty happy however that I got the opportunity to be in the first Alder Grove Academy.

—17-year-old male

This year of 2007-2008 was flipping crazy. So many different events took place during this year that I can't even explain half the details.

Well, what I can say was that it was a blast. I will never forget Mr. Rose. He pushed me to do things that I did not think I could do. He is also telling me to think about being an artist since I am pretty good.

This school helped a lot of kids and I was one of them.

—17-year-old male, Josh Pavlov [GR Postscript: Sadly, this student took his life in 2013.]

When I first came to this school I hated it so bad I never wanted to come to school. I really hated the uniforms but after I got used to them I really started to care about them. Nothing in this school was hard for me, but sometimes I did not try my best. I was excited once I took the program seriously and began earning metals.

I loved playing football and baseball and the whole academy started becoming a team. Unfortunately before the year ended, I got locked up for 33 days for some stupid reason. Mr. Rose however, did not give up on me. When I returned to class he got in my face and asked me if I had reached rock bottom yet? That really caused me to think about my life.

Mr. Rose, I just want to thank you for putting up with me. I really appreciated you letting me have my long hair. I know you really wanted me to get it cut. Thank you so much for everything.

—16-year-old Latino

"**Sophomore**, moving up to junior"—can't say much though. All I wanna say is that this was the best year of any year in my life. I have never learned so much in my life till this year.

I mean look at my past—of all the years I have been in school, I have been a failure. Not here!

I don't know if I want to stay here next year if there isn't going to be an academy. I love the way Mr. Rose teaches and I don't really want to go to Placer High...what can I say, I love it here.

—Anonymous Student

This year at the Alder Grove Academy was fun playing in the Mud Bowl (Turkey Bowl). I also liked it because I was the only cadet to make the Honor Roll in the third quarter.

I had a lot of good times here, like becoming a sergeant and having my own platoon. Taking Mr. Rose's tests he gave us was hard but fun and he taught me algebra, something I didn't know.

This year at the academy was—I can't believe it—great. I can't really believe it is over.

Mr. Rose, I could never do what I did without you. Thank you for everything.

—16-year-old Latino

Today is the last day of AGA. I remember a lot of good things and a lot of bad things. I remember the first few days of AGA—it was so much different than last year. A lot of memories were at the old site, like the first of everything about the academy. The new site has a lot of memories too, like the Turkey Bowl. We played football on a whole bunch of different fields. We had a great Christmas Party.

Unfortunately, we also had people in and out of juvenile hall. Some stupid kids snuck in drugs and cigarettes. I remember my best friend get wheeled out on a stretcher, and I also remember getting the best grades I've ever gotten. I remember all the drama and fights, and I mostly remember Mr. Rose and how he made my year here the best. I will never forget you, Mr. Rose. Finally I will never forget my fellow cadets who came and went throughout this year.

—17-year-old female

Well, it is the last day of school here at the academy. Here are my final thoughts. Not much has changed for me. I'm graduating tomorrow from here as a high school graduate.

I just keep thinking about how I'm going to live. Well I know I am planning on entering the military as an airborne infantryman and later an Army Ranger. This academy and the army helped me realize that this is the career for me.

I got a lot of knowledge from Mr. Rose and I want to thank him for helping me graduate. I did not think I could do it.

—18-year-old male [GR Postscript: This cadet went on to the U.S. Army and eventually became an Army Ranger.]

Today is the last day of school here at AGA. Woo hoo! I met the challenge. We all met the challenge—well, the ones who did not got thrown out. From way back at the first day of school till now, a lot has happened. I've changed a lot. I have made some mistakes, but I have learned from them.

Mr. Rose taught me a lot. He pushed us all so hard. I couldn't have done it without him.

—16-year-old female

I loved all the fun times I had in the Alder Grove Academy, including our runs with the army on every Monday and Friday. I loved when we raised the flag over by the PCOE administration office. I had fun writing our essays for this book. I liked how we went and played football everyday if we earned it.

Unfortunately, we moved to a stupid site. Afterward they found a place to play football until we trashed the field and got kicked off. I had fun when we did the Turkey Bowl and when Mr. Rose got tackled when we were practicing for the Turkey Bowl. I have had fun the whole school year especially playing baseball. I am glad I got kicked out of my old school cause if I hadn't, I would not have met Mr. Rose and probably would not have graduated from the eighth grade. Thanks for everything Mr. Rose. I am going to miss it here.

—16-year-old male

The roots of education are bitter,
but the fruit is sweet.

−Aristotle, Greek philosopher, teacher of
Alexander the Great (BC 384-BC 322).

CHAPTER 27

THE LAST DAY

I am proud of all of those who met the challenge the academy set for them. There are so many to thank–from cadet-gangsters ringing a Salvation Army bell at the post office on a rainy day to those who thought college was out of reach and were admitted. I've spoken about parents who didn't care but not enough about those who did, those who thank me, even today, for "saving" their kids. It pleases me to remind them that if their son or daughter hadn't wanted to change, my efforts would have meant little.

On my last day, I was touched when the probation office staff stopped to say goodbye—it brought back fifteen years-worth of wonderful memories. Though most couldn't believe I had chosen to retire, they also understood that for me, the new classroom management techniques held no allure.

As I expected, it was hard to leave the kids. I'd challenged them and they had risen to the occasion. Each of them held a special place in my heart. One of the cadets said that he had not only "made a friend, but a family" and that was how he would always think of the cadets and our staff.

My last day at AGA was close to my birthday so two of the students brought in a big birthday cake, chocolate milk, plates and forks. As we feasted, Goldie, on behalf of all the cadets, gave me a yearbook that included pictures of almost all of my cadets during the last year.

When we finished the cake and hugging one another, everyone filed out shouting, "Bye, Mr. Rose," "We will miss you," and "Don't forget us." I noticed that one cadet lingered. It was the one who had made a comment earlier about how we were all like a family. He had really turned his life around over the prior two years and had refused to return to his traditional school.

He looked me straight in the eye and shook my hand. "Mr. Rose, I have learned more from you in the last two years than in my entire life," he said. "I will never, ever forget you and I really hope you will come back and see me."

God, how I will miss teaching.

"The greatest battle you cadets will face in life is doing the right thing."

–Gary Rose

CHAPTER 28

FOR TEENS WHO DON'T GIVE A DAMN—ONE CADET'S MESSAGE

You know, it takes a lot to change someone, especially yourself if your train of thought is "I don't give a damn–nothing worse can happen in my life than what has already happened."

I've learned from personal experience that it helps a lot if you have hope for the better. If you know or even think that you can change your life, it *can* happen. The more you have a better outlook on things, the better that little seed inside your head can grow and expand to help you remember the good times.

Amazing things will start happening to you. Doors will open and windows will open, but it will not come to you on a silver platter. You have to *want* to change, and until you get rid of your negative outlook, it won't happen.

People, especially adults and family members, tried to tell me the same crap for years: *You have to stop doing this. You are never going to get anywhere.* Worse than that is hearing it from teachers, cops, probation officers and judges. No matter who it was that was telling me these things, I didn't want to listen even though it was the truth.

I don't know if other teenagers have the same outlook on life that I did, but when adults told me not to do something, it just made me rebel that much more. It was not because I hated them. It was because I wanted to accomplish things for myself, that I wanted independence. I wanted to feel like no one could touch me, that I was invincible. I wanted to hold onto this attitude even though I knew that someday I would have to face the consequences. Even if I didn't have to face legal consequences, I knew I was recreating a vicious cycle of "I don't give a shit."

If you can't break this cycle, it's going to ruin your life until you reach what Mr. Rose calls "hitting rock bottom." You have to somehow want to stop partying, cursing, and whatever. But you won't stop until you are honest with yourself and you *know* that what you are doing is wrong.

I told my friends that doing the wrong thing is like being in a wagon train. You have to choose between following the wagons you've always followed or breaking free and going down another more positive trail. A fresh start is what I am talking about.

It is so awesome to be able to change your life, to have a feeling of accomplishment and independence because you *do* give a shit and want what's right. It makes you feel like you're living the lyrics for the song *Can't Touch This*. Believe me, it is *so* much better than all the negativity that might be in your heart right now, negativity that you don't really want and certainly don't need.

No matter what people say and do to get in your way, you can always choose that fresh start and take the right path— that's what I did.

–Journal #5, 16-year-old female

PART IV

LOOKING BACK

MILITARY LIFE IN AUBURN'S MIDST, SUNDAY MAY 31, 2009

Alder Grove tackles some of area's most challenging students

By Gus Thomson Journal Staff Writer

The phone calls with The Question come in to Auburn's Alder Grove Academy and teacher Gary Rose once or twice a week. Parents may have seen the students on the former Alta Vista School grounds, dressed in their Army camouflage uniforms stiffly saluting the raising of the flag or taking part in exercises on the playground along Lincoln Way. They're wondering how their child could be part of what they've seen.

The answer Rose gives parents may be a bit off-putting. But it's true. To get into Alder Grove, their son or daughter need to get kicked out of school. Alder Grove is part of Placer County Office of Education's juvenile court and community schools system. Its 38 students are in grades 7 to 12 and are some of the toughest challenges for the local education system. They've been expelled from other schools for behavior or truancy problems. Some are referrals from the county Probation Department.

An ex-Milpitas police sergeant, Rose helped put the school program together about 2½ years ago and is currently the lone teacher. He said that the U.S. Army has been a partner, providing drill instruction and physical training three days a week the first year. The trainers are from the North Auburn Army recruitment center and more recently have been unable to devote the same amount of time because of the current demand for military jobs, he said.

Sandra Watson, director of the program, said one of the main objectives of Alder Grove is to help students get enough credits to return to the schools they came from. So far, 11 students have gone back to Chana and Placer high schools. The military side of instruction includes "digital" camouflage uniforms, boots, ranks from private to sergeant, awards in the form of pins that can be worn like medals, and an insignia featuring a Spartan helmet they wear on their sleeves.

Watson said that the military emphasis is about regaining high school students with a rigorous philosophy of instruction. It's not about channeling students into a military career, she said. "The recruiters are not allowed to recruit," Watson said. "Kids aren't able to make informed decisions. But they (Army recruiters) are there if they have questions." The school has had students enlist. Rose said five joined the military over the first two years and two more are due to join.

Sixteen-year-old Alex O'Gorman of Auburn has been an Alder Grove student since eighth grade, after ditching school and ending up punching a vice-principal. He's planning to join the Marines in July, when he turns 17, having been given parental permission. "I knew you'd be asking me that," O'Gorman said, with a smile, after being asked by a reporter whether pressure from the school or recruiters played into his decision.

"There's been no pressure at all. Very few are thinking of joining. We have fun and they don't recruit us—or brainwash us." O'Gorman said he's wanted to enlist since he was little ("Someone has to protect the country.") and the rigorous program at Alder Grove gave him an indication of what it would be like. "It makes you sure you want to do it," he said.

O'Gorman has risen in the ranks to staff sergeant. He takes pride in the toughness of the math curriculum and the fact that others want to go to his school. "But I tell them they don't want to be kicked out of school to be here," he said.

Taylor Satterlee, 15, of Auburn, has been in the program for about two months after cutting too many classes forced her out of Placer High. She hasn't missed a day at Alder Grove and is hoping to return to Placer High. "It's made me a stronger person," Satterlee said. "A lot of the kids here have been put through a lot at home and I've learned from that."

Satterlee traded in her regular Placer student garb of jeans and a T-shirt or a dress for Army cammies. "I'm a girly girl so people would think that I wouldn't like it," Satterlee said. "But when everyone wears military uniforms, it's less judgmental. It puts everyone together as just teens."

Rose said that for some students, he serves as a father figure as well as teacher. Office of Education figures show three out of four students in the community schools program come from socio-economically disadvantaged households.

The program will continue this coming year, with its location at Alta Vista on a year-to-year lease with the Auburn Union School District. "I know it's working," Rose said, recalling a student's return after "getting popped" and spending time in juvenile hall. "He walked to the front of the class and apologized to them," Rose said. "And then he came over, put his arms around me and said he was sorry."

On a recent school day, Rose was overseeing students as they took part in P.E., competing in a tug-of-war and then flag football. Other than the location and the number of gray shirts emblazoned with the word "Army" on them, it could have been any P.E. class in any school in Placer County. But in the frenzy of arms, legs, grins and grimaces, Rose subtly did his job of trying to shift careening lives back on course. Rose pointed to the tug-of-war. Each side won but he brought them back for one more match. "They have to learn that if they lose, they don't give up, they try again," Rose said.

The Journal's Gus Thomson can be reached at gust@goldcountrymedia.com or comment at Auburnjournal.com.

ALDER GROVE ACADEMY CADETS AND STUDENTS

By Alder Grove Academy Cadet Bobbsey Twin

Before I arrived at AGA, I did not feel very good about myself. I had no direction or goals and that is probably why I was escaping by both using and dealing drugs and cutting school. I hated school and that is why I usually skipped. I was not getting anything from the lessons and the teachers did not seem to care if we understood the material or not. They were just putting in their time and waiting for the next holiday.

I was attending Whitney High School and got caught with marijuana and charged with possession for sale. I was taken to court and put on probation for both a felony and misdemeanor. As I said, I did not see any future nor did I really give it any thought. I just wanted to party, use drugs and hang out with friends.

That, coupled with my poor attendance, got me expelled and sent to the Alder Grove Community School before we became an academy. We used to call it "cockroach high" because of the cockroaches that scurried on the walls when we started boxing everything to move to the second Alder Grove Academy.

Eventually, I started to change. First, Mr. Rose had already transferred from the juvenile hall and was in place as the teacher at Alder Grove Community School before I was sent there. I had made the choice already to stay clean and not get caught for any additional drug charges since I was on probation.

At first, when Mr. Rose told us that we would be changing the school into a military boot camp academy in partnership with the U.S. Army, I was like, "what?" I don't want to be in the army. But the way Mr. Rose and Ms. M approached the change and actually asked for our input, I started to see that it might be fun.

Mr. Rose allowed us initially to select the type of uniforms we would wear and since he was paying for it out of his own pocket, us girls selected a uniform (camouflage) that was different than the boys. He even bought us some ¾ length pants to use on cool physical training days. We came up with our own rules and possible consequences. We all got into it and I realized that we were now not just a bunch of screwed-up kids on probation, but we were starting to become a family.

I loved having to wear the camouflage and the physical training with the army got me in the best shape I had ever been in. Me and my best friend, who Mr. Rose called the Bobbsey Twins, loved not only doing our school work but polishing our boots, and playing sports with the guys. School was fun and not one of us wanted to miss a day of it. Even Easter break became a drag since we wanted to be back at the AGA.

Mr. Rose and the U.S. Army taught us lessons about leadership and accountability. I really took these lessons to heart and try to practice them today. I am no longer on probation and the AGA helped me become a better citizen.

The way Mr. Rose taught was totally different from any other teacher I ever had. Not only were the classes fun, but we found that the more challenging they were, the more we wanted to show him we could do it. We could earn medals but he made grades more important. He told us that once we hit 18 years old, society is not going to care about us—that we had to decide how we would run our lives. Over and over, when someone whined, he would say that same phrase about not changing until we reached rock bottom. He caused us to review our past behavior. I remember one time we had to write a five paragraph (minimum) essay on "Burning Bridges." He asked us to think about all the bridges we have either "burned" or damaged in our lives and if we thought we could go back and repair them.

I remember an essay contest he held where we could break up in teams of two and we competed for a $200 top cash prize for the best essay. He played a song for us entitled "The Eve of Destruction." We had to research the meaning of the various words in the song and the time period when the song was released. Chelsea and I won first place but Mr. Rose also had a second and third place prize and he took all of the winners to the Auburn Applebee's for dinner. Can you believe that? What other teacher would do that for his students? None that I ever had.

I was one of the original cadets at AGA-1 (Cockroach High), and I went through the two additional moves to AGA-2 and AGA-3. Altogether, I guess I was in the program for over 2 ½ years and I loved it. I had to get permission from Ms. Berry to stay after I met my rehab plan, because the AGA was my family and I did not want leave the other cadets, especially my best friend.

There was a funny thing that happened to me. It was the time that I was not paying attention on the baseball field and Jorge hit a high fly ball in my direction. I had just had my stomach pierced and was playing with the belly button when all of a sudden all the other cadets and Mr. Rose yelled my name. Then I had a bad pain on the top of my head where the softball hit me. I had tears in my eyes and everyone started laughing but then they all came to me to see if I was alright. After that I always tried to be alert. Football was a blast. The guys really got into it. Mr. Rose sometimes would have the boys go to the sidelines and it was girls vs. girls. I loved it.

After it rained, Mr. Rose would ask the girls if we wanted to play "fumble drills." What a stupid question! We all did! Girl vs. girl in the mud—what fun. I remember the big Mud Bowl we had. It had rained hard for days and as a reward for doing well on several weekly exams, Mr. Rose said that if we brought in clean clothes to change into, the girls would have a Mud Bowl football game. Oh my God! By the time the game was over, we were all covered in mud. It was everywhere and afterwards us ladies had to get cleaned up.

Ms. M. really got upset when she walked down the hallway to the girls bathroom after we had washed and cleaned up and she saw the bathroom covered in mud. She yelled to Mr. Rose to see what we had done and said that she was not going to clean it up. Because we were like a family, the neatest thing happened. Without Mr. Rose saying anything, a lot of the male cadets told Mr. Rose that they would clean it up and they did!

Another funny thing that I will always remember is the barbecue Mr. Rose and Ms. M had for us on the last day at AGA-1. Mr. Rose bought hamburger and hot dogs and other treats as did Ms. M and we were going to hold a final party at

Cockroach High. Kevin Ambers bragged about being a great BBQ chef and poured a ton of lighter fluid on the briquettes. Well, someone else had already put lighter fluid on the charcoal. In fact, if I remember correctly, several people put fluid on the grill. Kevin lit the match and the next thing we knew, he had singed his eyebrows off. The bad part was, he did not know it until we all started to laugh.

There were a ton of cadets at this point. When I first arrived at the old school before it was AGA, we only had about eight to ten kids, but by the time we had the BBQ and were leaving for the second AGA, we must have had nearly forty cadets. We all loved Mr. Rose and Ms. M. We could all go and talk to them anytime we needed to. We had to remember though that they would not just tell us what we wanted to hear and we may not like what they had to say, but we all respected them. The same thing could be said about the sergeants from the U.S. Army. They always offered to counsel us if we needed it.

How can I forget those days when Mr. McDaniel tried to teach us how to march on the basketball courts at AGA-3? It is not as easy as it seems. We constantly turned in the wrong direction and Mr. McDaniel would laugh and shake his head. He did not give up on us but we never really got it right.

One of the saddest moments was seeing my best friend (my "twin") being taken out to an ambulance after overdosing in the second AGA. She took a pill and had a bad reaction and I was so scared for her. I had never seen Mr. Rose be so angry because of it.

He went to the hospital after school to see my friend. She was sad for letting him down. Also, I remember how sad it was when we learned that another cadet's father had committed suicide. He had been teaching us computer skills and then did not show up. Later we learned why.

After leaving the third AGA in my junior year, I finished high school and graduated. The stuff I learned from Mr. Rose at the three AGAs made the rest of my high school education easy. I did not cut school and concentrated on keeping my grades up where I had them at AGA.

I am not married but do have a boyfriend. I have been doing a lot of traveling and relocating and since leaving the AGA program, I have lived in Wisconsin and Colorado where I am now located. At twenty-three, I still like to wander. I worked at a cellphone company and now work for a catering firm, but soon, my mother will be moving to New Mexico and my boyfriend and I will follow. Maybe someday I will decide to stay at one place and develop a career.

I honestly believe that if I had not been expelled and spent time with Mr. Rose at the AGA program, I would have lost out on having a productive life. The academy gave me direction which I needed. Mr. Rose and the rest of the teaching staff and the army provided the role models I needed. The way Mr. Rose taught us, the way he honestly showed he cared, the love both he and Ms. M. had for us was very, very special. It truly changed my whole outlook and life and as I said, it was hard to leave and go back to my traditional school. I learned responsibility, accountability and how to respect others.

We also learned to give back to the community and our parents. I remember the food drive we had and how we beat even Placer High School though they had a lot more students than we did. I remember the cadets ringing the bell with the Salvation Army one Christmas and the good feelings we all had. And how can anyone forget the great Thanksgiving and Christmas parties we had together as a family?

I did not know Brendt Volarvich personally but I remember the story of what he did (killing a California Highway Patrol Office) and the impact it had on Mr. Rose. He would point out how Brendt had destroyed his life and warned us to not go down that path.

I do have ideas about how teachers can help teens. Mr. Rose and Mr. McDaniel who used to substitute for Mr. Rose were easily the best two teachers I ever had. Why? Because they not only made the lessons fun, they showed us how what we learned related to us either then or would in the future. More importantly, they were real. In other words, they were not just putting in their time like some of the teachers I had in other schools. They truly wanted us to learn and be successful. The AGA, the way it was set up, was created to make us better students and future adults.

Having the military there with us gave us even more role models. They helped us remain focused on both our studies and physically. I feel that if more school districts had schools like the AGA, more at-risk kids would become success stories and turn their lives around like I did with my fellow cadets.

I really hope that other students having problems in their lives can learn from our book about how we turned our lives around. I cannot wait to attend a class reunion and see all of my former cadets again.

By Alder Grove Academy Cadet Sergeant

When I received a request from Mr. Rose to write something about my time at the Alder Grove Academy, I had just come from the probation department seeking a spot in a rehabilitation center. I have been in and out of various rehab facilities and was actually clean for eleven months before my contact with my family of drug users got me hooked again. Because I've recently had a daughter, I want to return to rehab to turn my life around first for myself, and secondly for my daughter.

Before I arrived in Mr. Rose's classroom, I saw myself as someone above the law. I was very defiant. When I first met Mr. Rose at the juvenile delinquent facility, I had been in and out of trouble. I was only in the seventh grade when I was charged with nine offences, mostly drug related, and assigned to C unit.

Brendt Volarvich's younger brother was with me in C-Unit. I was there when we found out that Brendt had killed a cop. I knew Brendt a little but he was older than me. At the time, I wondered what was going through Brendt's younger brother's mind knowing that he would never have a brother again, at least outside of visiting him in prison. I heard that Mr. Rose was considering quitting at the time and I am glad he didn't.

I remember when they finally thought that I was old enough to start going to Mr. Rose's classroom in A-unit with probation officers Mr. A and Mr. Reynolds. I was sad to learn that Mr. Reynolds passed away. I was at JDF on a lot of Christmas Eves when Mr. Rose and Mr. McDaniel would show up as Santa and his elf. It meant a lot to all of us who were in custody.

I did not like going to school but once I was in C-unit, it stopped me from getting into more trouble. I had already been suspended from my regular school so after my arrest, the school said that I could not come back. That is when I was contacted by Ms. Berry who told me that she was starting up a boot camp style school and asked if I was interested.

I told her I was all for the AGA since I had done well in another boot camp. I needed to go to a school that had structure. So I was at Cockroach High during the summer with Mr. Rose and Ms. M, while they got ready for the academy. I was proud of being one of the first at the academy when we chose our uniforms and broke up into squads. It was nice to be the academy's first sergeant. I loved the way Mr. Rose taught history and math. At first I didn't care about either one, but he made math easier for me to understand and I now love history.

I went with Mr. Rose to the City Hall meeting in uniform when PCOE decided to move us from the first academy at Cockroach High to the second location. I even remember when we were boxing up all of the books at Cockroach High and the cockroaches actually started to walk on the walls of the classrooms.

Ms. M was kind of like a step-mom to a lot of us. I loved the way she used to refer to some of that God-awful food we were delivered for lunch. It was nice when she got us some Top Ramen instead of mystery meat. If we thought that Mr. Rose was upset with us, we knew we could go to her and she would tell us what was wrong. It was like a family at both AGA-1 and 2.

After I arrived at the academy, I played the role Mr. Rose expected of me. In school I tried to be the best sergeant we had and to serve as an example to the other cadets, but in all honesty, when I was away from school, I was still "above the law," using drugs and doing things that I should not have been doing. Looking back, I was putting on a face I knew I needed to show when I was in the academy and attending school; at least I was not doing things that could get me into trouble.

The funniest thing that I can remember—gee, there was so many—was when Albert Torres caught a football over where there is now a community garden and in the process ran into a small tree. I also remember the time when we were all running together in our P/T clothes through the graveyard and we were told we could not do that anymore. When Mr. Rose decided we would run through the graveyard near AGA-2 because it was close to either Veteran's Day or Memorial Day, Mr. Rose told us about his father being buried there. I remember him standing over his dad's grave and saying, "Hi Dad, these are more cadets." He started to choke up so Alex and I walked Mr. Rose away from the group.

Some sad things that happened, happened after all of us left AGA and Mr. Rose went back to JDF - Albert Torres had back problems and got hooked on opiates. This seemed to always help his pain. Unfortunately, he died, though I'm not sure why. And of course, we were all shocked to learn that Josh hung himself.

Yes, if it wasn't for the AGA and Mr. Rose, I could have easily gotten into even worse predicaments than I am in now. I will tell you the truth. If it wasn't for Mr. Rose and AGA I would not have been able to remain focused enough to get my high school diploma. Because the school was so structured and run in an orderly fashion, it forced me to concentrate.

Fortunately I never got sent to prison and although I am on probation, that is better than parole. I need to get my life together especially with drugs and that is why I went to the probation department today. Mr. Rose told us to never give up and I think that now, with a kid, I have reached rock bottom and need to concentrate on my life and that will help my daughter's life. I still remember when he said to not bring a child into the world unless we know that we can provide them with more than we had when we grew up and that is what I want to do. I want to be clean forever, and go back to school and learn about how to be an air conditioning and heating technician.

In the next 5 years I hope to be clean and off probation. I hope to have attended HVAC school and have a good job for myself and my daughter. I want to be a better father than my father and the key is sobriety.

I think that teachers, police and parents can help teens who have challenges like mine with tough love! They have to keep their kids accountable and know what they are up to. When a parent just gives their kids money to get rid of them so that they can do their own thing, that doesn't help. They are just enabling us to do bad things because it seems like they do not care. Instead, you need to let your kids and students know that you care about them, but that you have rules and consequences for breaking those rules.

By Alder Grove Academy Cadet Chavo

I have to admit right up front that a few of us did not reach rock bottom for a long time, and I was probably one of the last. Mr. Rose repeatedly told us that unless we reached rock bottom we would never go in a positive direction—it took a long time to realize that he was right. As I write this, I am on parole after serving 2 ½ years in prison for several felonies including kidnapping, assault with a deadly weapon, transporting drugs and selling guns illegally.

You see, I was one of the original students who attended the Alder Grove Community School before it became an academy. I was a smart-ass who was full of myself. I was always partying using alcohol and drugs. I had no guidance at home and no idea of what life held for me. I really didn't care as long as I could party.

When Mr. Rose arrived at the school I was not excited since he seemed too strict for me. When he said we were going to become a military type academy, I wanted no part of it. I hated the idea of having to wear camouflage with black combat boots and not having long hair—my hair could not touch the collar of my uniform. It wasn't until I started to see a real change in the other cadets that I really started getting excited about wearing an army uniform and getting in shape. Two of the cadets were really close friends and they both told me that I had to take it seriously and serve as an example to some of the other cadets.

Before I knew it, I too liked wearing the uniform and competing for medals. It was fun rising in rank. The biggest turning point for me was when I was recognized by both Mr. Rose and Sgt. Howell and Sgt. Hewitt, who told me that I had leadership qualities and I just had to make an effort. Sure enough, I started rising in ranks myself. It was because of what they saw in me that caused me to push myself into becoming a leader. I started realizing that I was not a "shit-head" but actually, with some effort, I could do well in school and turn my life around.

I attended AGA-1 and AGA-2. The academy taught me to become a better listener and to try and put myself in the other person's shoes to understand where they are coming from. There was a feeling of us cadets becoming more than just fellow students. We formed a family. We helped each other succeed. We celebrated Thanksgiving and Christmas together which for some of us, was a first since many came from dysfunctional families.

There were so many funny things that occurred while in the two academies. We loved playing football and of course, all of us thought that the NFL had nothing on us. Someone threw a long pass to Albert Torres and he made a great catch only to turn and run into a tree. Fortunately, it was a small tree but it knocked him down.

Then there was the time that we were playing flag football and Damian tried to prevent me from catching the ball and we ran into each other. His shoulder hit me in the eye but, actually, I did not feel anything. I was just happy I caught the ball. Everyone started asking me if I was alright and what was wrong with my eye. Later, when we got back to the classroom, I had a huge shiner.

Mr. Rose was not a big fan of the second academy since we did not have a P/E field like the first academy. We had to do physical training and march with the army on the asphalt parking lot. We also had to walk over near the flag pole by the Placer County Office of Education, and after raising the U.S. flag, we marched in front of the library. Actually that started to be fun because people from the office and even people going to the library stopped and paused while we raised the flag. We were all kind of proud.

Another time, we decided to play two-handed touch football in the parking lot. Someone threw a pass to one of the cadets and he made a great catch. Unfortunately, after catching the ball he ran into the side panel of a new car and his knee dented the car. Instead of Mr. Rose getting mad, he called Ms. M and had one of us cadets bring him a camera. We found the owner of the car who was not very happy since she had just gotten her car out of the shop.

After taking some pictures, Mr. Rose had Ms. M send an email to his boss, Ms. Berry. She was upset once she saw the damage but Mr. Rose got what he wanted for us. After the accident, Ms. Berry got us bus tickets so that every other day, if we deserved it, we boarded buses that took all of us to a near-by park for P/E.

There were a few sad times at the AGA. Two of the worst was witnessing one of our female cadets having to be taken to the hospital from an overdose. Some cadet brought in some ecstasy I think, and she had a bad reaction. Mr. Rose got really upset and after the ambulance took her to the hospital, he made sure the police arrived to take the other cadet away. We later learned that after school, Mr. Rose went to the hospital and spent some time with the female cadet. That was pretty cool.

One of the cadets became one of my best friends in AGA-2. I was going on my second year at AGA and really started to like it. My attendance and grades were up and I started thinking about graduating high school and attending college. My friend's dad taught a computer class to us. But one day he did not show up. Neither my friend nor Mr. Rose or Ms. M knew what was up so Mr. Rose took the time slot and the class day went on. We learned later that my friend's dad had taken his own life. It was really painful to see my friend hurt so much.

For some of us it took longer to turn our lives around. It was sad to see some cadets re-offend and return to juvenile hall. When they returned, they had to apologize to their fellow cadets for letting the academy down. Actually, for some, it only took one apology and they stayed out of trouble. If you held rank and got in trouble or brought shame on the AGA, you lost your rank. You were told by Mr. Rose and army that you could re-earn it, but you really had to prove you deserved it.

The number of cadets continued to grow. At both AGA #1 and #2, it was almost wall-to-wall desks. I think however that this added to the feeling of us being a family. If someone started goofing off and pissing off Mr. Rose, us older cadets stepped in to make sure the cadet who was goofing off cleaned up their act.

Eventually, because I kept screwing up, I was taken out of my home and placed in a group home. I did not get to stay at AGA and that is when things started to go bad for me. It really hurt me to not be a part of the order and structure of the academy—it was like a family to me. I knew it had started to change me for the good—my grades and attendance were up and I was proud of my new me.

By age 18, I was running again with the wrong crowd. I was into drugs and one thing led to another. I did not get to graduate high school and seemed to have forgotten everything I had learned from the time I was in the academy. I was not accountable to anyone and since I did not have positive role models like Mr. Rose and the army to help me stay the course, I really screwed up.

A friend of mine and me got in a fight with a kid and my friend shot him in the ass. The cops were looking for us for attempted murder and robbery so we ran. In the process of running and feeling like we were invincible, we got involved with weapons and drugs.

When we finally got caught, the attempted murder charge was dropped but even with a plea deal I got sentenced to three years in prison. I did some of my time in Tracy and finished up in San Luis Obispo. While in prison, I had to share a cell with a serial killer who bragged about all the killings he did.

The time I spent at both AGAs was very special to me. I did not realize all the lessons I was being taught by Mr. Rose and the army and I didn't take them seriously until it was too late. But I always kept hearing Mr. Rose's haunting words— that until I reached rock bottom, all the BS in the world was not going to help me turn my life around.

Now, after prison and being placed on parole, I have sincerely reached rock bottom and am proud of what I have now become. I've had a few jobs as a carpenter where I can put together free-standing walls. I did have a good teacher while in prison who helped me eventually get my GED. Mr. Rose had taught me Algebra and basic math so well that the prison teacher had me teach the other inmates who were trying to earn their GED. I was really proud teaching guys twenty to forty years older than me.

In the next five years I hope to get my General Contractors license and specialize in building earth-friendly homes for the homeless. I have learned how cheaply a nice home can be constructed but unions are preventing this from happening. I know I want to give back to society.

To help students like me, we need a hell of a lot more schools run like AGA.

Yes, I know I screwed up big time, but I went downhill only after I was removed from AGA. Teachers have to show that they believe in their students and truly want them to succeed. We do not want to be told to do something for the sake of doing it. Instead, give us some choices and let us make our decisions. You have to show relevance of the subject matter and why we have to know it. That is how Mr. Rose did it and that is why so many of us liked coming to school. Let us be ourselves, but act as role models and show us the road to success.

The army and the AGA taught us how to get along as a team. We even had rival gang members in the academies and for the most part, we all got along because we were a family of cadets—students that no one else wanted to deal with.

Unfortunately, I was taken out of the academy and although I am not putting the blame on anyone but myself, my life changed for the worse when I left. That is why I feel so strongly about having more military type schools.

By Alder Grove Academy Cadet Evelyn Monroe

Before arriving at AGA I was a good person inside, but I kept making the same stupid mistakes. It finally caused me to attend AGA where my sister was already attending school. I guess what I am trying to say is that I was just another ordinary person when I arrived at AGA.

I loved going to school at Colfax High School. Everyone was my friend there. Nobody ever fought with each other, but that was probably because it was a small school and town so everyone pretty much knew each other already. My favorite subject was math. I saw a bright and beautiful future ahead of me. I knew that I wanted to be a nurse in the labor and delivery ward of some hospital.

After arriving at AGA, I felt like I wanted to see more of the world and live life to the fullest and to not continue to make stupid mistakes that would ruin my future. Mr. Rose somehow instilled that in us. He told us not to just look at our own little world or friends and family, but to explore beyond that.

For the twelve months I was at AGA, Mr. Rose taught me many amazing life lessons. He taught me how to be tough, which is extremely important to me since I am only five feet tall. Playing football and having to work out all the time at AGA made me not only physically stronger, but mentally as well. He also taught me how to appreciate life and all of its blessings. This means the most to me—learning to love myself and being thankful for everything really opened my eyes. He always seemed to have a police story that really related to things all of us were going through as teenagers. He didn't really judge us, but we all knew that he expected us to always give him our best effort.

The funniest experience I had at Alder Grove Academy was probably when Ronnie Jones would carry one of the smaller cadets across the field while playing football. Even though we all came from different parts of Placer County, different backgrounds and nationalities, the academy and Mr. Rose turned us into a family. He was "dad" and we were his kids. He told us what he expected from us, and he helped us reach those goals.

My saddest memory from AGA was when I got in my first and only fight with my boyfriend at the time. He was my first love, Emilio Ramirez. I cried in the lunchroom and ran to the bathroom. Mr. Rose told Ms. Jenny to follow me and see what was going on. She came in and told me everything would be alright and it turned out to be true. We all took care of each other.

Being in the AGA program changed my life for the better. I wouldn't be the person I am today if I did not go to the academy. When I was sent to AGA I already knew my sister was there so I was not afraid of going to a new school. I knew we had to wear uniforms which was ok with me since I did not have to decide each morning what to wear. My sister had already told me that Mr. Rose was tough but fair and that he was the best teacher she ever had. When I met Mr. Rose, he treated me as if I was already part of the academy family.

Today, I am a full time college student and I also have full custody of my beautiful and amazing baby sister, Julia. During the next five years, I want to continue my schooling and become a registered nurse. By that time I will be 22 years old. I also cannot wait to help my baby sister become a beautiful young woman. I may even add my amazing boyfriend to my little family.

I think it would help many teens if parents were more open with their kids and if teachers weren't so tough. Why can't more be like Mr. Rose? Though he joked and helped us have fun with our subjects, he held us accountable for our own actions. We learned there would be consequences for all of us if we screwed up.

By Alder Grove Academy Cadet Sleepy

First, I want to apologize for not doing a better job of staying in touch with Mr. Rose and the other cadets. I have gone back to both locations for AGA-2 and AGA-3 but the academies had relocated and then closed down. When I have talked to cadets, they always say good things about Mr. Rose and that he went back to teach in the juvenile detention facility after Alder Grove Academy reverted back to an ordinary court and community school.

I got expelled from Placer High School twice. The first time, I "did my time" at the Alder Grove continuation school. It was when I went back to Placer and got kicked out again—they said I extorted money from some kid—that I got sent to Alder Grove Academy. I regret pretty much every day of my life up to that point because I did not take education seriously.

The Alder Grove Academy was a shocker at first. Mr. Rose did not give me any slack and I needed constant motivation as well as the feeling that he never gave up on me. Mr. Rose and Ms. Berry used to rag on me since I always had a hard time staying awake in class. When they found out I was going into the army, they said, "Please, army, don't give him a tank. He'll lose it." The marching, the drills and the P/T and P/E was what woke me up most days. I also remember us going outside whether it was hot, cold or raining and Mr. Rose saying that "if the army can do it, we can do it."

It was really at this point that I started getting into it—the whole academy thing. We were assigned to different platoons and identified by colors. I can't remember the color of my platoon, but it created a family atmosphere based on competition. There was a lot of peer pressure put on us but that brought all of us together. Most of us came from bad homes and the academy became our home. Ms. M and Mr. Rose were like a second mom and dad and they held us to certain standards and demeanor. If we did something wrong deliberately, there were consequences not just for the person who broke a rule, but for the whole platoon or class.

To be honest, I disliked the recruiters at first because I thought that they were trying to brainwash us or just fill their quota. But they never tried to talk me into joining. They were really good at teaching us leadership which Mr. Rose also modeled for us.

Before I knew it, I was really getting involved with the whole army military structure of the academy. Little did I know that my ability to turn my life around at the AGA was due to this type of environment. I'm now 24 years old and I joined the army at 17. I didn't know anything about the military other than that my grandfather and my uncle served.

You see, the academy saved me. I had nothing going for me. I knew I wanted to go to college but I had no money. At home, besides family drug use and fighting, I had to grow up watching my mom deteriorate from Huntington's disease for most of my adolescence.

The U.S. Army was a big inspiration for me. I needed a career and since I was doing well in the AGA atmosphere, I asked Corporal Burubeltz if he regretted going into the U.S. Army. He said, "It was the best decision I ever made." That was all it took. At that moment I knew I wanted a military career and with his help, I enlisted in the army. Because life at home was unbearable for me, the U.S. Army seemed to be my way out.

I went to basic training to be a cavalry scout. Basically, we had all the same duties as an infantryman, but we were more like the security guards of the Department of Defense, meaning we observed and reported. I attended advanced individual training at Fort Knox, Kentucky, which is called OSET. Only a few combat military occupational specialists do this. My duty station for my entire 4-year enlistment was with the 2nd Brigade Combat Team, 3rd squadron 7th US Cavalry Regiment, 3rd Infantry Division out of Fort Stewart Georgia.

I was deployed to a place called Mosul, Iraq for 12 months in October 2009 to 2010. I was eighteen years old, fighting America's war and not really knowing why we were there in the first place. But once you do get there you are simply focused on one thing and that is to do whatever you have to do to keep breathing another day and make it home.

Your heart weighs heavy and your adrenaline never stops. I was in a Humvee when an improvised explosive device (IED) blew us off the road. Fortunately, the chemicals they used had spoiled and the blast was not powerful enough to kill any of us. There were a lot of firefights and contact as well. Except for losing a good portion of my hearing, I got back home with ten fingers and ten toes.

I was released from active duty in 2011. I thought I could always go back into the army if I needed to. I had never been in any trouble while I was in but when I tried to return, they would not take me back. The army was cutting back and after a year, I was homeless. My unemployment benefits paid my rent, but I had made an error in applying to the army for housing I was entitled to so I was screwed—I didn't have enough money to pay the bills. To make matters worse, it ruined my perfect credit score. I had earned that record because of what Mr. Rose taught us about personal finances. Someday, I'll get it back where it belongs.

I'm still homeless and trying to qualify for housing from the army. I was in a rehab facility for a time but after being caught drinking a beer in my room, I had to leave. To get back on track, I enlisted in the National Guard in 2013 where I attend drills every month. They are aware of me being homeless but there isn't much they can do.

I think that there should be more schools modeled after the AGA. Many kids had a rough life at home with no one to act as a role model. Here, we had Mr. Rose and the army staff working with us, challenging us, and all the time we could feel that they really cared about us. This school changed all our lives for the good. Without it, I do not think I would have graduated from high school nor entered the army. In spite of my other problems, I still have skills, education and a sense of accomplishment. That would not have happened without attending AGA.

Today, I want to take the time to say thank you to Mr. Rose and the Alder Grove Academy. Mr. Rose truly changed the path of my life forever, and for that I wish there was some way I could pay him back. I have no doubt that I would be dead or in jail if I hadn't received his guidance.

By Alder Grove Academy Cadet MooMoo

When I first attended AGA, I was a fuck-up. I did whatever I wanted to do. I didn't care about others and I didn't worry about consequences. I was first suspended and later expelled from E.V. Cain because of not attending school, getting into fights and, frankly, not giving a fuck about anything. I hated school and didn't see the reason for attending. Having a "don't give a damn attitude," I just didn't care about anything but having a good time.

When I first arrived at AGA-1, I was a little scared even though I knew at least one of the cadets. I wasn't sure what a military style school was and I heard that although Mr. Rose was fair, he didn't tolerate a bunch of screwing around. But once I got used to the order and discipline and the way Mr. Rose taught, I loved it there.

The army was a great addition. I loved the ranking structure and although I was out of shape, within a few weeks I noticed that I was getting stronger, losing weight, gaining muscle and in the best shape of my life. My grades started to improve because

I really wanted to become a Staff Sergeant. I think I only made corporal but I was proud of the type of student I had become.

I thought that if I could succeed in a military type school, then I could overcome anything. It really changed my life for the good—I had a purpose. I didn't want to skip school and get a demerit. I wanted to be with the other cadets who had become my brothers and sisters. Mr. Rose kept pounding on us about the bridges we had burned and the fact that until we reached rock bottom, we can say everything we think he wants to hear but he will know when we're bullshitting him. Though the army and Mr. Rose would be there for us, only we can actually change our lives.

I learned that I was the type of student that could only do better in school if there was order and structure. The cadets seemed to all come from broken homes with alcohol or drug problems and most of our traditional teachers didn't know how to deal with us. But with Mr. Rose and the AGA, we knew that not only would he not let us fail, but he would challenge us each and every day. He would set the bar and after we reached the bar, he would move it higher.

We loved it when Mr. Rose and the army challenged us, we became a team. For the most part, we helped each other out, especially those in our platoon. For some reason, it seemed that in AGA, we all acted a little more mature than in our traditional schools. I don't know if it was the uniforms, Mr. Rose, the army, or the chance to go up in rank or earn a medal, but we all seemed to act older together.

I attended AGA-1 starting in the eighth grade, and moved to AGA-2 where I really wanted to stay until I was able to graduate high school. But because I was in a foster home, they moved me to Placer High School where I graduated, but AGA was the best school I ever attended.

One of the funny things I remember is the way we used to put people in the garbage can as part of our initiation. That was so much fun. The Turkey Bowl and the cake was great. I am sorry that I broke my leg and was not able to play in the Mud Bowl. Everyone, including our girl cadets, loved it.

All of the P/E events were great especially when the army sergeants played with us. I remember that dreaded run up the "Hill" and the Ranger run with the army. I also remember us and Mr. Rose running with the army through the graveyard and afterwards we were asked to not do it again. So, we found the Hill up to the graveyard. That almost killed me. I also remember the P/T with the army when four of us guys had to do pushups together. That was hard, but as I said, I really started getting into shape.

I also remember when those of us who took the program seriously went into the bathroom and got our heads shaved. You probably couldn't do that today. But for us, it was more than an initiation, it was becoming part of the family atmosphere.

Two sad things happened while I was at AGA. One was when one of the girls overdosed and had to be taken out of the academy on a stretcher. Mr. Rose was upset when he learned of what happened and made sure the police were called. The other sad event was when we learned that a fellow cadet's father committed suicide.

Right now I work at Taco Bell but it's only temporary. Once I earn enough money, I want to first travel around the U.S. and then Europe. In AGA, Mr. Rose taught me so much about different wars and history that I really want to see the world. Once I am finished traveling, I want to attend a culinary arts school because I love to cook. I am not a parent, not married and not on probation.

If I had an opportunity to tell teachers and parents how to deal with juvenile delinquents, I'd say don't force your will on us. If you do, we will rebel and do just the opposite. If you want to reach us, do what Mr. Rose and the army did. Make it relevant to us and the lives we'll be living as adults. Mr. Rose was able to tell us real life stories about being a police sergeant that emphasized the consequences of doing some of the stupid things we were doing. And most of us didn't even think of it that way until he hit us with real life situations—that's what caused us to change. Like he used to say, only we can change, no one can force us to do it.

Without AGA and especially Mr. Rose, I think I would have continued to be a failure and probably in prison. Because I attended AGA and learned about discipline, respect, order and consequences, I believe it definitely changed me for the better. After I left and returned to a traditional high school, I realized that since I completed a tough program at AGA, I would succeed at Placer, and I did. I know how to respect people. I have matured. I have a different outlook on life thanks to being a cadet.

By Alder Grove Academy Cadet Ronnie Jones

Before I started at the academy, I was hard-headed, had a quick temper, would take no crap and was always fighting. I would not listen to anyone and I hated school.

In my junior year at Placer, one of my friends told me that another student had written "nigger" on the school grounds and I went after him. I asked him if he had written the word and he told me to get out of his space. I remember hitting him hard two times, knocking him to the ground where he was unconscious. I thought that the school administration would have called the police, but instead I was told that I was expelled there and then. I later learned that I was being sent to a military style boot camp school called Alder Grove Academy. But I didn't start out that way.

Up to the seventh grade, I was an A student. But things happened at home and I started to give up on school. My real dad disappeared from my life and my step-father took over as my role model. He was both verbally and physically abusive causing my mother to hide in her room. He told me to never come home from school if I avoided a fight. In other words, even if I did not start the fight, he expected me to finish it, and if he learned that I didn't, I would be abused also.

I wanted to be successful but did not see that happening. I started hating school, especially math and writing. I would not do homework and used any excuse to avoid showing up for school. With my grades failing and being so far behind in my school credits, I started drinking and smoking pot. I knew that the AGA was going to be my last stop and didn't think the program or the academy would help. I was over 80 credits behind and with my bad grades, I thought that I would never graduate much less pass a GED test.

At first at AGA, I thought Mr. Rose was a joke. He had all of these ideas that I could be successful, that he saw potential leadership skills in me. I soon learned that Mr. Rose taught from the heart and really cared about our success and so did Ms. M did. She was like a second mother to a lot of us cadets.

I realized that Mr. Rose, Ms. M and my new best friend Emily actually did give a shit about me and were pushing me to change my life. Mr. Rose pointed out that everyone has burned bridges but that it takes a man or woman to realize that they have reached rock bottom. He challenged all of us both physically and mentally. Even though his class was fast paced, he knew when some of us weren't understanding the lesson and would quickly change it so that it made sense.

After school I hung around with Emily. She helped me conform to school rules and concentrate on being successful. For the first time in my life, I could come to school and hang with my "family" and then go home and have other types of role models like Emily and her mom. I had the best of both worlds. I knew that I could always go to Mr. Rose like I could with Emily and that they would both care about me.

What I learned at the academy that was most important to me was that everyone with a little training can be a leader. Also, after becoming adults, we would be held accountable for our actions and, to prepare for that, we needed to learn to be held accountable at the AGA. The army also really impressed me with their lessons on leadership. The whole academy became a family and the other cadets were my equals, my brothers and sisters. It was because of the order, structure and discipline at the academy and the presence of the army that I knew I wanted to enlist. They did not ask me but I knew that I was the type of person who needed discipline and training to make it as a young adult. The academy and the staff helped me get my head on straight. They saved my life.

I attended what we refer to as AGA-3 at the old Alta Vista School. I was proud to wear our cadet uniform and proud of the day that Mr. Rose promoted me to the rank of sergeant. Man, I will never forget it.

The funniest thing that happened while I was at AGA would be the time the softball hit Kasey on the top of the head. We all started to laugh but looking back on it now, I guess should she could've really gotten hurt. I also remember all of the great softball and football games we had, even in the rain and snow. Mr. Rose used to say, "If the army is out in this weather, so can we." I also remember all the times we tried to teach Desi how to play football and how I had to walk her into the end zone as she was screaming and in a state of panic and the opposing team was chasing her. Good times! We were all proud of our uniforms and medals, our grades and what we were learning.

I wanted to stay at AGA until I graduated since I was doing so well there but then something sad happened. Mr. Rose confirmed that the Placer County Office of Education was closing the academy in spite of its success. Worse, we learned that Mr. Rose was so upset that he was asking for a transfer back to juvenile hall. He told us that it was because of his knees which we knew were bad. But we knew the real reason was that he was disappointed with the closing of the academy, especially because it helped so many of us.

After he left, the new teacher could not handle us. Any cadet who had met their rehab plan quickly left what was now the Alder Grove Community School. As soon as I could, I transferred to Chana. I had learned so much at AGA and earned so many credits that I was able to catch up with the other students and graduate with my high school diploma. I would never have accomplished that without AGA.

I left the U.S. Army after serving four years and receiving an honorable discharge. As an E5 Sergeant and logistic specialist, I served one tour of duty in Afghanistan where I experienced my first fire-fight. Honestly, it scared the hell out of me. But I survived and returned to the states.

I was tested in the army and afterwards. For the first time in my life I had money but I didn't know how to manage it and was too trusting. I gave a lot to my mom and then one day found that she had been taking some out of my account. I lost my best friend, Emily, over a stupid disagreement. On several occasions when I was feeling down in the army, I looked at my U.S. Army uniform and thought of the days I wore the AGA cadet uniform and how I handled all of the challenges there. I thought to myself that if I was able to succeed at AGA, then I could handle whatever the army or life threw at me.

Before I went to AGA, I did not know how to write an essay but I was able to write reports for the army that were outstanding. I also learned that some bridges can be rebuilt and I did that recently with Emily and my wife. I am a proud father and I will pass on to my son what I learned at AGA—that no matter had bad things may seem, you can make them better.

I am planning on attending Sierra College and then transferring to a four-year university. In the next five years, I hope to have a BA degree in Criminal Justice. With my experience in the army, I believe I would be an excellent Correctional Officer.

I think that if other students would read our book, they will see that they can overcome any hardships they face since we were able to. But teens do need help. No matter how bad things look, teachers need to be open to their students and not pre-judge us. You cannot assume that all students learn the same way. You can't just tell us to read a chapter in a book and do homework, because we won't. You have to make it interesting and show us why we need the information because we want to be challenged. Just don't give up on us.

I feel I became a success. I was fortunate to be sent to AGA and to be exposed to order, structure and discipline. AGA's leadership skills and accountability prepared me for the adult life I now enjoy with my family.

By Alder Grove Academy
Cadet Bryan Kale

I hope Mr. Rose hasn't sold his Dodge Ram Rumble Bee truck—seeing his truck lets us all know he is still around.

I was expelled from E.V. Cain a year after Delarosa was expelled. I was arrested and put on probation for theft of a skate board. Since attending AGA, I am proud to say that I have never been in trouble again. I really think that if I had not been sent to AGA, I was headed to prison—no doubt about it. I had no thoughts of the future and didn't care anyway.

I only attended AGA-2 for one year and then left to attend Placer High School. At first, when I learned that I was being sent to AGA, I was a little nervous although I knew several of the kids that were sent there. I noticed that they liked wearing the army uniforms and they were all getting in good shape. I was not sure if I would be able to keep up with them.

I had always hated school. Didn't see the point of going since I did not like my teachers and the subjects they were teaching didn't mean anything to me. Mr. Rose not only taught me algebra, English composition, science, and history, but he taught us things we needed to know when we became adults. I will always remember what he taught us about stocks and bonds and investing and what to watch out for when we are offered our first credit card.

The first day that I arrived at the academy, Mr. Rose told me that it was up to me to decide if I wanted to change my life. He said he and the army would be there to help, but ultimately I had to make the choice.

After he had that talk with me, I could see in the eyes of some of the cadets that something was up. Soon, I was initiated into AGA when they put me in a trash can. I didn't mind because I knew that this meant that I belonged to the family. I eventually even had my head shaved because I really wanted to be a true cadet. I loved P/E and the fact that we had to earn it made it all the more special. I know a lot of us were good in the classroom but we also wanted to go outside even in the rain, and participate with Mr. Rose and the army.

I loved the Turkey Bowl and the trophy we won on the winning team. I will never forget getting up in front of the class and showing off the cake that we won and then Fernando announcing that we had decided to share it with the rest of the class.

Sure, we had arguments and there were some cadets we did not like, but I had never attended a school where, for the most part, we all stuck together. Wearing the uniforms hid the fact if we came from poor families and did not have fancy clothes to wear. We did not worry about gangs because as Mr. Rose would say, the only gang colors we had were camouflage and that there was only one Alpha Male and he was it. But we didn't care because we were a team and we didn't want to let Mr. Rose down.

Mr. Rose taught me that even though I had burnt many bridges in my young life, I could go back and try to repair those bridges. Burning bridges was related to reaching rock bottom. If we did not care about hurting others and ourselves, we should just go ahead and burn bridges while we pretended we were trying to change our lives.

But he always saw through it. He'd sometimes get in our faces and say "don't bullshit a bull-shitter." He knew that until we changed our ways, we would continue to be fuckups and never become success stories. There were always consequences for our bullshit, like no donuts on Friday or a long run with the army up the hill to the graveyard. But even though he got mad at us for letting him down, he fought for us.

I remember that he was upset with the county for putting us at AGA-2 with no place to have P/E. He felt, and of course we agreed, that we needed some time each day to let off some steam. So instead, he decided to let us play touch or flag football in the parking lot which was full of cars, coming and going.

We had fun and the rules were strange, like you could run behind a car and then be opened for a pass. One day a cadet threw a pass to another cadet and he made a great catch but then smashed into a parked car hitting the side with his knee. He did not get hurt, but the car had a huge dent in it. Of course we all called out woo!!!! We thought that Mr. Rose was going to get in trouble and be mad at the same time. Instead, he smiled and asked for someone to get Ms. M's class camera. He took some pictures of the damage to the car. The owner came out and was a little upset with Mr. Rose, but Mr. Rose remained calm (must be because he used to be a cop) and gave the owner of the car Ms. Berry's phone number.

We learned later that he had assumed that sooner or later someone would complain or get hurt and that would cause the county to do something. He was right. Soon, we were all being bused twice a week to a dog park to play football or baseball.

There were other times when he really got upset with us. Some of the stupid cadets hated the food we got from lunch but instead of putting it in the trashcan, they would throw it up into the rafters in the room where Mr. Rose stored our weightlifting equipment. Soon we got a complaint that rats were breeding up in the rafters because of all of the food. I think we all had to run the Hill that day and I doubt we got donuts that Friday.

Currently, I am working with Delarosa at the local Taco Bell. I am not married, have no kids and not on probation. I have not been in trouble since I left AGA. The school showed me that I could succeed if I wanted to. Being able to get my grades up at AGA and also getting in shape made me stronger for when I started to attend Placer High. I knew I would get my high school diploma there since it was harder at AGA.

I am now attending Sierra College and majoring in auto mechanics but I will be changing my major. Although I haven't decided on my new major, after finishing college I hope to find a better job with better pay, an apartment or maybe a house and a car.

Teachers, administrators and police have to remember that teens are rebellious. Unless you say it the right way, just telling us over and over not to drink, smoke, or do drugs is a challenge to us to try it. Also, adults should know that we don't want to be treated like babies. Trying to make teens behave with rewards just causes them to use the system.

The AGA was totally different. There were rules and they were strictly enforced. We all had to earn our rewards which was usually our grades on Friday. The medals and stripes we put on our uniforms were special—none of us had experienced that before. I know I like uniforms and the rank and structure of AGA. I think everyone who is having problems fitting in at their traditional schools should go through a program like AGA. I was sad to hear it had been shut down.

By Alder Grove Academy Cadet Hronis

My sister Brooke and I both got expelled at the same time from Placer High School for attendance problems. Our mom was a single mom trying to provide for me, my sister, and our brother. Because she worked nights, we were not supervised so basically my sister and I stayed out late, partied, and slept in the next day. To hell with school.

We were both sent to Alder Grove Court and Community School. It was a joke. The school was in Dewitt Center, an old army building that had nasty brown water in the both the faucets and toilets. Thank God we had bottled water to drink. The food was also nasty and a lot of times none of us students ate it. Ms. M used to call it mystery meat. Our attendance still sucked since we continued to party at night and my sister and I saw no need to go to school.

Alder Grove had a ton of teachers before Mr. Rose arrived. I can't think of the names of most of them, but the worst was a male teacher who had us do nothing but art. Art, art, and more art. He also had us do crossword puzzles that were for second graders. One day we were excited to hear he had been removed.

So my sister and I showed up for class the next day and there was Mr. Rose. As soon as he spoke and told us what he expected from us, I knew that, as he often said, "There was a new sheriff in town." He told us that he had learned about some of the prior behavior in the class and that any students who continued to cause problems would soon be removed.

Mr. Rose was so handsome and funny that my sister and I wanted to get him together with our mother, but that never happened. He initially made me nervous because I did not think I could do the work he said we would be doing.

Remember, neither my sister nor I took school seriously and now Mr. Rose said we would be learning algebra, English, science and history and NO art!

What a complete difference! We had to take weekly tests. He would get in our face and challenge us to do the best we could. I started loving school. My sister and I would go home and tell our mother that we were actually learning things. We talked about history and great literature. Our mom was glad that we were showing up for school on time.

Then one day Mr. Rose told us that he had been asked by Ms. Berry, who was like our second mom, to create a military style boot camp school that would be called the Alder Grove Academy. He wanted to know how we felt about that and wearing military uniforms called BDUs. My sister and I thought that would be cool. It would sure make it easier to get ready in the morning, especially because there were still times that my sister and I stayed out late and partied.

We would also be wearing black combat boots and Mr. McDaniel would teach us how to get them real shiny. When we got them, he made it fun showing us how to polish them. Because Mr. McDaniel looked like Santa Claus, we used to kid each other that "Santa Claus" was teaching us how to polish shoes.

After we got our uniforms, we had to make a presentation to the school administration. When the supervisor and an attorney came over to Alder Grove, several students got up and explained why we wanted Alder Grove to become a military style school. After they left, Mr. Rose told us how proud he was about our presentation and gave a ton of money to Ms. M. to go pick up pizzas for us.

That day we learned that Ms. Berry got permission to have the academy and we would become the Alder Grove

Academy. Mr. Rose, who bought the first BDUs with his own money, told us that now we all had to dress in one uniform so the boys gave in and we all agreed to wear the tiger BDUs.

What we did not know was that Mr. Rose had finally got a budget from PCOE and was ordering a ton of equipment, plus he and Jorge Silva went to Big 5 Sporting Goods and worked out a deal for our combat boots. They also picked up a ping-pong table, a punching bag and other sports equipment. He ordered black and white P/T clothing and on the day our baseball hats arrived with our mascot on the front, I have to admit, I loved it. We were part of something big, something that had never happened in Auburn before.

My sister really got into it and she became the first female sergeant in charge of the Blue Platoon. I think we had three platoons at the start but boy, the academy got bigger and bigger. A lot of our friends heard from about it and wanted to attend. Sadly, you had to be expelled or referred by probation to attend the academy. Stupid huh?

We were ready. We all had our uniforms and now we were going to meet the soldiers from the U.S. Army that would train us. Sgt. Howell and Sgt. Hewitt really made an impression on us. They were both in great physical shape and had so much energy for our new academy. They taught us leadership, accountability, and respect. They got us all in great shape. We ran, did exercises, running competitions and drills. And when lunch time came, we were all starving to death because the army had drilled us—we were in the best shape we had ever been in.

Yes, sometimes my sister and I would show up without the required uniform and had to pay the consequences, but we were all part of a huge family. Things were fun. For anyone reading our book, it is hard to explain what happened to me and my sister. We actually wanted to have better lives, to become better people. The challenges that Mr. Rose and the army threw at us was exactly what we needed. We had no direction at home. Here at AGA, there was order, structure and if we did not go along with the program, there were consequences, just like the adult world Mr. Rose was preparing us to enter.

Both my sister and I attended AGA-1 and AGA-2 for almost two years. These were the best years of my life and I will never forget the time I spent at AGA. The funniest thing I remember was when we were playing P/E and Damian and Oscar banged into me going for the ball and I got a bloody nose. I couldn't stop bleeding, yet I was laughing the whole time. Of course, the time Albert crashed into the tree was funny.

When Mr. McDaniel or Sgt. Howell and Sgt. Hewitt took us to what we called the parade field by Bell Road to teach us marching, God but we were awful. It was so funny seeing people turn in the wrong direction. I know it sounds weird but marching in a straight line is harder than it seems. I was proud to stand at attention and have Sgt. Hewitt or Sgt. Howell inspect us. Yes, even then I would sometimes have the wrong uniform and had to get down and do pushups. But at the same time, seeing all of us cadets standing in formation made me proud.

Our mom told my sister and me that she was seeing a difference in us. Brooke and I didn't see it but she did.

Eventually Ms. Berry told me that I needed to go back to my traditional school because I had been at AGA for too long. I knew I needed to leave but it was my family. I had raised my grades to the highest they had ever been and I earned them. The work was hard and challenging but now I had to see if I could do it at another school.

I owe everything to Mr. Rose and the time I spent at the AGA. Ms. Berry and Ms. M probably don't realize it, but they helped make me into the woman I am today. I am now married and have a beautiful daughter. I am a stay-at-home mom and my husband and I would like to have two more children. After that I would like to return to school and attend college.

I did not know Brendt Volarvich personally, only the trouble he got himself into. I can tell that it still bothers Mr. Rose. The open letter Brendt wrote to us from death row was both sad and inspiring.

My advice for teachers is to make their classes relevant to their students. Show enthusiasm, be prepared to teach. Realize that we all learn differently but at the same time, we want to be challenged. I agree with my sister that we need more schools like AGA. It changed our lives and I cannot wait until my daughter reaches a certain age when I can sit down and read "OUR" book about me and her auntie as cadets. I really hope that other students who read our book get inspired to change their lives.

Our mom died a few years ago and I know that she was proud of my sister and me. That could not have happened without AGA.

By Alder Grove Academy Cadet Twin A, a Female Sergeant

Before I arrived at Mr. Rose's class and before it became the Alder Grove Academy, I was lost. My sister, our brother and I were left at home alone at night since our mom worked the night shift. My sister and I pretty much did whatever we wanted to do and school was the last thing on our minds. Because of this, we got thrown out of Placer High School due to our lack of attendance.

When we arrived at Alder Grove, the teacher who was there was a joke. All he had us do was art and crossword puzzles. Even though my sister and I knew we had to change our attitude and show up for school to be able to return to Placer High, we were not learning anything, so why go to school?

Then Mr. Rose arrived. At first I thought, "Man, this guy is serious." I was really nervous. When he introduced himself and said he was a former cop, I knew that things were going to be a whole lot different at Alder Grove. Before I knew it, school became fun. I loved all of the subjects he taught. He definitely got my attention by making all of the classes relevant to my future.

For once in my life, I had direction. The way the class was run gave all of us the structure we needed. Mr. Rose became like my father, strict but fair and he brought passion to the classroom. When he would teach history it was like we were reliving it. It is because of Mr. Rose that I started exploring a future career in archaeology and anthropology. Now we had a teacher who really cared about whether we understood the material or not. He did not come in and put his feet on the desk and read a newspaper after assigning us some boring crap to read. No, instead he challenged us and showed us how what we were learning would be needed when we got older.

After only a few weeks, we came to class and Mr. Rose had not written our daily agenda on the board. Instead, it said TBA (To Be Announced). Of course we were just high school kids and could not wait to see what he had planned. Some of us tried to get the information out of Ms. M but she would not tell us other than to say we would love it.

In our classroom, even before we became an academy, Mr. Rose treated us like young adults and we appreciated it. He had two big coffee pots in the back of the room where eventually we would have a board showing all of the platoons. One coffee pot had coffee (Mr. Rose *loves* coffee) and the other had hot water for either hot chocolate or Top Ramen. Even then we had rules. If you wanted coffee, you had better get it before class and be in your seat when he was ready to start. Sometimes Ms. M would bring in home baked goodies and before long the whole class seemed like a family away from home.

On this day however, Mr. Rose told us about a meeting he had with his boss, Ms. Berry. He said that over the spring break (he still said Easter vacation because he hated being politically correct), he had been working on a project to make Alder Grove into a military style boot camp school. Some kids initially said, "hell no" but I have to say, I was really interested in what this was. I remember him turning on his computer and with a projector showed us various styles of camouflage that we would be wearing instead of our normal street clothes. Of course, that started an argument because the girls wanted the green tiger striped uniforms and most of the boys wanted the Digital Uniforms that the army was considering wearing.

He then outlined what he envisioned as the rules and regulations. He talked about platoons and a ranking structure and I can honestly tell you that I knew I was going to love it. I always thought about making a career in the army and now, with all of us wearing uniforms and working with Sgt. Howell and Sgt. Hewitt, I knew I would be part of something big.

You see, at a normal school, girls like me had to spend time getting ready each morning, deciding what to wear etc. But now, all my sister and I had to do was get up, put on some make-up if we wanted to, and then put on our BDUs (Battle Dress Uniforms). I forgot, we also had to wear black combat boots that had to be shined.

Mr. Rose told us that he was going out on a limb since, unknown to Ms. Berry, he would go out and purchase the types of BDUs we wanted to wear. When they arrived, Mr. Rose had Ms. M hand them out to us girls and we all ran to the bathrooms to put them on. I loved them. We all looked so professional. I was part of something new, a new style of school that I never dreamed about before.

Mr. McDaniel who always subbed for Mr. Rose, came in to show us how to spit shine our combat boots. McDaniel offered us gift certificates for the best polished boots and I actually won it a few times.

Those in the class that were good at art (you would have thought it was all of us due to the other teacher) were asked to come up with a design for a patch showing a Spartan as our mascot. It would be on our uniform and our P/T clothing as well as our baseball hats. Mr. Rose said that he would not order these items however, until we got official permission from the Placer County Office of Education.

Most of us were so excited because school had become fun. We had to do our normal work—algebra, English, science, and history—but once that was completed, we worked on how to make Alder Grove Community School into the Alder Grove Academy.

Mr. Rose felt that since it was our school, we should be the ones to convince the school big shots to approve it. When they arrived, some of us told them why we wanted the school to become an academy. We told them that we needed the order and structure the new school would provide and how proud we were wearing BDUs.

Within one hour, Ms. M got a phone call from Ms. Berry saying that the school administration was impressed and we could become an academy.

Sgt. Howell and Sgt. Hewitt helped us learn leadership and accountability. We were not very good at marching at first, but I took it so seriously that I was promoted to Sergeant of the Blue Platoon. We started out with only three platoons, but soon, more and more kids came to AGA and we had six platoons.

My mother was so proud of me and my sister. Our attendance was no longer an issue and she loved hearing our stories about what we were doing in school. This was very different from before when we would come home and say we learned nothing at school.

I was honored when Mr. Rose asked me and Damian to go with him and Ms. Berry to the Auburn City Council meeting to get approval to move AGA-1 to a new location near the post office. I did not have to speak but I was so proud sitting there in my BDU and shined boots.

I attended both AGA-1 and 2 and am so proud to be one of the original cadets of AGA. If it were not for Mr. Rose and the AGA, who knows what would have happened to me and my sister? We learned leadership, accountability, dependability, respect and how to handle challenges. That was exactly what most of us needed.

I was doing so well that I asked Ms. Berry if I could leave and attend school at Colfax High School. I don't know why I was so stupid because after I left and started at Colfax High School, within five months I asked to return to AGA. It was home and I needed to return.

My mother's health continued to fail yet she still worked. Because she was absent, however, me and my sister, being a little weak, started partying again. We showed up late for school or cut classes. Ms. Berry started picking us up at home and bringing us to school (usually after stopping at Starbucks). But once we got to the school, there was a feeling that we were all together to learn and most of us looked forward to what the day held.

After two years at the first two AGA's and before the move to AGA-3, Ms. Berry felt that we needed to return to our traditional school. I eventually went to Chana Continuation High where I graduated high school, something I would never have accomplished without Mr. Rose and the time I attended AGA

One of the saddest things I remember at AGA was when one of the fellow cadets learned that his father had committed suicide. The funniest thing was when we were playing football and Albert Torres caught a long pass and when he turned around, he ran into a tree. Fortunately it was a small tree and it bent when he hit it. Everyone laughed so hard. There are so many great memories from both AGA's.

Although she was sick, my mom worked hard. She had Hepatitis C and sadly, eventually she passed away. Before she died, she was very happy about how my sister and I had turned our lives around. Initially, it destroyed our family to lose her, but I am happy to say that eventually it made us all a lot stronger and we are now very close.

Currently I am working as a care provider in Placerville and helping my uncle start up his new curb painting business. Eventually I want to return to college and go after my degree in either archeology or anthropology. I am not married nor on probation. I live with my boyfriend and I act as the step-mom for his three children.

The time I spent at AGA inspired my passion for learning, something I did not have until I met Mr. Rose and AGA. I could say the same thing for my sister. She also graduated high school and I am so proud of the young lady and mother she has become.

School administrators need to know that a lot of kids, especially those of us that were becoming or were juvenile delinquents, need a place like AGA to feel we belong. We want to be challenged and to learn but we want teachers to make it relevant like Mr. Rose did. Don't give up on us. I hope that those that read our book will see that they, too, can become successful and overcome the problems they may be having night now.

Thank you, Mr. Rose.

By Alder Grove Academy Cadet Bobby

When I first arrived at AGA, I looked at myself as someone who wasn't worth much. My family always tried to make me see it differently but deep down inside, I always felt that way. I thought I was a pawn of sorts, a person to be moved wherever and whenever someone wanted to.

I felt that school was a pointless thing. The teachers only repeated the same material over and over again and they really didn't seem to care about their students very much. School was something that I dreaded to my bones. I would come up with any excuse I could not to go to school. This resulted in many days of poor attendance. I was credit deficient and yes, most of it was my fault, but I felt that school was a waste of my time. This would change once I was sent to the Alder Grove Academy. Boy, would it change.

It was when I was in the second year of the AGA program. On that day Mr. Rose promoted me to sergeant and gave me my sergeant stripes indicating my new rank. I held my stripes tightly between my fingers. I could hear Mr. Rose speaking but I couldn't make out every word he was saying. For the first time in my life, someone besides my family thought me deserving and worthy of something special. That day I felt pride in myself like I belonged to something instead of being an outsider.

You see, by this time I had started to turn my goal-less life around. All of us cadets started off initially as "new booties" as Mr. Rose used to refer to us. If he thought you were taking the academy program seriously, you were promoted to private and had your first stripes on your U.S. Army uniform. We all wanted to earn medals to put on our military uniforms, but holding rank was really something special.

Medals were important since they showed that you did something above and beyond what other cadets did. You could earn one for good attendance, community service, honor roll, having improved the most, or for leadership. But, once you started putting your rank on your uniform, there was a new sense of pride.

At first, we wore the old army uniforms that were green and we had to polish our combat boots This was actually fun since we competed with each other for a reward either from the army staff or Mr. McDaniel who taught all of us how to polish our boots. We had to stand at attention and either Mr. McDaniel or the army would determine who had the best shined boots. It may seem like something stupid but we were becoming not only a team, but a family.

Mr. Rose was our "father" and the other people of the academy—Mr. McDaniel, Tom Grayson, Ms. M, Ms. Jenny and Ms. Berry—really cared about our success.

When they learned of my promotion, all of them were very proud of me and that meant a lot. Mr. Rose and the AGA program taught me the value of having pride in yourself. If you don't have that pride you can't rise to your true potential. I won't lie, it took a while for that to get that through my thick skull but when it did, I held on and have never let go of that lesson.

Mr. Rose also taught me the value of school, what it can do for you and how it makes you a better person. That lesson helped me through the rest of my high school career and into my college years. I remember the day that he gave us an assignment in which we had to recall the times we burned bridges in our life. That brought back a lot of bad memories to a lot of us, but more importantly, we had to explain how we were going to repair those bridges.

If we were going to learn a new subject and we were having trouble learning it, he always reminded us that, like babies, we had to crawl before we could stand. We laughed when he asked us to remember how often we fell on our asses when we learned to ride a bike or skate.

For a time, Mr. McDaniel was the seventh and eighth grade teacher in one classroom and Mr. Rose had the older students. Mr. McDaniel taught me so much about U.S. Government and I earned an American flag to wear on my uniform. Eventually Mr. McDaniel had to leave—perhaps due to money problems at the education department—and we all had to go into Mr. Rose's classroom. It was wall-to-wall cadets and I now had to learn algebra with the older students.

Mr. Rose made it fun by making jokes about some of the rules you must follow in algebra. It was almost like John Madden football. He made bombing sounds when clearing parentheses and he'd talk about how the "x" was "pissed off" if there was a number next to it. He also showed us how it applied to our current and future lives.

I spent a total of almost three years in the program. I know we changed locations a few times and the best location by far was our last location. It was an abandoned elementary school and it had a lot of basketball courts (which we used as our marching grounds with either Tom Grayson or Mr. McDaniel). It also had a football field that we used for both football, soccer, softball and Frisbee. Sergeants Howell and Hewlitt and Corporal B would use the football field for our P/T. We seemed to run a lot and before I knew it, I was getting into the best shape of my life.

We had become a family. Sometimes we fought among ourselves, which really got Mr. Rose angry but for the most part we never really had problems. We celebrated when a cadet was singled out for doing something great and if we screwed up, we all suffered the consequences, which made us stronger as a team.

Fridays was our exam day. When we got there, we changed into our uniforms and joined our platoons to raise the flag. We had an honor guard who would raise the flag and then we all marched back to the classroom where Mr. Rose had coffee, chocolate and donuts ready for us. He treated us as adults if we deserved it and Fridays were our day to show him what we had learned during the week.

I remember that he sometimes wore a 49ers black shirt that said, "Don't tell me—show me!" In other words, don't tell him how smart we thought we were but show him by passing the long exam. Those exams were long. Each exam had a section of what we covered during the week so you would find at least ten questions on algebra, government, economics, U.S./world history, English, and science. There were at least fifty questions. Mr. Rose said that the purpose was to show us how to take a long exam like the high school exit exam and later college entrance exams. No one complained. We drank our coffee and ate our donuts and took the weekly exam.

The saddest time for me would have to be when Mr. Rose was hurt and then had to leave the school. The class had just been let out and Mr. Rose had seen one of the students messing around in the bushes behind the school and had gone to confront him. I remember standing in the parking lot with my mom and the other staff talking when I heard something that made me look over to the side stairs that led down to the basketball court area. I saw Mr. Rose drop to his knees holding onto the rail of the stairs and the student running down the stairs to get away.

Ms. M hurried over and called for the police. The student apparently had drugs on him and Mr. Rose found them. The student slapped Mr. Rose's hand and Mr. Rose lost his balance. We all knew that Mr. Rose had had a ton of knee surgeries so this was not good.

I was holding a notebook at the time. I dropped it and started to run toward the stairs. I jumped down the stairs to chase the other student but my mother yelled at me to stop. I can remember feeling rage at what happened and still do to this day when I look back on it. It hurt even more when we heard and saw an ambulance come to the school to transport Mr. Rose to the hospital. We were all surprised when he showed up for work the next day on crutches. Almost all of the cadets asked him how he was feeling. After all, he was our father.

The saddest day however, was when we were all in the classroom—there must have been between forty to fifty cadets at this time—and you could see that Ms. M and Ms.

Jenny were upset. Mr. Rose told us that PCOE had decided to no longer have AGA as a military style school. Instead it would just be a community school. Then Mr. Rose said that he had requested a transfer back to juvenile hall where he had come from. Since the AGA was gone, so was he.

We were all shocked. Many of our girl cadets cried. Some of us protested and said that this was not right. None of us wanted to return to our traditional schools. We had become a family over the years and nearly all of us had made big changes in our lives only to be abandoned. After a lot of us complained, Mr. Rose told us how proud he was about how all of us met his challenges, how he was honored to have been our teacher and that we would always be in his heart. He told us that now we all had to "cut the apron strings" and prepare to re-enter our traditional schools, that they could offer us much more than AGA did. He challenged us to see it through without him, but sadly, the new school was terrible and most of us decided we'd rather be at our regular school.

I feel that my life turned around and became much better thanks to knowing Mr. Rose and being a part of the AGA program. I now have pride in myself and my life. I hold my head high and face each challenge with confidence. He challenged us in AGA and that experience has prepared me for any obstacles I may face in the future.

I did not know Brendt Volarvich personally but Mr. Rose often talked about him to point out how we needed to really question our behavior and choices. I know that it hurt Mr. Rose after learning that one of his students had killed a police officer.

I am currently in search of a job and am attending a community college. I am studying to be a computer programmer and am thinking of branching into either video game design or cyber security. I hope to finish my schooling and possibly either join a computer programming company or even go into work for myself by fixing broken down computers.

After my own experiences being an at-risk youth, I believe that it would help

Students like me to have more structure and more entertaining lessons. Also, students need to know why they are being taught the subject matter and how it will help them in their future.

By Alder Grove Academy Cadet Noe Perez

As Mr. Rose knows, I was deported to Mexico. This is how my life is going since the last time I saw Mr. Rose and the other cadets. Things didn't go right or wrong. I just let time pass. I'm always trying to make a difference in the world and I just need the right people to connect with, those who follow law and want peace.

All the time I spent in juvenile court and in boot-camp can probably make a whole new book. In fact, you could probably make another book in which all of us former cadets could write about what we are doing now.

For me, I got married and I have a son four years old. But I am now alone without my wife or son because I am poor and I don't have any money. My ex-wife left me for someone else who has money. I am happy though now that I have you guys to talk to.

I don't have school papers though I need them down here so I can become a teacher, maybe an English teacher.

But my papers are in Crystal Creek or Placer County and I have no time, money or ability to get them. Unfortunately, I signed my deportation papers too quickly and did not think at the time that I might need my school records. I am not sure what to do.

By Alder Grove Academy Cadet Naomi

Before I arrived at AGA, I saw myself as a carefree teenage girl who would figure life out after I was done partying. I knew I wasn't a bad person, however, I knew I was a very irresponsible one. Before I arrived at Alder Grove Academy, I went to school to see my friends and then ditch the rest of my classes because I had better shit to do. I had it all figured out. I was going to get married to my then boyfriend, go to massage school, and live happily ever after.

When I first arrived at AGA, I still found myself ditching class although it was harder because my probation officer always came to find me. One day however, Albert and I were in the army's office, talking to the army sergeants about our lives and how we wanted our lives to turn out. That is when I realized it was time for me to stop acting like a rude bitch to everyone that was trying to help me and finally grow up.

Being at AGA taught me to take responsibility for my own actions. For instance, if you did something wrong, you had to do push-ups (I hated push-ups). But by making me do them, I thought twice before doing something wrong again.

Also, Mr. Rose helped me believe in myself. We had to run a mile in a specific time to qualify for the army and earn a medal to be worn on our uniform. I never thought I could do it but with Mr. Rose's help and the encouragement from the other cadets, I was able to make it. It may not seem like much, but crossing that finish line boosted my confidence forever. I knew I was capable of anything as long as I never quit trying.

I attended the Alder Grove Community School before Mr. Rose came and turned it into the academy. I was there for two years. The funniest thing that happened was on Albert's birthday. I baked him a cake that looked like a giant penis and Ms. M (very smart lady) made me show her before I could share it with the class, and her face was priceless. The saddest thing was seeing some friends I grew to know and love doing drugs. No matter how much I tried to tell then not too, they "knew better" and continued when school was not in session.

I got married in 2013 to an amazing man. We have two beautiful children, a boy two years old, and a girl who is three. I am a bartender and we live in Montana. During the next five years I plan on moving to Idaho, buy a house, and finally go to massage school! I do believe I owe a lot of my current success to the Alder Grove Academy. I learned so much about myself there and made life-long friendships. My experiences at Alder Grove Academy made me a more confident woman.

Sadly, we have lost some of our cadets and that has made me see life as the precious gift it is. Mr. Rose and I may have bumped heads but he helped me know whatever I choose to do in life, I can do it as long as I never give up and keep running. Teenagers need structure and rules and a positive role model. If a teenager respects you, like we all did Mr. Rose, you will try harder to not let him or yourself down.

By Alder Grove Academy Cadet Pavel

Before I arrived at AGA, I thought that I was at rock bottom. I had no direction and I didn't care. My brother was already in jail and I didn't want to end up there but I really did not know what I was doing with my life.

I was called into a large room when I was in the eighth grade at E.V. Cain. There were a lot of people there but I only had my mom. These people were going to decide if I would be expelled from school. If they agreed, I would not be able to graduate with my classmates and I would not be attending Placer High School. I don't remember too much about the meeting but there was a Sheriff's Deputy there and during the meeting he asked me if I was related to a man with my brother's name. I said I was and he said that he thought so since he had seen him in jail. I am sure that his statement about knowing my brother and had an impact on the group deciding my fate.

I was told that I would be expelled and that I would be sent to a military boot camp school called the Alder Grove Academy. I would not be attending Placer with my friends. To be honest with you, I was scared. It was hard living with just my mom and my brother being in jail. Here I was, still in the eighth grade, and now I was being sent to a military school with a bunch of older, bigger high school students. Also, I was overweight. How was I going to be able run, do exercises, all the stuff a military school was going to demand from me?

At least this boot camp school was a school where I could come home after school and be with my mom. Some schools I heard of required you to stay overnight for a long time.

What I remember first about the Alder Grove Academy is how Mr. Rose joked with us—he told us that we would be successful or he would kill us! Then he would add, "With love in my heart." All of us knew that he was serious, that he would always be there for us. The AGA became my family of friends and Mr. Rose held us together. I felt safe, I felt appreciated. I looked up to Mr. Rose as a role model. Remember, I only had my mom at home. Now I had Mr. Rose, Sergeant Howell, and Sergeant Hewitt.

The most important things I learned were discipline and team work, and about ranks, medals, and consequences. The way the AGA was set up—and I attended all three of them until I left to attend Placer High School—was very structured and I, like most of the students, needed that. The army taught us leadership and the way we were formed into different platoons and held rank reinforced that. I was so proud when I got promoted and earned a medal. In fact, Mr. Rose might remember I won more medals that anyone in AGA.

I also remember the consequences if we did something wrong, like running up the dreaded hill at AGA-2 (the fishbowl), or losing P/E. I also remember the day when Mr. Rose got upset with two of the cadets for being rude and forgetting their uniforms. He put them on the platoon that reported only to him. He called it the PMP—Positive Motivation Platoon. He had Ms. M go out and buy all of us McDonald hamburgers, fries and shakes and while all of us were eating outside, he had the two cadets that violated the rules pull weeds with him. No one else ever wanted to be in the PMP!

Bottom line, I learned that in life there are rules and consequences. Don't operate outside the rules because if you get caught, you face the consequences. I loved all the police stories Mr. Rose told us about people he had to arrest for violating the law and the consequences they faced. None of us will never forget those stories, especially what happened to Brendt Volarvich.

I was with the AGA program from the start until just before it closed down. I remember Ms. Berry telling me that I needed to start going to school at Placer High School even though she allowed me to stay many years. I remember Mr. Rose telling us that he was honored that some of us wanted to stay in AGA although we could return to our traditional high school. No one, including me, wanted to leave the other cadets and Mr. Rose. But Mr. Rose always stressed that AGA could never compete with traditional high schools because they had so much more to offer so I left AGA. My mother, to this day, says that the AGA was the best thing that ever happened to me.

The funniest thing that I can remember while attending AGA was Kasey being hit on the head by a softball that I hit. I remember swinging and hitting the ball and it really went high. When it started coming down everyone yelled at Kasey to catch it, but she was playing with her belly button and the ball hit her on the top of the head. I felt bad because I had a crush on her. I also will never forget the Turkey Bowl (which our platoon won) and the Mud Bowl. It was also fun doing training with the army and playing football with them. And when we participated in the food drive, we collected more food than Placer High School. It was always nice when Mr. Rose offered us cash for a good job.

Once a week Tom Grayson would come into the class and we would tell him if there was a new cadet. He would ask the new cadet to identify themselves and if they did not stand, and most did not, he would yell at them and tell them to stand. They got scared and of course, all of us would laugh. After they said their name and answered some questions, they started to sit down. Then Tom would yell at them asking them who gave them permission to sit down. Of course when it was all over, Tom would make friends with them and tell them it was an initiation. Usually, after this new cadet went through the initiation, he/she was the first person to tell Tom when a new "bootie" arrived at AGA.

The saddest thing was when we learned that a father of one of the cadet's committed suicide. Oh, and the time that one of the girls overdosed. Because I had a crush on her, I felt bad seeing her taken away from AGA on a hospital stretcher. I went with Mr. Rose after school to see her, but the hospital would only let him in.

My life is absolutely better because of the AGA program. Mr. Rose used to ask us if we had burned any bridges and if so, could we repair them?

Mr. Rose and the army taught us how stupid gang affiliation was and what leadership really meant. He taught us not only what was in the textbooks but how it related to real life. He taught us investment basics, how to use a checkbook, and what to watch out for when using credit cards. When he got mad at us, we knew we earned it and most of us were sad for letting him down. But the next day, there he was bright and early ready to challenge us again. It was my home away from home. He and Sergeant Howell and Sergeant Hewitt taught us that to earn respect, we must show respect and I see it every day in school and in my relationships.

I am not married, don't have any children and I have never been on probation. As a full time student at Sierra College majoring in business, my plan is to earn not only my BA but an MBA. I will be the first one in my family to accomplish this. Over the next five years I want to earn my degrees, find a great job and get married. I never, ever, had this much ambition in my life and my mom will tell you that I changed because of AGA and Mr. Rose.

Schools should realize that most of us "at-risk" students have had a tough life already and we respond to order and structure as long as it is backed up by a caring teacher, not a phony teacher who always tries to be nice. We see through bribery (offering us a candy or cup of Starbucks) for following some rules. Instead, we want to be challenged and earn whatever reward we might receive. Mr. Rose would bring in donuts and coffee especially on Fridays, but we HAD TO EARN IT! He would tell us that teachers who gave us rewards for just following the rules would be setting us up for failure when we became adults.

He would ask us what would happen if we continued to not follow the rules at our future jobs—we knew that we would be fired. So, in his classroom, our grades were our rewards as well as an "atta boy," extra PE time, or higher rank. That is what made the academy so special to us.

By Alder Grove Academy Cadet Brittany

Before I arrived in Mr. Rose's classroom, I thought of myself as an awful person. I had been kicked out of Placer High School and, although I had dreams, I did not see them as realistic. I did not like going to school. I had a very hard time learning and comprehending the information that I was being taught. Part of the reason I was sent to Alder Grove Academy was because I hadn't been going to school. I did not see myself graduating from high school and I had actually thought about dropping out of school and just getting a job.

After I arrived at the academy, the subject that I most struggled with was math. I remember sitting in class with Mr. Rose and a light bulb went off when he was teaching a math lesson. I suddenly understood what was being taught. For the first time in my life, I was excited to take a math test because I knew that I would know all the answers. He made algebra and related math topics fun and then challenged us to see if we really understood the material during our weekly Friday exams.

In Mr. Rose's class, I learned to be open to alternative teaching styles and that, when I listen, I will most likely hear something that will help me. This was important for me because I had tried for so long to be a good student, and here I was in alternative education and I was learning to become a great student.

I believe I spent six months at the third Alder Grove Academy up at Alta Vista School. I liked wearing the army uniforms. It made it easier to get ready for school especially being a female. We all looked alike in class and we never had any gang problems.

The funniest thing that happened was when we were playing baseball and I was batting and no one thought I would hit the ball. Not only did I hit the ball, I hit a home run. It was such an ego boost. I loved it! We all had to earn physical education and I would get mad if for some reason, we lost the chance of going outside.

I remember when Mr. Rose would introduce us to a new concept and someone would say that it was hard. He would just stand there and wait for the rest of us to ask him to bring it on, to show him we were ready for the challenge. No other teacher ever did that to me. P/T and P/E was so much fun even though it was physically tough. I got into the best shape of my life at AGA.

I do feel like my life would be different if I had not encountered Mr. Rose. He taught me how to be open to learning and that is something that I am forever grateful for. He challenged us in ways we had never been challenged. He was the coach and the exam was the enemy—we learned to defeat the enemy by passing the weekly exams. I was so proud of my turnaround; getting a medal for academic achievement was frosting on the cake.

Also, Ms. M was there as our "mother." If we had any type of a problem that we did not want to share with Mr. Rose, we knew we could go to her and she would support us. You could not put anything over on Ms. M. Though I am sure she sometimes consulted with Mr. Rose, none of us girls ever felt that she betrayed us. Sometimes, when we wanted to have a party or pot luck, we felt that it was better to approach Ms. M, especially if Mr. Rose was upset over something. She knew when to approach him, and we often got our way when she smoothed things over.

The saddest thing that happened was when Mr. Rose left Alder Grove Academy. I remember several students started to cry. Some of the guys wanted to go to their traditional schools immediately. Mr. Rose told us that change is hard to handle and he personally hated change. He told us to give the next teacher a chance, but we did not like the fact that it was not going to be a military style school. It really sucked since we were all doing so well.

If I had not gone to Alder Grove, I would not have been able to see that I was full of potential. After I left Alder Grove, I had the opportunity to go back to Placer High School. I re-entered Placer as a sophomore and maintained 3.9 GPA till my senior year when I graduated in 2012 with Honors!

If I had not learned how to be present at school, I would not have been able to achieve all that I have achieved thus far.

Today I have a job as a personal stylist. I create wardrobes for a number of my high-profile clients. I do not have any children and am not on probation. I am a few months away from graduating from Sierra College with an AS Degree in Social and Behavioral Sciences. When I am finished at Sierra College, I will transfer to SCU Long Beach and major in fashion design and textiles.

During the next five years, I would like to graduate from a four-year college, have a fun job, a great home in Southern California or New York. I would just like to live my life happily and comfortably. I don't need to be filthy rich, but I would like to have available funds in case of emergencies and to be able to travel and go anywhere without worrying about finances. Mr. Rose always stressed that we should be prepared for the worst so when it happens we are not surprised.

Most of us had terrible childhoods/families, and we all had a bad attitude about school, teachers, and cops. I think that if teachers were to care a little more about students rather than their paycheck, students would be more successful. I think that when teachers are passionate about what they do, it makes learning a better experience. When someone is passionate about their job, it comes across as being more caring. I think that being caring is the best way to help students be more successful. But I also believe that with some students, it is necessary to be a little harder.

This paper has really been fun to write. It brought back so many memories about one of the most important times of my life.

By Alder Grove Community School Student Crash

I was in a class with Mr. Rose when I attended the Alder Grove Community School after the closing of the academy.

When I found out that Mr. Rose and his former cadets were going to write a book about their experiences in the academy, I really wanted to be in his book. I believed Mr. Rose pretty much ran the Alder Grove Community School like he ran the Alder Grove Academy. We did not have to wear uniforms although I think that would have been great. But the classroom had structure and each of us were taught discipline and accountability.

Before I met Mr. Rose, I looked at myself as a failure. I did not want to go to school because I thought it was pointless and I didn't see any sort of future for myself. I did not know what I was going to do once I got out of school, and I really didn't care.

Then I met Mr. Rose. He taught me so many valuable lessons, lessons that changed my point of view about myself and life. He actually cared about all of us. He did not make it easy academically but he taught all subjects in a way that even the slowest person in our classroom would eventually get it. If he was trying to teach a concept in Algebra and he could tell some of us didn't understand it, he would come up with a new way of teaching us the concept that we could understand.

One of the courses he taught that we valued was about personal finance and investing. Man, I wanted to run out and start investing immediately, but I wasn't eighteen yet. He taught me useful things like psychology and interesting subjects like marine biology. But the best part was that he treated us like adults. Other teachers I had had in the past seemed to just go through the motions. They did not have a passion for their job. It was as if they became teachers so they could have a three-month vacation and a week off for Thanksgiving and two weeks for Christmas.

Can you believe that when we arrived sleepily for class, our teacher had already fixed us imported coffee to help us prepare for his first lesson? He treated us like college kids and we loved it.

As I said, this was after the academy closed and we weren't a military style boot camp school. Still, Mr. Rose and Ms. Lum always talked about how successful that program had been. So, when I first met Mr. Rose and he said we were going to change things at Alder Grove Community School and make it somewhat like the academy, I was all in. It would turn out to be the best years of my life. You see, before Mr. Rose arrived, the school was out of control. The teachers that were at the school before Mr. Rose treated us like babies. The work they gave us was for elementary kids. Most of us did not take anything they said seriously and many of us did not do the work. That changed when Mr. Rose arrived.

Mr. Rose had some of us put a large piece of paper on the back wall. The paper on the wall listed our names and next to it was a one. He told us that even though we would not have ranks, we would be assigned a number depending on how well we did in class, followed the rules, and took care of each other. We all started at step one.

You did not have to be the smartest person in the class to rise in your steps, but if he felt you were not giving your best effort, your chances of reaching step five were, as he often said, "slim to none." We had a lot of rules and man, if you did not follow those rules you got demoted a step or two and even then, there were further consequences.

Next, he re-arranged the desks in a stadium like manner or an arc. We could sit in whatever desk we wanted until after the first week when some of us got moved up from first to second step. Once that happened the highest steps got to sit in the back row and the first steppers had to sit in the front.

One day, Mr. Rose really messed with our minds. He seemed to be in a good mood but he had this grin on his face meaning that something was about to happen. Ms. Lum came at the beginning of each class when Mr. Rose would go over the agenda for the day. On this day, he said that he was proud of all of us and that he and Ms. Lum had decided to try something different with the step assignments. He led us to the back room where there were boxes of new desks that rolled and turned and was a lot more comfortable than the old wooden desk. Mr. Rose had some of us open the boxes and assemble these new desks. When Mr. Rose came in the next day, we were all sitting in these new desks screwing around, using them like bumper cars. Mr. Rose got pissed. We all stopped screwing around and he said that as of that day, if you were a fifth stepper, you got the new desks, but once you lost your fifth step, you got a lousy wooden desk again.

When we had coffee and donuts, he would put the boxes of donuts out so that we could see the different types, but he always allowed the female students to go first regardless of their steps. Then it was the boys' turn but fifth steppers got first choice and so on. God those were great times.

Oh, we also had to earn P/E. In other words, it was not a given each day. We had to all work as a team and get our work done or we did not get the right to go outside. P/E had never been part of the curriculum until Mr. Rose came so for all of us, including the girls, we loved going outside and playing football or baseball.

Man, we had some great games out there and Mr. Rose said that the girls "played for blood." We only had a few injuries and it forced us to work as a team, although sometimes some idiots in the class acted out and Mr. Rose got upset and we had to go back inside.

It was so cool to celebrate as a class when Mr. Rose got his doctorate. It really motivated me to go onto college/ university once I get out of high school. Now I could call my teacher "doctor."

I'm not sure what the funniest time was because we had so many and it would be hard to choose from, but the saddest is easy. That was the day we learned that Mr. Rose was leaving. That was a hard goodbye. Though I knew it wasn't goodbye forever, it really hurt all of us. He had done so much for us. He was having problems with his feet and knees—we knew he was in pain but every day he was there.

He was also upset over some new teaching methods the education office was forcing on us called PBIS. At the start, they did not make us use PBIS because the system we had was working. I liked coming to school. Most of us did. None of us liked PBIS and we pretty much rebelled. This was probably why he decided to retire.

After Mr. Rose retired and left Alder Grove, I transferred out and went to Chana Continuation High School. A lot of us never thought we could pass the high school exit exam or get a high school diploma, but I passed my exit exam the very first time. Before coming to Alder Grove, that would never had happened.

Mr. Rose has inspired me to do more with my life and actually make money. Within the next five years I plan to get a job, my own apartment, and work on meeting the weight requirement for the army so I can enlist.

I feel that teachers, parents, and the police should not give up on us. Some of us may seem to be screw-ups and most of us were, but given the right opportunities we, too, can change and become productive adults. Having Mr. Rose made it easy for most of us and we will never forget him. Also, I feel that the county needs to have more military style boot camp schools. Even though our Alder Grove was not an academy, the things Mr. Rose and Ms. Lum did that were similar made most of us success stories.

By Alder Grove Community School Student Goldie Locks

I attended the Alder Grove Community School after the Alder Grove Academy closed. Mr. Rose came back and taught at the school. When I heard that Mr. Rose was writing a book about the other academies, I asked him if I could be included in the book since, upon his arrival at the non-military Alder Grove, he still pretty much ran it the same way.

I am what most people call a former delinquent. I never wanted to go to school, never wanted to do any school work—I just wanted to get drunk and get high. I always imagined a rich future for myself. Yet, with all the drinking I did, I just saw myself slowly going down a different direction and it was going to be bad.

So, after I made the decision to bring contraband to school and I got caught, my life got back on a positive track. That may sound confusing but it was because of being caught with contraband that I was expelled from my traditional school and got sent to the Alder Grove Community School and ran into Mr. Rose. I immediately I bonded with Mr. Rose. He seemed to get along with all of my former classmates and I felt like many of them, that my family away from home was Alder Grove Community School.

One of the things I loved was the way Mr. Rose interacted with everyone in the class. He was an amazing teacher. When I arrived, I had straight F's. Mr. Rose helped me raise my grades eventually to straight A's!

Also, when I arrived, everyone had a nickname and the class and Mr. Rose called me "Goldie Locks." For the entire year I was at the Alder Grove Community School, Mr. Rose helped me change not just my bad attitude but my whole outlook on life.

Mr. Rose set up his classes like his former academy classes in that we were rated in the classroom. In other words, if you exhibited Level Four or Level Five behavior, you got the best desks and responsibilities like greeting people who arrived at our school, answering the phones, and helping with lunch

Everyone started out as a Level One. If you did a good job and Mr. Rose felt like you deserved to be raised to a higher level, you were promoted to Level Two and so on. All of us, regardless of our level, had to work as a team or we would all suffer the consequences but the Level Fives had to take care of the class. You could get demoted if you failed to live up to the standards of a Level Five.

Mr. Rose would bring in donuts on Fridays if we all deserved it. We also had coffee and hot water for chocolate each day and he ran the classroom like a junior college. We had to bring in our own coffee mugs and if we left them out and did not clean them, Mr. Rose would throw them in the garbage can. We all learned quickly to follow the rules.

We also had to earn the right to have physical exercise. It was not part of the normal curriculum, but Mr. Rose felt that being cooped up all day long in a portable classroom was too much. So, even in the rain, if we deserved it, we got to go outside and play either football or baseball.

On Fridays when we took our weekly exam, he often wore a black shirt that had a SF 49ers logo on it and the words, "Don't Tell Me, Show Me." This meant to us that we could tell him how smart we were, but until we showed him on our weekly exam, it was all words—just bullshit.

In class at Alder Grove, Mr. Rose had us watch *Gridiron Gang, Dangerous Minds, Stand and Deliver* and *Gifted Hands*. Watching these movies together went a long way in motivating us to succeed and to write in our journals every week. I found this not only relaxing, but it was nice to share our inner thoughts with Mr. Rose. He never judged us and we could not wait to get them back and see what notes or words of encouragement he gave us.

Celebrating Christmas and Thanksgiving together in the classroom before our vacation was special to all of us. Many of us came from families that did not participate in celebrating these holidays either for lack of money or because they had a terrible family. One time we all participated in a Secret Santa event. It was so great when Mr. McDaniel arrived in the backroom with Ms. Lum and then appeared as Santa to the class. Here we were, all expelled students, some on probation, and we were celebrating Christmas together. Sadly, one of the students confessed to me, this was the best Christmas she ever had.

Though I may not have known Brendt (now on death row in San Quentin), we all knew how Mr. Rose felt he failed to bond with Brendt. After reading Brendt's open letter to all of us, I could see that Mr. Rose really did care about all of his students.

GARY ROSE, PH.D.

The saddest part of my life as a student came when we learned that Mr. Rose had decided to retire. He was the greatest teacher I ever had and my role model. All of us looked at him as our dad and now he was leaving us. Many students really got upset and had a hard time dealing with his eventual departure. To them, it felt like they were being abandoned again.

The school administrators tried to introduce a new program called PBIS after Mr. Rose left and we all hated it. It made us feel like babies. Ms. Lum tried to run the school the same way as Mr. Rose but it was not the same.

Just a year ago, I left Alder Grove knowing Mr. Rose helped me a lot. I now attend Chana High School and can finally say I feel on track again, THE RIGHT TRACK! There are several other Alder Grove students with me at Chana. We see each other every day and they are my brothers and sisters—all because we went through the Alder Grove environment together. We would have loved to finish our education with Mr. Rose at Alder Grove, but because he taught us self-discipline and how to handle tough problems, we're all doing well at Chana.

How did the structure and order of Alder Grove help me? That is easy. If I had never met Mr. Rose, I wouldn't feel as satisfied with myself as I do. When I look at my present life, I realize my experiences at Alder Grove and the way he forced us to be accountable for our actions all affected my life in a positive way.

In the next few years I want to attend college. I want to major in both culinary arts and art. I went through a very abusive childhood so I never got to follow my dreams and reach for what I wanted. Mr. Rose taught me to never give up and always reach for my dreams. Those of us who constantly hurt need someone to comfort and understand them, and this is what Mr. Rose did for us.

It is funny how life works out sometimes. I violated the law by bringing contraband onto my traditional school grounds. I got expelled. I was sent to Alder Grove Community School, hating school and with failing grades. Now I am ready to enter college, and all because of the time I spent at Alder Grove with Mr. Rose.

By Brendt Volarvich,
Former Juvenile Delinquent Facility Student–
An Open Letter for Mr. Rose's Students

Dear Fellows:

As most of you already know, I never cared about school and never paid one iota of attention while in school. Hell, basically I was a drug addict with a fifth grade education by the time I went to Placer County Juvie.

No teacher had ever gotten through to me or interested me in anything until Mr. Rose. This was before his military school that many of you got to attend, yet he was able to reach me by his unique style of teaching. He taught me how to understand basic math, algebra, and introduction to geometry as well as essay writing. All of his teaching helped me pass my GED a couple of months after I was released from juvenile hall.

It is not just Mr. Rose's teaching though, that was important. He actually gave a shit! A couple of years after I left the hall for the last time, Mr. Rose saw my case in the news and immediately knew who I was. He felt as if he had failed as a teacher. But it wasn't his fault. I assured him of that when he actually came to Death Row to see me. It's no one's fault but my own, my own failure.

I truly believe that if I had I been through Mr. Rose's military academy, I could have been helped, possibly to the extent of turning my life completely around before I ruined it and took an innocent man's life.

I believe in Mr. Rose and his ideas. He wants to help kids like me, like you, and like us. And he wants to help other teachers and parents to turn us around because it is hard for us to do it by ourselves as we all know.

Troubled teens are often unwilling to listen to a "normie" (normal) adult. I was like that. I've got to admit it's hard to say what teachers should have told me because I know I never listened. I was so hard-headed and stubborn and stupid.

Now, I would tell a parent to be tough, but that often backfires, so would being too soft and nice. I would say that teachers and parents should try to find someone like me who's made serious mistakes and introduce the troubled teen to that person. Hopefully, the teen will realize that his life is at risk and that people like me are an example of what every at-risk teen must learn *not to be.*

This is why I hope you will all work with Mr. Rose on his and your book. Who knows? You may be able to save lives here! Isn't it worth it to do whatever is necessary and damn any personal gain or excuses?

I believe it is! If you look inside yourselves and really think about the long-term benefits and implications in getting your book published and sold to as many teachers and students as possible—hopefully, Mr. Rose's ideas could be implemented on a large scale—Wow!!!!

You have to help in any way you can. Tell everyone you know to read your book and learn from your stories.

Remember, Mr. Rose always believed in us and tried to help us change into productive men and women.

It's too late for me to make that change, but it's not too late for you and other young people like you.

By Jaylynn,
A Former Student, Now Incarcerated
The Circle is Complete

Hi, my name is Jaylynn and I am a 21 years old female incarcerated in Placer County jail. You can imagine my surprise when I learned that my favorite teacher from the time I was incarcerated in the Placer County Juvenile Detention Facility, would now be my instructor in pursuit of my GED.

As I said, I first met Mr. Rose (now Dr. Rose) around September 2011. I had been arrested for drug paraphernalia. I was 16 years old at the time. It was my second stay in juvenile hall. I was also pregnant.

Mr. Rose was a very nice teacher who really seemed to care that we not only got an education, but would use this new knowledge to change our lives and improve our adult futures. Of course, now that you know I am an adult and back in confinement, I guess you can say that I didn't use my knowledge wisely.

Now that I am an adult, to have him in my life again was extremely surprising but also exciting. I knew deep inside that he would help me gain my GED and I could change my life for me and my son.

It is my hope that my contribution to Mr. Rose's book will save at least one other at-risk person from ending up like I have—in jail and not home raising my son.

Fortunately for me, I was never locked up over Christmas as a juvenile but I will be now that I am an adult in our county's jail. You see, I was eventually released from custody in October 2011 and was placed in the Placer County Drug Court program which I was proud to complete. But, in 2016, after having my baby, I got arrested again, this time as an adult offender and off to the Placer County Jail I went.

Now I am locked up again. My charges this time are for identity theft and conspiracy. My son lives with my mother who is his legal guardian. It really hurts when my mother brings him to jail for visitation and I only have 20-30 minutes to be with him. You can't imagine what it feels like when they leave and I am alone. I am counting down the days until my release.

The first time I attended the GED prep course and was again with Dr. Rose, I have to admit that I was nervous and also embarrassed. I did not know how he would treat me after all of these years. I had already learned so much from him in the past while in juvenile hall and that knowledge has stuck with me to this day. Would he accept me when he saw me now in county jail? He always told us that until we hit rock bottom and sincerely dedicated ourselves to turning our lives around, we would probably continue to re-offend and would never be successful. I guess this is what happened to me.

When he saw me that first day in our GED class, he had a big smile on his face and walked up to me to see what I had been doing all these years. Of course, the red coveralls printed with "PCSO Inmate" kind of gave it away.

I told him I had a son and he was concerned as to who was raising him while I was incarcerated. He was warm and sincere and never hinted that he was judging me.

The class began and I instantly felt as if I was back in my classroom at juvenile hall. His teaching style had not changed. He was teaching us what we needed to know to pass our GED exam, those portions dealing with social studies and English language arts. He not only taught us the concepts of what we needed to recall for the test, but also, when possible, techniques and strategies to use to conserve time. He is a teacher who always gets to the point. He is a no-bull-shit type of teacher who makes learning fun. Though his lessons are very structured (which is what I need in an instructor), he still uses a lot of humor to get his point across.

Within a few weeks, he told me that I was ready to take both sections of the GED exam. Since I had already passed the math and science sections, if I passed the two remaining exams, I would earn my GED. The day before the exam, before he left for the day, he gave me a final pep-talk, telling me to follow his strategies and I would be successful.

He was right! I passed both sections with flying colors and have now earned my GED. He has inspired me to start taking college courses in pursuit of a career for myself and my son. I am also considering cosmetology. I could hardly wait to call my mom and let her know that I now have my GED.

One day while the other female inmates were arriving from the different tanks (cell blocks) for class, Dr. Rose told me that he had just realized that I was the first student that he had had from the "old days" at juvenile hall who has become an adult and one of his students again.

In our GED class, he had read a few sections of the rough draft of "Hitting Rock Bottom" and everyone in our class can't wait to get a copy.

To my surprise and excitement, he asked if I would like to be included in his book since I had "made the circle complete."

I could hardly wait to tell my story in hopes that juvenile females heading in the wrong direction might actually turn their lives around after reading what I have to say.

Now that you have read my story, I hope that you will "hit rock bottom" long before I did and start a productive life. If any of my story helped, then I am excited for you. You, too, can do it!

RECOLLECTIONS OF THE ALDER GROVE ACADEMY STAFF

By Joan Berry,
Retired, Director of Alternative Education,
Placer County Office of Education

Before the Alder Grove Academy ("AGA") started, there were several successful military schools in California for high-risk students. The Sacramento County Office of Education operated one of those schools which was located on the closed Mather Air Force Base in Sacramento.

Throughout Placer County, we had several students struggling with truancy, lack of motivation, and problems with following school rules who were referred to our Court and Community School programs from local school districts and the Probation Department.

The students came with a referral and a rehabilitation plan. They could only return to their districts if the plan was satisfied by the students and approved by the districts. The student was given one year to complete the plan and if they did not complete it, we had to develop a new plan.

Until the AGA was formed, many students who did not meet their rehabilitation plans and failed to become eligible to return to their districts were "lost" in the system—in other words, they could be on the street. The purpose of the AGA was to keep these students in school.

Mr. Rose and I, two additional teachers and two Roseville Police officers—all of whom were concerned with truancy—visited the Mather Academy and basically liked what we saw. Students in the 7th to the 12th grade attended class in military uniforms and a retired army officer and military personnel ran the school while several civilian instructors worked in the classrooms.

When we were given the opportunity to interview a few of their cadets, we were very impressed with the stories they told about how the order and structure of their school, with its emphasis on military discipline, helped them turn their lives around.

Very soon after our visit to the Mather Academy, I asked Mr. Rose, who had recently earned his doctorate, to prepare a proposal to introduce the concept of a military school to the Placer County Superintendent of Schools and the Placer County School Board (PCOE). The proposal was accepted, and we opened Alder Grove Academy the following semester.

Dr. Rose not only designed an effective program but was a perfect fit as the teacher in charge. AGA was a huge responsibility and undertaking. Dr. Rose was and is a natural-born teacher, a "rough around the edges" and caring cop. With his background in financial planning, he taught senior economics and all required math classes. This included lessons in how to balance a checkbook, buy a home, invest in the stock market for retirement, and buy a car.

He loved to challenge his students and even though the program was highly structured, the cadets loved him and his teaching aid, Ms. Michelle Segarra. When we had to approach the Auburn City Council for approval to move from the first AGA site to a building in the City of Auburn, we brought two proud, uniformed cadets, one of whom spoke to the council requesting approval.

We started our first AGA in an old army barracks used during World War II. I remember how Dr. Rose, without my knowledge, bought some camouflage uniforms to see if his students would like wearing them. He also purchased combat boots and I remember showing up at the site one afternoon and seeing the future cadets polishing their boots with Mr. Paul McDaniel. This later became a ritual with the army—the cadet with the best polished boots got a reward.

The program went extremely well. I don't recall the cost of the uniforms but I remember Dr. Rose making deals with uniform companies and our local sporting goods store to get the best and cheapest equipment for his cadets. The use of uniforms immediately resolved gang color and clothing issues. As Dr. Rose would tell his cadets—some of whom were from rival gangs—the only gang colors would be the U.S. Army camouflage uniforms.

Based on cadet feedback, we knew the students felt they were unconditionally accepted and the entire staff cared about their success. They were welcome to come into school ahead of schedule to have coffee, eat something and polish their boots, which they thoroughly enjoyed. Dr. Rose chose to show up before school, many times as early as 5 a.m. As a result, some students started to show up at 6 a.m. Many of them felt they belonged in a schoolroom for the first time in their lives.

The academy was structured. Each morning the platoons would march to a flagpole and raise the U.S. flag. From there they returned to their classroom, grabbed a cup of coffee or chocolate and had to be in their seats in time for Dr. Rose's lectures. Amazingly, each morning when Ms. M called the role, the count was always high—and these were kids who previously had truancy and punctuality problems!

The cadets were assigned to a platoon and each platoon had a ranking system. With help from the army staff, AGA held ceremonies to present awards and promotions with the entire class in attendance. The cadets all loved the recognition. In addition to rising in rank, each individual student could also earn medals to wear on their uniforms. Often, when I visited the various academy sites, cadets would approach me to show off their medals or announce that they had been "promoted."

The US Army partnership added a strong component to the program. The students responded to the military regimen and rewards system for doing their best. The army never tried to recruit students, but many of the cadets wanted a career in the military so it was good exposure for them. They knew that if they stuck with the program and graduated from high school without committing any future criminal offenses, they could reach their goal.

This is why many cadets wanted to stay in AGA rather than return to their local high schools. If the student was taking responsibility for their education and were serious about succeeding at AGA, I worked with the school districts or probation department to make it possible for them to remain.

The U.S. Army staff provided training in leadership and accountability to supplement what Dr. Rose and the teaching staff were trying to instill in the cadets. In addition, the army managed the cadets' physical training and team building programs, both of which were very important to these at-risk kids. At times, when the army volunteers could get away from their recruiting office, they showed up at the AGA and played sports with the cadets. In addition, the U.S. Army staff was there to counsel any cadet that requested to meet with them.

I remember how excited several of the cadets were about marching in their first parade. I cannot remember the holiday but I recall seeing the photos of Dr. Rose, Tom Grayson and Paul McDaniel leading our cadets in their parade around the City of Auburn. The cadets loved the response of the crowd as they passed by.

I observed Dr. Rose's classroom often. For a period of time I transported two truant girls directly to the door of the classroom and would have a cup of coffee once we arrived. This gave me the opportunity to observe the program, including the army personnel, our special education teacher, and teaching staff. Dr. Rose ran his classroom like clockwork. Each day, he taught Algebra, English, Earth Science, U.S./ World History, and Economics. When the army was not on site, Dr. Rose also taught physical education.

By the time the AGA moved to its third location, there were 42 cadets. With a larger number of 7th and 8th graders, I assigned a second teacher to assist Dr. Rose. Later, that teacher had to be reassigned and Paul McDaniel temporarily took over the second classroom.

Dr. Rose felt that since he was running the academy similar to a college classroom, then his cadets should have the option to have a cup of coffee or hot chocolate in the morning. On Fridays, he would bring in dozens of donuts for all to enjoy. Even giving out donuts was organized. Regardless of rank or platoon, female cadets were always first. Then the remainder of the cadets could get their donuts based on the overall score of their individual platoon. This stressed accountability. During test time, the students were totally engaged and wanted to do well. It was good to see them working for rank and extra privileges. Many cadets told me that being at the academy was like being a member of a family.

When the PCOE moved the school closer to the main office, the color guard (cadets led by the army and Dr. Rose) raised the US flag each morning while the other cadets stood at attention. It was a pleasure to see them engaged and proud of their duty. Many of the staff and visiting public would come out and watch them. After the raising of the flag, the army either conducted physical training or marching drills with the cadets.

It was after the AGA moved to the old Alta Vista school site for AGA-3 that I decided to retire. Sometime after my departure, state and county education policy changed. Although we had previously referred local students to out-of-the area community schools, the new policy mandated that students should remain in their home communities and, where possible, in their local schools. Education authorities believed that this was a more positive approach and encouraged assimilation into a student's community.

Many of the students attending AGA were from Roseville, Lincoln, Granite Bay and even two or three from foster homes in North Tahoe. A few had to catch several buses in the early morning hours just to make it to the academy on time.

Because of the new trend of keeping students closer to home, AGA was closed. The AGA students were placed in district high schools, continuation high school programs or, if necessary, community schools located closer to their hometowns. The local districts worked to provide their high-risk students alternative programs within their home districts.

Watching the Alternative Education program at AGA was difficult. However, the administration decided that giving the students an opportunity to succeed in their own communities was much more important.

In my opinion, the AGA was highly successful. The fact that many cadets turned their lives around while or because of attending the AGA program was and still is very special to me. The AGA concept demonstrated that for many at-risk students order, structure, and an empathetic teaching staff can turn kids around and help them reach goals that once seemed out of reach.

By Tom Grayson,
Former Instructor, Alder Grove Academy

After providing intervention and educational services to at-risk teens at Success High School, Adelante High School, Juvenile Drug Court, Chana High School, Alder Grove Community School, and the Placer County Peer Court, I was honored when Mr. Rose asked me to work at the Alder Grove Academy. The program was impressive and I liked Mr. Rose's enthusiasm and dedication to youth. I was also honored that he saw something in me that he felt could make a difference in the lives of these young people. That was definitely a train I wanted to be on.

I received my degree at the school of hard knocks. I grew up in Brooklyn, New York and left home by the age of 14. My life experiences allowed me to identify and understand young people who took a dark and negative path. I knew what it meant to feel as if no one was listening and to have nowhere to go, to think that loneliness and hopelessness is your destiny.

As a young adult, I started working with young people in my church. In the Air Force and as a civilian, I worked in my off-hours with the same troubled population. My goal was to help at-risk teens realize that they were worthy of a life filled with promise. I wanted to help them understand that they are stronger and wiser than they ever give themselves credit for, to introduce them to the concept of life skills, to the knowledge that they could make healthy choices that would lead to have a healthy life filled with unlimited possibilities.

Many of the cadets at AGA were lost—their young lives were out of control and they had no self-discipline or resources. They came to the program searching for meaning and purpose. The program offered these young people a consistent, supportive plan with clear and simple expectations. They sensed that it was providing the structure and support they needed as well as the self-acceptance they longed for. Our goal was to help them understand that failure can be used as a motivational tool to achieve success, and to embrace the fact that they did not need to hide behind drugs, alcohol, and gangs to succeed.

One of the most important techniques we used at AGA was listening. Cadets were allowed to use street language to express themselves. This gave us the opportunity to understand a lot of their pain and fear and not let social standards get in the way. Unfortunately, in a traditional school setting, the social and academic expectation that the student express himself in a particular way will often cause the young person to not even be understood let alone listen. With the help of Mr. Rose's educational instruction, cadets learned how to increase their emotional vocabulary so that they could better express their frustrations and fears, verbally and in writing. As the cadets' self-understanding increased, so did their ability to articulate those feelings in a socially appropriate way.

We provided basic life skills information and engaged them in team building activities that helped them to model what they were learning. When cadets were overwhelmed with certain problems, we taught them to identify the problems and what they should do. "What happened?" was the first key question. Then they needed to understand what part they played in what had occurred, whether playing that part was helping or hindering them, and what were they going to do next?

Cadets learned how to work through the pain in their lives and the shame associated with their choices and life circumstances. Often, they concluded, "this shit has to stop." They also learned to celebrate their accomplishments, something many of them had never experienced. Often when a cadet gave a correct answer or made a positive choice in class I would ask the class to give them a round of applause. This encouraged the other cadets to feel compassion for their fellow students and raised the self-esteem of the student who received the applause.

They learned that "success" could mean that they got locked up in Juvenile Detention, or it could mean that they graduated from high school. It could mean that they were a gang member or they could be employed with a career. We encouraged them to believe that they always had the ability and energy to do the right thing, make a positive choice, set goals for themselves, and to achieve those goals while staying out of harm's way.

The cadets came to the academy as individuals and had never worked together before. My goals were to teach them how to work as a team, the meaning of discipline and to have fun without being self-destructive. You have to remember, most of these young people were using illegal drugs and were starting to participate in gang activities. Working together in a healthy way was a new concept and experience.

Physical education was a revelation to cadets who had no concept of working with others for a healthy purpose. Most of the cadets never had the opportunity to belong to anything except, in some cases, a gang. Few had ever been on a sports team of any kind. We developed several obstacle courses and used very physical team building activities to encourage healthy physical exercise. As the cadets became more active, they developed a greater sense of physical and psychological self-esteem and empowerment. They came to believe in themselves more and more. Though the short-term goal was to enjoy the moment, the long-term goal was to develop awareness about the benefits of a healthy lifestyle.

One of my fondest memories is watching the cadets when they marched in the Veterans Day Parade. They had worked hard to prepare and could not believe that they were in the Parade. They marched so proudly—it was a marker, a celebration in their new-found abilities which encouraged their self-esteem and willingness to work as a group.

The academy staff never treated cadets as though relapse was a failure. Instead, it was a learning moment—a moment when the staff could help them identify what they could do differently. I credit the success of the program to the total commitment of the amazingly qualified teaching and support staff at the academy. They provided clear expectations of the cadets, were consistently available to provide support, and reinforced each cadet's belief in his ability to be successful. By overlooking the cadets' rough edges of language and physical appearance, they were able to focus on the cadets' needs.

If I was going to advise teachers, police, or parents, I would suggest that they listen to the young person in front of them.

Just listen. You have no idea what they have been through or what hurts. Let them tell you, without interruption, and without judgement. Our young people want people to listen to them. They want you to listen to their pain, their goals, and their fears, without judgment or opinion, because it is important to them. They want the same respect that adults demand from teens. Though we all have fears and pain, we have to remember that most adults have life skills that help them to cope while teens, troubled or not, are just being introduced to those skills.

It broke my heart when the program was terminated because of the time and energy the staff had invested to develop a meaningful and very successful program. It was sad to think that the program was not going to be there for the many at-risk teens who would follow. The staff and the army volunteers had become role models and the only people in whom these kids felt they could safely confide.

I frequently see young adults in the community that I worked with who were at the academy. They often become emotional and thank me for being a part of their life. They tell me about attending vocational training, seeking higher education, or military experience, and that if it were not for the academy, they would be in jail or dead. We had the highest graduation rate of any alternative education program in Placer County. The credit for that goes to each cadet who found out they were worth fighting for.

It was an honor to work with Gary Rose and the team at the academy. I will always be as grateful for the courage and perseverance the cadets shared with me as I am for the opportunity to have helped them on their way.

By Tobrin Hewlitt,
U.S. Army, Retired and Alder
Grove Academy Volunteer

Working with troubled youth is a challenge and it takes a dedicated group of educators and support staff to make a difference. Most of the students who were going to attend Alder Grove Academy didn't have a support structure at home. I don't believe these students had ever been held accountable for their actions. Under the circumstances, I couldn't turn down an opportunity to put on my pretend drill sergeant hat. I, too, wanted to help them establish a work ethic that would make them successful in the future.

What was most satisfying to me was being available to them—I discovered how important it was to them to learn about someone else's life. I spoke with a few one-on-one. I tried to tell them that the direction they were headed in was going to destroy them. Like a hamster in a wheel, they were running nowhere and if they wanted to change, they would have to get off that wheel. The choice, I told them, was "to do the hard right over the easy wrong." We tied this into the academy's overall environment where cadets had to take responsibility not only for themselves but also for the others in their platoon and class.

I remember how terrible the cadets were at first about executing commands. What is your right and what is your left? It was like the army's basic training—people march in the wrong direction and don't realize it until they see the rest of their squad walking towards them.

At the start of the program, we not only led the physical training program but also presented lectures on leadership and accountability. Over time, the cadets became better at executing commands and feeling motivated. Hopefully, learning to march and lead drills and ceremonies gave them a sense of leadership and accomplishment. I know that Sgt. Howell and I were very proud and excited to see the cadets march in their first parade.

The first academy was in a former army barrack and Mr. Rose got permission to use a large field near the former Sheriff's Department. That was an ideal spot because we were able to do close order drills, run rallies, and a lot of physical activities. But the building was too old to occupy and the academy had to move to a different location that didn't have an area appropriate for physical fitness.

At the second AGA site, there was only a busy parking lot. Sgt. Howell and I scouted the adjacent landscape and found two veteran cemeteries. They looked like safe places to run and sing cadence without bothering the neighborhood. Neither Mr. Rose nor we thought that anyone would object to a bunch of students dressed in identical P/T sports clothing running through a cemetery. But after a time, I was surprised to find out that someone visiting one of the cemeteries complained. I probably got heated and called it a bunch of BS, but we explained it as best we could to the cadets so that they could see how a professional person should respond to a negative.

After being removed from those locations, Sergeant Howell and I found what the cadets called, "The Hill." Actually it was the road we had marched on when we had gone to one of the cemeteries. Since it was a public roadway, we used it for P/T. We did the best we could but the location was not conducive to physical fitness. We did however, have a flag detail and every morning, whether we were there or not, the cadets would march from the academy to the Placer County Office of Education Administration building and raise the flag.

I was proud of what we tried to accomplish with the cadets. My fellow army volunteers did it to be a part of the community, to reach out to at-risk youth, to help them understand the benefits of military principles and build a foundation for success. We tried to mentor the cadets as we would mentor our own soldiers.

I joined the army to help people. I believe that our mentorship and guidance resonated with some of the students and they became better citizens because of it. We never encouraged any of the cadets to enter the military; yet several of the cadets enlisted. It was rewarding to see how these at-risk students seemed to excel academically in a military style environment. They liked the order, structure and guidance that they were often lacking in their home life.

Unfortunately, after the academy moved to its third location, the U.S. economy entered a recession. Every day, our local recruiting office had individuals parked outside before we opened seeking a career with the army, which they probably would not have considered if the economy had been better. This drained our resources and sadly, each week, it seemed that we had to cancel our commitment to the academy.

Eventually, Sgt. Howell and the other army staff that worked in partnership with the Alder Grove Academy were informed that the academy was going to close and again become a court and community school.

My experience with the Alder Grove Academy has led me to believe there is a population that could benefit from boot camp style schools. The structure, responsibility and accountability, discipline, leadership and mentorship that are instilled through military training can be great tools for at-risk teens who want an opportunity to succeed.

I hope that the cadets' stories inspire other students, even those that are not "at-risk," to believe they, too, have a future. If teens can share their stories about overcoming obstacles, they can inspire one another. But educators also have something to learn from the cadets' stories. School administrators should consider the template that Mr. Rose and the Placer County Office of Education put in place at the Alder Grove Academy for at-risk students. Clearly, unless these children have the opportunity to learn about order, structure, discipline, accountability, team work and leadership from caring, demanding, and consistent adults, they are unlikely to succeed in adulthood.

By Ronald Howell,
U.S. Army and Alder Grove Academy Volunteer

When I first met Mr. Rose when he came into our recruiting office in Auburn and explained the purpose of the Alder Grove Academy, I was enthusiastic and excited to have a chance to mentor young men and women and try to have an impact of their lives. They were at risk-youth and for some, it was their last chance before entering the judicial system or, in some cases, being allow back into a public school if they met the requirements set by either their traditional schools or the juvenile department. I was a Sergeant and thus needed to get approval up the ladder, any my commander officer was equally excited about giving back to the community.

Unfortunately, before the partnership between the AGA and the U.S. Army took place officially, that commanding officer left and Sgt. Hewitt became my supervisor. He was stoked about the idea and thus the stage was set. I knew it was going to be a challenge both for Sgt. Hewitt and me, but we were very much up to it. I myself had difficulty in school and thought that this would be a great chance and opportunity to reach out and help when others may had given up on these youth. I also believed that my life experience, both prior and in my present position in the Army, would relate to the students and they would be more susceptible to listening and hopefully learning from my own experiences.

I never had any reservations of what types of students that would be attending the academy. I had several meetings with Mr. Rose and his main teaching assistant, Michelle, and they gave me an accurate picture of the type of students we would be dealing with and some of the charges they faced. Both Sgt. Hewitt and I had a lot of experience dealing with young adults who desired to enter the military and the baggage some of them had. Sadly, we had to turn many away from their chosen career because they waited too long to turn their life around. Here was a chance that I could intervene before it was too late, and help them reach the goals they had set with the help of both our intervention and that of Mr. Rose and the teaching staff.

Actually there was a great sense of accomplishment witnessing these young men and women turn them education and lives around while adjusting to an environment very similar to the military—order, structure and when necessary, discipline. They got the benefit of getting in great physical shape and showed that they too could do well in school with a little more direction and empathy by the teaching staff.

Just being with the students daily, making visits during school for lunch and also their physical training days. Drill and ceremony was also fun. Teaching them drill movements and making them work as one team and unit was a first for many of them.

As Sgt. Hewitt and I developed their trust, they would confide in us about having problems and issues not only at school but personal as well. After time they opened up more and more talking about their problems and really listening and taking advice. We, along with the teaching staff became their role models. Sadly, for some, they had no one else to talk too and looked forward to the days that Sgt. Hewitt and I were there.

In addition, Mr. Rose and Michelle would tip us off if they felt that one of the cadets might need to talk about something due to their temperament in class. Usually all if took was for Sgt. Hewitt and I to take them away from the classroom, and hold an informal counseling session with them. Some were struggling with gangs attempted to recruit them and we talked about the disadvantages of them making the wrong decision.

These students, including the female cadets, liked the competition during physical training, whether it was tug-a-war, races, or who could do the most push-ups, sit-ups and mile runs. In the first year of the AGA, we did not have the demands to be at our recruiting office and therefore we could stop by at the AGA and play P/E with the cadets, thus furthering our bonding.

Unfortunately the economy started to tank and more and more individuals started showing up at the office trying to enlist in the military. This was obviously our military duty and we began having problems meeting our obligation to be at the AGA.

Like SFC Hewitt mentioned in his input for our book, I can't remember any particular student since it has been years. I do recall a few of the cadets, on their own, enlisting in the Army, but overall just being there with them when they were having problems and issues not only at school but personally as well, we got to know they but time has passed. After time, they opened up more and more, talking about their problems and really listening and taking advice from us. I know we saved more than a few from information we received from the teaching staff over the years.

P/T days were always exciting. The cadets were all at different levels of physical fitness so were tried to ensure we made it challenging for everyone but also motivating and still fun at the same time. Some of the male students I will always remember, wanted to challenge us in sprints and running and other activities and most failed in those challenges. They took it in stride and became more focused when we conducted P/T, wanting to get in great shape. Some of them would come up to us and tell us that they continued to run and do exercises on their own because they wanted to get in good shape. When it came to drills, just teaching them the basic movements at first was a task in itself. But after time, they all became one unit and worked as a team. Most learned the formations drill and movements and after a while didn't need much guidance from us. They worked really hard and not only impressed us but they also gained a since of pride within themselves. Mr. Rose had them broken up in platoons identified by colored armed bands and that really worked well during competition etc. At one point we had a lot of cadets, well over 40 I believe and there were at least 6 platoons.

Working with Mr. Rose, we helped select the platoon sergeants and corporals. They had to either totally impress us with their work effort both in class or outside of class, or they had to submit a letter as to why they wanted to hold rank and Sgt. Hewitt and I conducted interviews.

We had an awards ceremony each time someone got promoted or earned a metal provided by the teaching staff.

I just remembered that at the beginning of the AGA, Mr. Rose wanted to match- up those that had high academic abilities with those that appear to be struggling so I offered the idea of a "battle buddy." Two people were paired up and they helped each other in both academics and in P/T etc.

I know there were two reasons we picked this spot. One was that it was a safe location for us to run and two, I really wanted it to sink in their heads that if they kept on the same path they and directions they were heading, they themselves could end up there.

The first AGA that Mr. Rose called cockroach high, had an ideal "parade ground" consisting of a large grass field to conduct P/T and drill and ceremony. These kids needed to get their energy out there and with both P/T and P/E (when they earned it), the field was great.

When the AGA relocated to the AGA near the post office, there was no place for either P/T or P/E. I know it really got Mr. Rose upset and he use to improvise by conducting P/E in the crowded parking lot, until a student caused damage to a parked car while playing football.

Because of the lack of a P/T field, Sgt. Hewitt and I checked out the nearby area for a place that might be more suitable. The graveyard looked like a good place. Sometimes we ran at the older cemetery and sometimes we ran up the hill to the new site. It had been sometime since Sgt. Hewitt and I had been in Basic Training so we had to try and remember how to count cadence.

As far as being asked to leave it, didn't really bother me too much and I don't fully understood why. Someone contacted Mr. Rose after a run, and said that the cemetery staff had received a complaint about a lot of kids dressed in black (P/E clothing) were running in the cemetery and they were scared.

I'm sure that if we had time to explain why we were there they would have understood and let us return if we wanted to. Just didn't have much time, since as I said, the economy caused us to stay at the recruiting office longer, thus not much time for running. Mr. Rose did what he could to cover for us.

I just wanted each student to understand that we have consequences for our actions and that even though we have all made bad choices it doesn't mean that we can't bounce back from those choices and make something of ourselves. Also, we wanted to ensure that they developed a good work ethic and that they knew they would be held accountable for their own actions to an even greater extend as adults and would not be able to blame others for their shortfalls.

I was so very proud and I could see that it was also important to the students when they presented us with the trophies. There was such a sense of pride knowing where most of them started in the beginning of the AGA and where they were at these last days of the Academy. I knew from Mr. Rose and Michelle that we had a huge success rate and that most were returning back to their traditional schools and moving on, hopefully, with a new sense of pride and accomplishments and goals. You could see it in most of their eyes and smiles that they had a new look on the future of what it had in store for them. I still always take the trophy they gave me and place it in all my Army offices on display for those to see. Of course it always gets noticed in which I happily tell the story of the AGA, the cadets, and those fun days and how proud I myself was of being a part of something great.

Like SFC Hewitt stated, we all joined the Army to help people, that's what we do. As Senior Noncommissioned Officers we mentor, lead and give guidance. I just hope that the students gained some of these traits from our days at the AGA and now are also able to help others with their experiences making them better students, citizens and parents themselves.

I personally believe more at-risk students could learn from this type of school and military type of curriculum. This is definitely something most public schools don't teach. I agree 100% percent with SFC Hewitt when he said that "The structure, responsibility, accountability, discipline, leadership, mentorship that is instilled through military training and was used at the AGA, can be great tools to push students to a path of success". Many of these cadets were lost and heading in the wrong direction. We, as well as Mr. Rose and teaching staff, did not want to lose them.

I recommend that other teachers, education administrators, students and especially other at- risk youth, need to read this book and see how our cadets overcame their obstacles and became success stories. I am really looking forward to attending our first "class reunion" so that I can personally tell them how proud I am of them.

By Paul T. McDaniel,
Former Substitute Teacher for Placer County Juvenile Delinquent Facility and Alder Grove Academy

My name is Paul McDaniel. I am a retired United States Air Force (USAF) non-commissioned officer (NCO) who served from the early 1950s through the middle of the

1970s. I had many assignments and performed in several different capacities. One of my major assignments was that of a military training instructor where I spend four years as an Air Force Instructor in the NCO Academy program. My primary duty was teaching military tactics as well as the subjects that are a part of the military life.

After the military, I worked in the USAF civil service system at McClellan Air Logistics Center, McClellan Air Force Base in California in the field of logistics. In 1999 I retired from that position and after a few months at home with my wife, decided that I needed some activity or outlet.

Since I had taught for four years in the military, my wife suggested that I become a high school substitute teacher. I had a master's degree and acquired a substitute teacher's permit.

I applied for a teaching position as a substitute teacher with the Placer County Office of Education (PCOE) and was soon working at the county's juvenile hall. This is where I met Gary Rose. We were from similar backgrounds—while I had been a member of the military, Gary was a retired police sergeant from a Bay Area police agency. We shared views about our nation's at-risk youth and both of us believed that their lives could be improved if they understood what it means to be accountable.

Mr. Rose was asked to form the county's first military style academy program for young people in Placer County who were on probation and asked me to help him design the program, especially in regard to the military portion.

This was near and dear to my heart. With some help from the United States Army sergeants from the local recruiting station, we soon had a program designed to teach basic drills and ceremonies, military inspection procedures and honors for dignitaries. I was very excited as I had always loved military drills and ceremonies, and had not been on the drill pad as a drill instructor for well over forty years. I loved the challenge and was surprised to discover I'd never forgotten what I'd learned and taught years before.

I especially enjoyed watching the students perform daily on the drill pad and, with each day and week, saw them gain more proficiency. During AGA-3, I had designed a drill competition exercise and was waiting for the opportunity to put it in effect when the PCOE decided to scrap the AGA program. I could not believe it when it happened.

Many local high school principals did not want these students to return to their campuses. To discourage the return of these students, the PCOE required that students take a course about the U.S. government and pass an exam about the Constitution in order to qualify to return to the original school. At the time it was an eighth grade requirement. Sadly, most adult American citizens would not be able to pass the same test.

Unfortunately, there was no money in the PCOE budget to hire anyone to teach this course. And because Mr. Rose had his hands full with forty-two cadets, I volunteered to create and teach a three-month class prepare students for the exam.

I took a dozen eighth graders with me to a second classroom and there I taught them about the origin of the U.S. Constitution, government structure and processes, voting rights, the Electoral College and more.

We had daily quizzes, weekly and monthly exams and a final where each student was required to achieve an 80% score to pass. I am proud to say that the overall score for these dozen eighth-graders was 82%. It's important to know that many of these students read and comprehended far below their grade level. Some were the offspring of parents who were here illegally and English was not spoken at home. Nevertheless, they overcame these obstacles and passed. All the students in the program were accepted back into their local high school and all have since progressed and are working toward becoming productive members of our society.

I would like to add that I presented all the students in this program with a lapel pin of an American flag which they all wore on their cadet uniforms with a great deal of pride. I often see many of these former students in Auburn and it's very rewarding to see them enjoy productive lives. Some are advancing with further education and some are in the U.S. military.

PCOE decided that the AGA program was not needed and perhaps too expensive. I believe that those who decided to shut down the program either knew little about it or its military dimension. The administrators' rejection was in sharp contrast to the students' respect for the quasi-military environment.

In my opinion, the administration complaints about the cost of the program were not well-founded. It was especially interesting to me that many parents and their children routinely visited the academy and asked Mr. Rose and the teaching staff how they could get their son or daughter enrolled. Sadly, the staff had informed them that to attend the academy their son/daughter would have to commit a crime and be placed on probation or be expelled from a county school. The parents were shocked to hear this.

I am proud to have participated in the Alder Grove Academy program and very sad that it was discontinued.

By Michelle Segarra,
Senior Teaching Assistant, Alder Grove Academy, Placer County Office of Education

The three years I spent at the Alder Grove Academy were the best years of my working life—I wouldn't change it for the world!

After watching three different teachers come and go in eight weeks at the Alder Grove Community School, I had informed Ms. Berry that I would try to convince Gary Rose to transfer from the Juvenile Delinquent Facility ("JDF" or the "hall") to the community school.

I was probably the happiest person on earth when our Director, Joan Berry, told me that he had agreed to come to our school to finish out the year. To help entice him to make the change, I told Gary that I would do all of the paperwork as long as he controlled the class which was completely out of control!

Admittedly, he was not very excited about moving to Alder Grove Community School since he always felt that juvenile hall was a good fit for him—he often called it home. He even had a nickname for his students, the "A-Unit Animals." This was not a put-down. He told his JDF class that animals have to learn to survive by being alert, willing to learn, adapt and overcome. And this is what he taught his students, basing his lesson plans on what they would need to understand in order to survive as adults.

Before Gary arrived, we had fights among boys and girls, students who were disrespectful to teachers, as well as girls trying to sneak off with boys to some other part of the building. Profanity was rampant and I am sure that some of the kids were probably bringing in drugs and alcohol.

Without a probation officer on site, we also had rival gangs who strutted their stuff without fear of punishment. Attendance was terrible and the kids hated the food. Sadly, the teachers could not relate to the students and the students, in turn, rebelled against their authority.

Having worked with Gary at the hall, I believed that he was exactly what the classroom and students needed. He was a former police sergeant and had a commanding presence and although he could be tough, he was very fair. The students would know how they stood with him. Gary's teaching skills were so good that I used to tell Ms. Berry's secretary that if the power went out, all the county needed to do was deliver some sand and give Gary a stick and he could successfully engage the class.

I will always remember that first day. Gary got to the Alder Grove Community School shortly after I arrived. I had already given him a "heads up" regarding some of our problem children. All he wanted to know was where they were sitting. On the whiteboard he wrote out the day's agenda. When I pointed out that he had not included physical education ("P/E"), he said the class had to earn it—it would be up to them even on the first day.

Instead of yelling, screaming and laughing as they normally did, they were quiet and wary. With the exception of those that knew him from the hall, most shied away. He engaged in small talk with students he recognized but for the most part, he sat at this desk looking at his lesson plan. Some were not happy that a cop would be their teacher if they had ever been hassled by the police.

Finally, the time had come for him to start class. The front door had a terrible buzzer sound that blasted into the classroom, so it would be very easy for him to know who was late. He stood up in front of the class and some of the students continued to talk. He stared at the talkers. They looked up, realizing that this was not a teacher to take lightly.

He asked, "Are you through?"

One tried to be cute and said yes.

"Hey," Gary replied, "if you want to continue, go ahead. We can just get out of class later."

A few other students yelled at the offenders to be quiet. Now the stage was set.

Gary erased the agenda on the board and said that today, they would just talk. He told them about his past experiences as a policeman and teacher. Then he instructed everyone to get out a piece of paper, fold the paper into rows and then write algebra, English, history, science, and math in the rows and to put an "A" next to each course.

As of that moment, he told them, each had earned an "A" and would soon realize how hard it was to maintain that grade. It was up to them. Whatever grade they received at the end of the quarter, they earned it. I had no doubt that on that first day, Gary was in total control of the class.

Sometime later, when Gary was asked to start a military boot-camp style high school, I was game and so were many of the students. With PowerPoint slides, Gary showed the class the uniforms and rules that he envisioned for what would become the Alder Grove Academy. Of course, when it came to uniforms, the girls wanted something different from the boys. Gary told them that for the time being, he would allow them to have different uniforms, but if the academy was approved, they would again vote on one uniform.

He also asked them to decide on a mascot. Because they had recently seen the movie "300" and had studied Spartan culture in their history class, they easily agreed on a Spartan as mascot. The students who were good artists drew a version of their mascot that could be used for a patch on their uniforms, training clothing and our baseball hats. Gary paid for the first uniforms, patches and stripes out of his own pocket.

Once we received PCOE's approval, the news of the Alder Grove Academy spread like wildfire. Parents called and dropped in at our office begging to enroll their kids. Unfortunately, the student had to be expelled from their comprehensive high school or referred by probation to be able to qualify for enrollment.

We had a lot of girls in the academy and I saw a need for the girls to have some time away from the boys. Gary agreed. After Friday's weekly test, Gary and I separated the girls from the boys and I took the girls to another room or outside and let the boys talk with Gary.

These sessions gave the girls the opportunity to talk about growing up and to bond among themselves. Of course, I heard things that I did not want to hear and let them know that as a school employee, if I thought that they were in danger, I would have to report it. Overall, however, I was thrilled to be able to give some guidance to the girls and they appeared to benefit from those hours.

All the cadets loved to have potluck lunches as well as a Halloween and Christmas Party. Although Gary would act like he wasn't interested, he was waiting for the cadets to come to him as a team and convince him they should be able to have a party. As Gary intended, this resulted in increasing the cadets' ability to work together.

The academy moved three different times. Each site had its pluses and minuses, but the number of cadets continued to increase. At one time we had 42 cadets made up of males and females, special education students, rival gangs and a few kids who had mental problems. But somehow we made it work. Many students refused to return to their traditional schools and asked permission to stay. Although Ms. Berry was happy to have them stay, Mr. Rose convinced some that they needed to return to their traditional schools for greater educational opportunities and to graduate with their friends.

It was a very sad time when the economy began to collapse, our funding diminished, and the army had less and less time to participate. The army personnel who so generously had offered their time had been important role models for all the cadets.

In a way, I was like the Mother Hen and Gary was the Father Goose. We did everything we could to help our cadets survive the most difficult years of their lives. Some of them didn't make it—Albert, Jose, and Josh, who are included in this book's dedication—come to mind. Others survived but still struggle in their adult lives with addiction and dysfunction. I like to think that the majority now lead happy and productive lives and that Gary and I helped them along the way.

CALIFORNIA DEPARTMENT OF JUSTICE, 2015 REPORT, CRIMINAL JUSTICE STATISTICS CENTER

Nationally there was an estimated 1,024,000 number of juvenile arrests. 53,500 were of a violent nature.

- 800 homicides
- 3,300 rapes
- 19,400 robberies
- 30,100 aggravated assaults
- 234,220 property crimes

IN CALIFORNIA DURING 2015

In 2015, the State of California provided data on reported juvenile arrests made by law enforcement agencies. In summary, of 71,923 juveniles arrested:

- Felony arrests accounted for 29.7 percent (21,381).
- Misdemeanor arrests accounted for 58.2 percent (41,848).

- Status offense arrests accounted for 12.1 percent (8,694) (e.g., runaways, truancy, etc.)

Eight out of ten juveniles arrested (80.7 percent) were referred to county juvenile probation departments. Of the 71,923 arrested:

Referred to County Juvenile Probation:	58,020 or 80.7%
Counseled and Released:	12,973 or 18.0%
Juveniles Made Wards of the Court:	64.5 percent (nearly two-thirds)
Of Juveniles Tried as Adults:	88.0 percent were convicted
Of Juveniles Tried as Adults, those sent to prison or the California Youth Authority	59.6%

Males Arrests in 2015 totaled 51,693:

- Felony arrests accounted for 34.6 percent (17,879).
  - Violent felony offenses accounted for 33.1 percent (5,918).
  - Property felony offenses accounted for 31.5 percent (5,631).
- Misdemeanor arrests accounted for 55.0 percent (28,420).

- Status arrests accounted for 10.4 percent (5,394).

Female Arrests in 2015 totaled 20,230:

- Felony arrests accounted for 17.3 percent (3,502).
- Violent offenses accounted for 40.6 percent (1,423).
- Property offenses accounted for 30.1 percent (1,054).
- Misdemeanor arrests accounted for 66.4 percent (13,428).
- Status arrests accounted for 16.3 percent (3,300).

In 2015, of the 21,381 juvenile felony arrests reported:

- 34.3 percent (7,341) were for violent offenses.
- 31.3 percent (6,685) were for property offenses.
- 7.2 percent (1,533) were for drug offenses.
- 27.2 percent (5,822) were for all other felony offenses.

In 2015, of the 8,694 status offenses reported:

- Truancy violations accounted for 13.5 percent (1,174).
- Runaways accounted for 34.5 percent (2,998).
- Curfew violations accounted for 22.1 percent (1,918).
- Incorrigible offenses accounted for 8.8 percent (767).
- "Other" status offenses accounted for 21.1 percent (1,837).

PART V

A FINAL WARNING

Discipline is a necessity, as a regulator of society, so that those who break its rules may be taught the necessity of obeying them.

–ENGINEER LOCKHART,
Santa Fe Employees' Magazine, July, 1909

Once again I could not expel my desire to teach versus retirement, so I applied and was successful in being offered a part-time teaching position with the Placer School for Adults. My students this time would be incarcerated adults (female and male) who were pursuing their GED certificates in hopes that this achievement might inspired some of them to live a life without criminal consequences.

During my introduction at the beginning of each six-week course, I explain with pride and honor, the students I have had the privilege of teaching over the years; especially those cadets that attended the Alder Grove Academies. It never fails that after explaining how the academy ran and its methodology consisting of order, structure and discipline, how many adult offenders, both male and female, felt that such a school might have helped them avoid the present circumstances they find themselves today.

After reading a few passages from the rough draft of the manuscript, many offered to add their stories to the end of the book, in hopes that those readers who still are not convinced that they need to change, might reconsider a life change after they learned what life was really like in jail and prison.

The following additional material was offered freely by inmates serving time in hopes that their stories can motivate you to change the at-risk lifestyle you are leading.

White Female Inmate

If you are reading this part of Dr. Rose's book, perhaps you are not convinced that a life of crime is the shits! I am a female who is willingly sharing my experience hoping that young girls and women would think twice before committing a crime. This place is HELL! I lost confidence in the system. It seems that crack-heads who have more than 20 prior arrests get released, but a person incarcerated for DUI (driving while intoxicated) are punished more severely. I mean it seems like people booked into jail for DUI in this county get less time than murderers.

But enough whining. You want to be locked up? Great! Look what is waiting for you. First, there is not a lot of hygiene. You will wear bras and underwear of other people you don't know or ever met. You will wear red coveralls. You will become programmed into when to go to bed and when to wake up. You don't get a choice of what to watch on our communal television. Sometimes the inmates take a vote, but other times it is whatever the deputies want to watch.

Our tank (cell block) is always cold and in my opinion you never get sufficient warm clothing. You better always be on the lookout for your personals because other females will steal your stuff.

You want to make a phone call? That will cost you .40 cents a minute. By the way, don't think your so-called friends will "keep in touch." They won't write to you and don't hold your breath if you think they will come to see you.

Visitation hours are limited and you only get 30 minutes to visit anyway. Some of the deputies are ok, but some are assholes. Nearly everywhere you go (with only a few exceptions) you will be shacked up like you are a murderer. I am in for a DUI, but I am treated just like our inmate murderers. I am shacked just like them.

The medical care is in-sufficient. When it is time to eat, you get 15 minutes and you must then turn in your tray. Don't like the food being served, too bad. You do not get a choice of the menu.

You want a nice long hot shower? Forget it! You get 5 maybe 10 minutes and there is no privacy.

You are surrounded by a lot of crazy females coming and going and you NEVER turn your back on anyone. So, if this is the life you want to live, you are a crazy female.

21-year old Latino Male Inmate

Dr. Rose has been my teacher for the past 6 weeks in the Placer County Jail here in Roseville. In addition to earning extra days off (which won't help me since I will be sentenced to prison soon), I attended his Social Studies/English Language Arts GED prep class since I only needed to pass the Social Studies portion to earn my GED.

During the time, he has taught us, he has referred to a military style boot camp school that he created addressing at-risk students that were headed in the wrong direction.

I would like to take the time to reach out to those who are reading this book and perhaps are going down the wrong path as rough as mine has been.

At a young age, you, like me, perceive things in which we think is cool. Once you are in your cell, it doesn't feel cool anymore I can tell you.

Knowing that your mother is hurting because her 18-year-old son is locked up, well, you don't know how you feel a sense of emptiness inside. Now I am 21 years old and I just finished my recent trial. I am waiting for the soon to be announced sentencing this Friday of a 19-year prison term. This is all because I didn't want to stay home. I didn't want to follow the rules of my parents. I didn't want to go to school.

The big thing I learned and want to pass on to those of you reading my entry into this book is acceptance. What I mean by this is that you must learn to accept the rules of your mother and father. You must also learn to accept the consequences of your actions. You must be accountable for your actions.

For those of you incarcerated as I am, accept the fact that the situation you are in can only change if you want it too. Don't let the time (sentence) you are facing defeat you. Make the time you are incarcerated as productive as you can.

Dr. Rose makes all of us participate when you are in his class. As he tells us, there are no free rides in his classroom, but honestly, no one wants to leave. He makes the classes so exciting and relevant that he has inspired me to start taking on-line college classes so that I will have a career when I am finally released. This is what I mean about making your time served productive.

You see, when I was younger, I always seemed to focus on the negative more than the positive. I look back and see how ungrateful I was. Now I find the good in all bad situations. You might think that I am maybe a little optimistic but it seems to help me pass time. I wish I was out and could point out to you how beautiful life is or can be. How colorful our world is and how it is not so bad outside the walls of prison or jail.

When Dr. Rose explained how the boot camp school was, I thought to myself how much I would've changed if I had had the opportunity to attend such a school.

You young offenders must take advantage of the options you have right now to be successful in life. Dr. Rose helped me pass the Social Studies test and I must say it was honestly the biggest accomplishment of my life. The test for me seemed impossible since there is so much history to remember, but Dr. Rose made it seem simple for us. I believe that anything now is possible.

For you, a successful life is possible. Never give us! Only you can take the first step to re-directing your life. No one else can do it for you. It is not too late to change. Once you hit rock bottom, you can only go up.

21-year old White Female Inmate

I am a white young female inmate housed in the Roseville County Jail. I just turned 21 years old and here I am, unable to step outside and feel the fresh air; unable to have the freedom to do what I want to do.

As soon as you enter the jail population as a female, be prepared to having your body violated. You will undergo strip searches down to nothing and told to put someone else's clothes on including underwear.

You will be unable to have control of anything starting from what to wear, what to eat, where you can go, what to read, where to sleep, what time you get up or go to bed, when you can shave, shower, make phone calls, turning on or off lights. And, worse of all, you do not have a say into who your cellmate will be. She could be as crazy as a loon, or even a female predator, you never know.

Friends? What friends? I cannot wait to get out of here and confront them. They all said they would write and visit. Bullshit!

As you grow older and choose your way of life and the lifestyle you choose is the life of a criminal, get ready for never being able to set goals. You will be asked to join gangs or form allegiances to cover your back and it is always for a price.

So please, listen to me and turn your life around. Only you can control where you end up. Don't get into the criminal justice system. You will have a very hard time getting out of it. I hope the little bit I have shared here helps someone.

Black Female Inmate

Thank God for Jesus. If it were not for him, I would have a hard time enduring the life inside the jail walls. You lose your identity as a human being in here. You are no more than an animal and are not treated with any respect. Yes, I have violated the law and supposedly I am now a burden or problem to society, but I am still a female and would hope to be treated as such.

So, young lady, you too want to become a criminal. Here is what you must get use too:

First, you are restricted from your privacy. You are always being watched; by the deputies personally; cameras everywhere; and your female inmates. You will be talked to like a child; supposedly by being talked to as a child, we are supposed to judge this as friendlier. It is supposed to eliminate feelings and emotions.

As you can tell by my opening sentence, I personally stick close to God so that he can remind me that I am a human and I do matter. Despite my past, I would encourage any young lady that is headed in the wrong direction to find Jesus Christ. As a higher power, I believe that that is the only way to live with a purposeful meaning to this world, and live "free" internally. I also realize that because I am locked up physically, with Jesus I am free mentally and that means more to me than anything: my sanity.

I have learned to love and appreciate the smallest, simplest things in life, and humble and endure trials, with a great expectation of liberty, freedom, and a bright light at the end of my journey.

I truly believe that I can do ALL things through Christ, who strengthens me.

White Male Inmate

Should any of you not believe the contents of this book you are reading, let me assure you it is not a lie. At age 11, a fatal accident with my dad's gun resulted in a 5-year term in the California Youth Authority which, by the end of my sentence, I was brainwashed and committed to a street gang that seemed larger than life.

At a young age, you need something to look up to; something to believe in and it must be something larger than yourself. Since mine was gangs, which led to violence, drugs, and sex and a disregard to education, I grew up a screw-up!

You see, earlier in my life when I did attend school, I was an honor student. That turned to a period of my life where I was always standing in front of a judge saying, "Yes, your Honor", "No, your Honor." "Yes I was here last month your Honor." I started not carrying about my future and funny thing, that future runs up on you fast.

I have been incarcerated 21 years of my 32 years alive. I have been in juvenile hall, CYA, jail and prison. I am now facing another 18 months. As of this writing however, I have never accumulated 6 months of freedom in between sentencings. Five years in, one month out. Three years in, two months out etc. Now at 32 years old I must do something, accomplish something in my life. Education seems to be the key to everything and I continue to strive for more.

If only I had applied myself at a younger age or woke up and decided to change, perhaps I would not be here. If you wake up after reading this book and sincerely and honestly decide to make a change, then you will be making the choice to live a normal life. By taking the time to buckle down now and make the commitment to change, you will be the master of your own destiny!

Don't consider change and here is what you can expect: juvenile hall, CYA, prison, life on drugs, violence, gangs, watching your friends die and attending their funerals. And, you better face the possible outcome of you being the next to die.

I ran with the wrong crowd. I have seen my friends die either by drug overdose or being jumped, shot or killed by random violence.

In prison, you NEVER turn your back on anyone lest being a victim of a sexual assault or being stabbed. You will always be hungry and you cannot just get up and go to your refrigerator.

You will be lonely. The prison system is always looking for new criminals but trust me, you don't want to be here.

You can avoid this trap by just making a little effort now. Finding someone to believe in and trust is the key. If you don't have it in a mother or father, there are always role models that you can use. You can choose to free yourself from what I call the shackles of destruction that will bind you and hold you for years at a time.

If I had one positive teacher or opportunity to meet someone to act as my role model, who inspired me to tell others of what to expect if they continue down the spiral they are on, I think I could have changed and made correct choices. Instead I have hurt my love ones, my family, myself. It appears from your journals that you lucked out and had Dr. Rose as your teacher and his support personnel that really cared about your welfare.

Your friends? Don't count on your friends. Watch out for them since many will want to drag you down so that they will not feel lonely. Instead they will help you fall into that trap I talked about.

Dr. Rose has complimented me on my writing ability and even encouraged me to self-publish. He even went out and bought me a book to aid me in my goal. Not too many teachers would do that, especially for a criminal.

I am 32 years old but feel much older. Currently I am doing an 18-months stretch (time) and go out of my way to avoid any type of trouble that could result in more time. I have even asked for a transfer to a new tank (sell) to help me avoid fights or things that could get me into more trouble.

I am finally ready to make a change. But for you, this change can come now before you are locked up like me. Yes, you can change RIGHT NOW! Don't wait another day. It is never too late.

Latina Female Inmate

I am currently locked up in the Placer County Jail here in Roseville. I'm from Sacramento. I am sure some of the other female inmates would agree that it is gross in having to wear other people's underwear. In addition, I have very long hair and it is very hard to have enough time to care for it when you are locked up.

Visitation is only for 30 minutes on Fridays from 6-6:30; that is it. I have four kids and that is not enough time to visit with my children.

The food here is not so good. The menu never changes. If you are lucky you'll get a good "bunkie" (someone you have to share the cell with). You have no privacy. It is not a place I would want my children to experience.

Sadly, I have been incarcerated in other counties; one of them being Sacramento county since that is where I am from. In that county, you could find yourself down (kept in your cell) for 23 hours a day. Most of the officers there are assholes. You see, you have a button in your cell which you are told are to be used for emergencies ONLY! If you push that button and it is not an emergency, they'll treat you differently. But if you really have an emergency, they take their time to get to you. It is really sad. The food there is shitty as well.

I have also served time in Los Angeles (Lynwood). It is better than Sacramento and Placer County, I can tell you that. The food is a hell of a lot better. You get better commissary food and you're out of your cells 6 hours a day, which is not too bad.

The one thing I didn't like was going to court. It was a whole day process. You would leave Lynwood at 4 A.M. and get transferred to the county where you were caught. You are placed in a holding cell which is always filthy. You would not return until later (about 6 P.M.) and I am telling you, you start becoming crazy.

The only good part of this ordeal is that that county seems to only make you serve 10% of your sentence

I have also been to Yolo County. That county is better than the last three (Sacramento, Placer and L.A.) They have carpet, vending machines, soda machines, and microwave ovens. You are out of your cell most of the time. The food and commissary is good also.

But let me tell you young ladies, especially you Latinas. Jail life is something that I would never wish on my enemies. Don't end up like me. Wasting my life behind bars, not being home with my children and family. Is this what you want?

Older White Male Inmate

So, you still think you want to be in jail or worse, prison? You and maybe some of your friends might think it is cool; that you will be together just hanging out. Well, let me tell you what you will face if you continue to screw up. It is NOT FUN inside the walls of an institution!

You do not have choices. They are made for you since you have shown society that you do not know how to make proper choices. The prison system will decide when and what you eat. The food is normally the cheapest they can get and at times, tastes like garbage. You eat or you go hungry.

Privacy? There is none! Everything you do is watched. Have to take a crap? If you are in a tank with a private toilet, you will still be watched by everyone.

Safety? Sure, if the guards are watching but they cannot be around all the time. You must be careful not to upset other inmates around you because how long does it take for a couple of inmates to beat the shit out of you or worse?

But the hardest part at least for me, is not knowing what is going on with those you care about outside the walls of the institution to your love ones and people you care about.

What you hear may not be the truth, but what can you do about it? It took me a year to find out that I was basically stabbed in the back by people who supposedly cared about me, but instead these were the people who put me in here.

You may think of yourself as a badass and an alpha male. I got news for you. In jail and prison, you are surrounded by alpha males and some of them cannot wait for fresh meat to arrive so that they can show the prison population what a badass they are.

Do yourself a favor. Stay in school. Follow the rules set by your parents or guardians. No matter how bad your current situation seems to be, it is still a hell of a lot better than inside the joint.

White Female Inmate

If you are a female on the outs (freedom) and think that you can handle life inside of bars, let me explain to you what it is really like inside here. The diet (food heavy with carbohydrates and sodium) that you are served and the lack of daily exercise are the two big lows of being in jail. Basically, you end up extremely overweight which leads to depression and lack of energy.

One of the obvious setbacks is breaking of hearts of your family members. They must struggle without you and it is all your fault. Sometimes you hurt your loves ones and friends so deeply that they move on without you. You may never see or hear from some of them again and let me tell you, abandonment really hurts.

So, to cut to the chase, get your mind straight. Ignore the game and everyone in it. Cut your losses and never look back. Get out of the mess you might currently be in while you still can. It is too painful to yourself and everyone else you love to sit in a jail cell and realize that you literally gambled your whole life away on cheap highs or unnecessary risks.

29-year old White Male Inmate

I am currently 29 years old and doing time in jail facing a 4-year prison term. I have been coming in and out of this jail (Placer County) since I was 20 years old. Let me tell you that I am one child out of four who was thought to be the golden child.

I got all A's and B's in a well-respected high school, and I even was a volunteer in law enforcement. I never got into trouble and was very successful as a student.

At age 19, I started hanging out with the "cool kids" and this is when my life turned. You see, I'm not here in jail facing prison, for using drugs or stealing. I'm here because I met someone on a dating app who ended up only being 17 years old.

Even though I didn't send any pictures or even meet up with this person, I still committed a crime. Because I was a "goodie two shoe", and I was involved in law enforcement, no one wanted to hang-out with me. So, I started hanging with younger people; people who looked up to me and "needed" me.

However, I never socially matured because I wanted to be accepted and therefore adopted into the younger generation. This began a snowball effect. While I never molested or had sex with anyone, my behavior became risky and interpreted by others as inappropriate, for the lack of a better word.

But now, looking back on that behavior, I realize that a 20-year old shouldn't have been hanging out with another under 18 years old, and at 29 years old, I shouldn't have been drinking with anyone under 21.

I have ruined my life just because I wanted to be accepted by others. Now I'm about to go to prison for 4 years just for talking to a 17-year old.

For you reading this document, I'm not accepted here. I sit in my cell for 21 hours a day. I get to talk to friends only if I want to pay .37 cents a minute, or for a 30-minute visit twice a week. Take if from someone who is educated and no one ever thought would be in jail.

Instead of trying to fit in, if I would have had the opportunity to attend something like Dr. Rose's military school, your academy, I think I would have been more focused on academics versus myself. I would have turned my energy and goals to obtaining rank in the academy and developed strong friendship with the other cadets.

But because I let my self-esteem get the better of me, I'm now in a revolving penal system; a system I may never get out of. I've wasted half of my 20's locked up. I have lost the job I had on the outs.

What I needed was the structured disciplinary environment that apparently, the academy offered to its students. This I feel, would have made a huge difference in how I turned out.

Dr. Rose pounded all of us male inmates during our six-weeks together to stop whining and get our heads out of our asses in order to succeed. He pointed out that compared to one of his earlier students who is on death row in San Quintin, we still have a chance to make a better life for ourselves and that has motivated a lot of us.

38-year old White Female Inmate

If I could sit down with you regardless of whether you are a male or female, I would try to set you straight about the life ahead of you if you want to be a criminal.

First, you do not have freedom. Every minute of every day is programmed for you. In our jail, you wake up at 5 A.M.; no sleeping in for you. You get slop for breakfast, lunch and dinner. You eat what is on the menu or starve. It is up to you.

Women inmates are the worse. Many of my fellow female inmates do not clean up after themselves. You can imagine what the shared toilets look like.

I do not get any visits because it became too hard for my children. Yes, I am a mom and it sucks not having my children with me or me being a part of their life.

I am sure some of the other females who have written entries for Dr. Rose's book have pointed out that when you arrive, you lose the clothing you were wearing. It is replaced with other people's bras and underwear and unless you are classified as a trouble maker of something else, you will wear red coveralls. You get a choice of wearing tennis shoes or rubber sandals.

If you have a drug problem which I have had my whole life, get help. I finally figured this out. Better late than never, but this will be my fourth prison term.

I was sent to prison for women on April 14, 2016 for drug sales and was back in on June 30, 2016 for drug sales and now face a 7-year prison term. I'm 38 years old and just wish I would have asked for help or probation would have made me attend rehab instead of watching me fall apart. But, that said, it was ultimately my choice that got me here. This is NOT where you want to come!

White Male Inmate

How, why or when did I mess up my life? I could say I came from a broken family. I could even say that I used drugs at a young age. I guess I could say that I did not apply myself in school or just that at the age of 16 I tried to commit suicide. All of these apply to me and now I am doing time in jail.

At age 20-25 I got into a relationship with a girl for seven years. I did not appreciate her or the child that we had. I messed that up myself. I guess the old saying of "you don't know what you got till it's gone" applies to me and my life.

Now I am a 290 registrant (sex offender) since 2003. In 2004 I got sentenced to my first California Department jail and prison.

I should have applied myself in life just like in 2003 I should have stayed in jail and fought my case longer, pointing out that I was a drug addict and alcoholic and perhaps get my sentence reduced or even dismissed.

Hearing about the school that Dr. Rose managed, I feel that if I had had the opportunity to attend such a school where structure and discipline and skills to make me a success later in life were constantly taught, maybe I would not be in the situation I am in now.

Only you can decide to change your life. Don't mess it up like I did please! When you hit rock bottom, you will know. You will remember all of the bridges you burnt along the way, all the people you hurt…but there is still time to turn your life around.

Older White Male Inmate

For you reading this book here is my input. Let me start off by saying I have used drugs and drank alcohol a lot, and because of that, I always end up getting arrested by the cops. I usually don't want to go to jail so I resist arrest which compounds my charges.

Right now, I am facing 6-years plus 4 prison priors for 10 years for resisting arrest. That is a long time.

You see, my and my ex. (girlfriend) use to fight. She would fight with me and call the cops. She lied a lot of the time and I ended up with 3 years in prison my first term. After that I got one year added for the last term.

It didn't help when the last time my ex-girlfriend told the cops I threatened to kill her, and because of that, I can't get on the stand in my trial without admitting to my prior commitments.

In other words, no matter what the District Attorney charges me with, all of my priors can be used against me so, I have no chance to live my life without the cops on my back.

You youngsters reading this book, is this the life you want to live? I sure hope you can get it right and lead a good life.

Something I want to add on is that Dr. Rose's teaching has given me hope that someone (maybe a 1/3 of the world) cares about us and he is in that 1/3 of the world. He has prepared me to take and pass the Social Studies and English Language Arts GED exam and once I complete that than it is on to the Math and Science portions. Successfully passing my GED exams will go a long way towards me straightening out my life.

48-year old White Male Inmate

For you who are reading this, I've been a product of the system for my entire life. I was deemed a ward of the court at the age of 11 and I am now 48 years old. I started running the streets skipping school, and running away from home because I didn't want to listen to my parents or any authority figure for that matter.

Once I got caught up in the system (juvenile court) it became a vicious cycle; in and out of handcuffs; in and out of institutions. I graduated from one hell hole to the next until it became a normal way of life to me. I knew nothing else.

Juvenile hall back to the streets and drugs; foster care to group homes; then back to the streets and drugs.

Eventually the court had enough of me and sent me first to the Boy's Ranch and later to the California Youth Authority. If you, the reader, do not know what the California Youth Authority is, it is basically a prison for juveniles like I had become.

Then one birthday I became an adult and the cycle now included a cycle of one state prison to the next. I have been incarcerated over 28 years of my life.

Listening to what the military academy was like as described by Dr. Rose, I real feel that if I had attended such a school when I was younger, it would have definitely helped me go in a different direction. You see, you may be like me and most of the other inmates in prison. We fuck up and make terrible choices in our lives. One screw up leads to another and since no one has taught us to be accountable for our actions, on we go from one crime to another. Hearing about how many of his cadets turned their lives around caused me to dream about how I would have turned out given the same opportunity.

So, for all those cadets who have become successful, I congratulate you. If I had become a cadet, maybe it would have saved a lot of grief for myself and my family.

"I will never promise you anything that
I cannot deliver."

"Success follows practice and experience.
Even the great Joe Montana and Jerry Rice
practiced to become Hall of Famers"

–GARY ROSE

EPILOGUE

The old saying that *time does not stop for anyone*, applies to the memories that stirred inside me, reading the journals of my former cadets who have now reached adulthood. From cadets. they have become mothers and fathers, nurses, welders, carpenters, painters, hostesses, college and university students, hairdressers, laborers, and members of our Armed Forces, to name a few professions. But before *hitting rock bottom* and making a conscious decision to turn their lives around, they were all heading in the wrong direction.

My cadets came from various high schools, continuation schools and our local junior high. Showing up for enrollment for their first day, they wore civilian clothes with most of the males showing what I called "butt cleavage" and girls showing a little too much skin. Many had hygiene issues and even though they were accompanied by parents, only the teaching staff, noticed.

Some wore gang colors or shirts displaying inappropriate subject matter. Some wore ankle monitors that had to be plugged in during class and on a few occasions, we, as a class, went out of range, setting off the alarms, precipitating that response of the probation department.

Alternative Education, you got to love it or it will tear you apart. Over the years I had been asked many times, how I could teach the students I had for such a long time. The answer was easy. A typical student coming from a functional home with loving parents, who act as excellent role models, who value education, come to school prepared to follow the rules of the school and classroom. They want to learn and their parents are very supportive of the teaching staff.

At-risk students generally do not have this going for them. For the most part, they hated school. Many suffered from physical/sexual or mental abuse. Some lived in poverty, were homeless, experienced gang violence and the ravage of drug use. Many were more mature than their age, because of living on the streets. With no adult supervision, the ran with the wrong crowd and thus began a series of making wrong choices.

Some, having no structured family, turned to gang membership as an alternative. Anger management, resistance to authority, disrespect, assaultive behavior, swearing, became the norm.

They are labeled "at-risk," meaning that if they do not change the direction they are going, they are "at-risk" of not graduating high school and possibly even worse, ending up in the criminal justice system.

So why did I teach at-risk students for so long? Because I loved the challenge of helping them not just overcome the effects of what I have alluded to above, but also to show them that they can be successful.

For 15 years, I saw so many juvenile delinquents go through juvenile court system, and with a fairly accurate ability, I could predict who would end up in state prison someday.

When Joan Berry hired me, and assigned me to juvenile hall, it felt like an extension of being in law enforcement again. Similarly, to the time I taught in our local high school in Milpitas, I was once again up in front of a classroom of students hoping to mold their minds and help them graduate high school.

Starting the Alder Grove Academy allowed me to continue to use the methodologies I used successfully in juvenile hall with student that would remain with me for at least six weeks. The Alder Grove Academy was the last chance for many of the cadets. If they were successful, they would be able to return to their traditional school and graduate with their peers. If they were not, they would either stay with me at the academy or reach adulthood and move on to Adult Education.

Others who were court referred, faced being sent to state sponsored boot camp correctional facilities or the California Youth Authority to serve a sentence.

So with this in mind, every morning at 4 A.M., I was up, showered, shaved and dressed in my black BDU and shiny black boots and left for another day with my cadets.

Some of the cadets had to travel 90 minutes each direction to reach the academy. Their parents either could not provide transportation or did not have a car. Free breakfast and lunch were served at the academy and the teaching staff realized that for many, this was the only food they would have for the day.

I do not want to leave you with the impression that the academy solved all of their problems and that my students, donning military uniforms, miraculously transformed into success stories. Even at the academy some tried to rebel against the system that was set up to help them.

One cadet who wore an ankle monitor, went home one day and somehow removed it. Then, my boy genius, concluded that if he stacked beer cans around the monitor, this would prevent that probation office from tracking him.

Probation came to the academy asking me if I have any information about his whereabouts and told me about the beer can experiment. Little did my cadet realize that the monitor showed that he never moved in his home, and that necessitated probations response.

Periodically, probation officers came to the academy for random drug testing. The student was escorted to their respective bathroom and then surrender a vial of fresh urine.

On one occasion, the student handed the vial to the probation officer who immediately noticed that something was wrong. The average body temperature is 98.6 degrees, but the urine in the bottle was very cold. It was determined that while the probation officer stood outside the stall, the student removed tank cover of the toilet and retrieved a secreted bottle of someone else's urine for the urine test.

It was a cat-and-mouse game with some of the cadets that did not take the program seriously. The teaching staff heard rumors that drugs (marijuana) was being hidden in the bathrooms and that students would retrieve the stash when they went to the head (bathroom). So, leaving Ms. M in charge of my classroom, I searched the bathroom, initially finding nothing. Then, prior to leaving the area, I decided to check the garbage can inside the bathroom. After removing the lining, there I found a lid of grass. We did not have time to stake out the bathroom and determine who the guilty party was, but I felt validated that I got one of them.

Then there was the day one of our popular female cadet came to school with a homemade cake she had made for Albert. Fortunately, she had to pass Ms. M who initially was so excited to see a student make something for someone else. You can imagine her surprise when she looked at a penis shaped cake with frosting.

Even during lunch, held in a classroom we called the mess hall, the cadets still needed to be under constant supervision. It was not just for the obvious reasons such as throwing food, swearing, intimidation, bullying, but also for inappropriate flirtation. What do I mean? A female cadet simulating oral sex with a banana for an example.

Somedays you can feel tension in the air as soon as the students were assembled. Quickly my staff and I tried to learn the reason for the tension and address it before blows could be delivered.

Uniforms eliminated the problem of students displaying gang colors. But you still had to watch for some of the hardcore members who would wear their colors in their socks. It also helped some cadets who, in their traditional schools, could not help but standout, since they had to wear hand-me-downs while their more wealthy peers, wore $200 tennis shoes. The female cadets loved the fact in the morning, there was no need to decide what to wear. A little make-up and they were ready for school.

Cellphones did not become a problem until AGA 2 and AGA 3 when the use of cellphones became part of the American way of life. To stop it, we instituted a procedure where all phones had to be turned in at the beginning of the day. This was met with resistance by a few who hit them on their body which then necessitated clothing searches.

I finally decided that this was taking too much time out of our morning and daily activities, so instead, I went against my supervisor's rule and allow them to keep their phone but with a caveat. If their phone went off during class or disturbed me and the class in anyway, the phone was surrendered and their parents were called to pick it up after school.

My rationale for the insubordination was validated when one day, most of my students' phones went off at the same time. Apparently a gang member had walked onto the Placer High School campus allegedly armed with a gun looking for person who was actually in my classroom. We were able to lockdown the school even before the police department and the county office was able to notify us. I also realized that colleges allow their students to keep their phones as long as they are courteous to others, and since I was teaching my students in a fashion similar to junior college, that is how I sold it to them.

"Choices matter and poor choices led to poor outcomes."

"The greatest battle you cadets will face in life
is doing the right thing."

"Right now society has an obligation to take care of you because
you are juveniles. But soon, when you hit eighteen-years-old,
all bets are off. It will be up to you, and you alone to survive."

All of us have burned bridges in our lives,
but can you go back and repair them?"

"As different or alike that you all maybe,
each of you are the masters of change."

"There are three skills that are the foundation for teaching,
accountability-order, structure and discipline."

"Without adults who can demonstrate accountability in
daily life, most children have no idea that accountability is a
sustaining principle for healthy personal growth."

OTHER BOOKS
by Gary J. Rose, Ph.D.

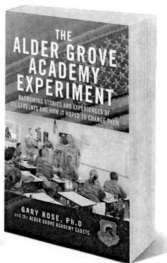

AVAILABLE AT:
Amazon and other fine bookstores
and online venues.

CPSIA information can be obtained
at www.ICGtesting.com
Printed in the USA
LVOW11*1000080617
537346LV00007B/3/P

·